Heritage and War

Heritage and War

Ethical Issues

Edited by
WILLIAM BÜLOW, HELEN FROWE,
DEREK MATRAVERS, AND
JOSHUA LEWIS THOMAS

OXFORD
UNIVERSITY PRESS

Great Clarendon Street, Oxford, OX2 6DP,
United Kingdom

Oxford University Press is a department of the University of Oxford.
It furthers the University's objective of excellence in research, scholarship,
and education by publishing worldwide. Oxford is a registered trade mark of
Oxford University Press in the UK and in certain other countries

© the several contributors 2023

The moral rights of the authors have been asserted

First Edition published in 2023

All rights reserved. No part of this publication may be reproduced, stored in
a retrieval system, or transmitted, in any form or by any means, without the
prior permission in writing of Oxford University Press, or as expressly permitted
by law, by licence or under terms agreed with the appropriate reprographics
rights organization. Enquiries concerning reproduction outside the scope of the
above should be sent to the Rights Department, Oxford University Press, at the
address above

You must not circulate this work in any other form
and you must impose this same condition on any acquirer

Published in the United States of America by Oxford University Press
198 Madison Avenue, New York, NY 10016, United States of America

British Library Cataloguing in Publication Data
Data available

Library of Congress Control Number: 2022947179

ISBN 978-0-19-286264-8

DOI: 10.1093/oso/9780192862648.001.0001

Printed and bound by
CPI Group (UK) Ltd, Croydon, CR0 4YY

Links to third party websites are provided by Oxford in good faith and
for information only. Oxford disclaims any responsibility for the materials
contained in any third party website referenced in this work.

Contents

Acknowledgements	vii
List of Contributors	ix

1. Heritage and War: An Introduction   1
   Helen Frowe and Derek Matravers

2. Seeking Sanctuary: The Pre-History of Cultural Heritage in the Ethics of War   12
   Tuukka Kaikkonen and Cian O'Driscoll

3. Conflicts in Heritage Protection   33
   Helen Frowe and Derek Matravers

4. Killing for Culture   51
   Bashshar Haydar

5. Cultural Icons and Reasons of Culture   72
   Dale Dorsey

6. Cultural Heritage Protection and the Reconciliation Thesis   92
   William Bülow and Joshua Lewis Thomas

7. Responding to Cultural Wrongs in Palestine and Israel   113
   Victor Tadros

8. When Damage Becomes Memorial   133
   Carolyn Korsmeyer

9. Architecture and Cultural Memory   153
   Robert Hopkins

10. Heritage Tourism after Conflict: Starting Philosophical Thoughts   174
    Penelope Bernard and Simon Kirchin

11. Stoics on Stuff: Stoic Consolations on the Destruction of Cultural Heritage in War   195
    Nancy Sherman

Index   213

Acknowledgements

This collection of essays is one of the outputs of the 'Heritage in War' project, funded by the Arts and Humanities Research Council and co-hosted by the Open University and Stockholm University. The project was co-directed by Helen Frowe and Derek Matravers, ably assisted by postdoctoral researchers William Bülow and Joshua Lewis Thomas. We are very grateful to the AHRC for their support. We are also grateful to anonymous readers for OUP for helpful comments on the shape of the volume.

We benefitted from discussions with a wide range of people and organisations during the lifetime of the project. We are grateful to members of the UK Blue Shield, the United States Military Academy at West Point, the American University of Beirut, the British Museum, the Norwegian Ministry of Defence, the Institute for Futures Studies and Tel Aviv University. We owe special thanks to the members of our Core Research Group, who met regularly to share their expertise: Andreas Brekke Carlsson, Jeremy Musson, Jonathan Parry, Gerald Lang, Tim Purbrick, Massimo Renzo, Emma Cunliffe, Dacia Viejo Rose and Victor Tadros. We are also very grateful to the members of our advisory board: Nancy Sherman, Yitzhak Benbaji, Greg Reichberg, Scott Parsons, Adil Ahmad Haque, Mark Vlasic and Bashshar Haydar.

We organised various events as part of this project, often with the help of our project partners. Thanks to all those who participated: Maamoun Abdulkarim, Amr Al-Azm, Kay Andrews, Anna Bergqvist, Yitzhak Benbaji, Penelope Bernard, John Bold, Samuel Bruce, Ruth Chang, Rory Cox, Tobit Curteis, Dale Dorsey, Rasa Davidaviciute, Cécile Fabre, Lucie Fusade, David Garrard, Lisa Giombini, Bashar Haydar, Moshe Halbertal, Richard Holton, Jann Kleffner, Simon Kirchin, Joakim Kreutz, Martin Hamilton, Robert Hopkins, Nick Howe, Laura Jones, Eliav Lieblich, John McGuiness, Cristina Menegazzi, James Mock, Veronique Munoz-Darde, Andreas Pantazatos, Jonathan Peterson, Elizabeth Pye, Michael Rainsborough, Frederik Rosén, Laurie Rush, Idit Shafran-Gittleman, St John Simpson, Sebastian Rey, Constantine Sandis, Elizabeth Scarbrough, Jacques Shumacher, Daniel Statman, Peter Stone, Victor Tadros, Erin L. Thompson, Jonathan Tubb, Corine Wegener, and Jonathan Wolff. We are also very grateful to members of the Norwegian Defence Ethics Council for hosting a series of very helpful meetings. Special thanks are owed to Lynn Meskell, Frederik Rosén, and Tim Purbrick for their various engagements with our work.

List of Contributors

Penelope Bernard is Project Manager on the Medieval Animal Heritage East Kent project at Canterbury Christ Church University. She is an archaeologist, heritage consultant, and former school teacher. She is currently co-leading a project on eco-heritage and well-being at Canterbury Christ Church University, supported by the UK Heritage Lottery Fund.

William Bülow is a senior researcher at the Centre for Research Ethics & Bioethics at Uppsala University. He works primarily in legal philosophy and applied ethics. He was previously a postdoctoral research fellow at the Stockholm Centre for the Ethics of War and Peace where he worked within the AHCR-funded Heritage in War Project.

Dale Dorsey is Dean's Professor of Philosophy at the University of Kansas. His work in normative ethics typically revolves around the intersection between prudence, normativity, and morality. His most recent book is *A Theory of Prudence* (2021), and he is currently working on a manuscript that explores the intrinsic value of human fellowship.

Helen Frowe is Professor of Practical Philosophy and Knut and Alice Wallenberg Scholar at Stockholm University, where she directs the Stockholm Centre for the Ethics of War and Peace. Her books include *Defensive Killing* (2014) and *The Ethics of War and Peace: An Introduction* (2011). She co-directed the AHRC project on Heritage in War alongside Derek Matravers.

Bashshar Haydar is Professor of Philosophy and the Mohammad Atallah Chair of Ethics at the American University of Beirut. He works on various topics in normative and applied ethics, focusing on the question of allocating the burdens of harm alleviation. He also works on aesthetic value and the connection of the latter to moral and cognitive values.

Robert Hopkins is Professor of Philosophy at New York University. He works in aesthetics and the philosophy of mind. He has published on picture perception, the imagination, memory, and the aesthetics of the visual arts. He is the author of *Picture, Image and Experience* (1998) and is now working on a book on experiential imagining, which, title aside, is almost complete.

Tuukka Kaikkonen is a PhD candidate in International Relations at the Coral Bell School of Asia and Pacific Affairs, Australian National University. His PhD research takes place at the intersection of the ethics of war, international political theory, and moral philosophy, particularly in relation to questions of moral luck, moral responsibility, and the ethics of war.

Simon Kirchin is Professor of Philosophy at the University of Kent. He works mainly in ethics and the philosophy of value. He is the author of *Thick Evaluation* (2017) and *Metaethics* (2012) and has edited and co-edited several collections.

Carolyn Korsmeyer is Research Professor of Philosophy, University at Buffalo, SUNY. Her research explores aesthetic aspects of emotion and the senses, including the artistic arousal of aversive affective states. These interests are pursued in *Making Sense of Taste: Food and Philosophy* and in *Savoring Disgust: The Foul and the Fair in Aesthetics*. In *Things: In Touch with the Past*, she argues that touch plays an often-overlooked role in the apprehension of old artefacts.

Derek Matravers is Professor of Philosophy at The Open University and a Fellow of Churchill College, Cambridge. He has written *Art and Emotion* (1998), *Introducing Philosophy of Art: Eight Case Studies* (2013), *Fiction and Narrative* (2014), and *Empathy* (2017). He is the author of numerous articles in aesthetics, ethics, and the philosophy of mind. He co-directed the AHRC project on Heritage in War alongside Helen Frowe.

Cian O'Driscoll is Professor of International Relations at the Coral Bell School of Asia and Pacific Affairs, Australian National University. His research focuses on the ethics of war, with a particular emphasis on the just war tradition. He has published two monographs, including, most recently, *Victory: The Triumph and Tragedy of Just War* (Oxford University Press, 2019), three edited volumes, and numerous journal articles.

Nancy Sherman is distinguished University Professor and Professor of Philosophy at Georgetown University. Her most recent book is *Stoic Wisdom: Ancient Lessons for Modern Resilience* (2021). Other books include *Afterwar*, *The Untold War* (a *NYT* editors' pick), *Stoic Warriors*, *Making a Necessity of Virtue*, and *The Fabric of Character*. She is the editor of *Critical Essays on the Classics: Aristotle's Ethics*. She has written over 60 articles in the area of ethics, military ethics, the history of moral philosophy, ancient ethics, the emotions, moral psychology, and psychoanalysis.

Victor Tadros is Professor of Criminal Law and Legal Theory, Warwick University. His books include *Criminal Responsibility*, *The Ends of Harm*, *Wrongs and Crimes*, and *To Do, To Die, To Reason Why*, all with Oxford University Press. He has held a Leverhulme Major Research Fellowship and is a Fellow of the British Academy.

Joshua Lewis Thomas is an Associate Lecturer at the Open University. Prior to this he worked as a postdoctoral research fellow within the AHCR-funded Heritage in War Project. He completed his PhD at the University of Sheffield and his primary research interests lie in value theory and applied ethics.

1
Heritage and War

An Introduction

Helen Frowe and Derek Matravers

1. Stones and Lives

As readers may recall, by 2017 the so-called Islamic State in Syria (ISIS) had been making international headlines for its destruction of world-renowned cultural heritage sites across Iraq, Syria and Libya. Groups affiliated with ISIS released videos showing devastating attacks on, for example, the ancient sites of Palmyra and Nimrud, and the widespread destruction of artefacts in the Mosul Museum. There were reports that terrorist groups were drawing funds from the organised looting of archaeological sites (Watson 2015).[1] In 2012, a group linked to al-Qaeda destroyed ancient tombs in Timbuktu in what became the first instance of heritage destruction to be prosecuted as a war crime by the International Criminal Court. These events gave rise to calls for greater protection for cultural heritage in war, ranging from pleas for training for locals trying to remove or protect threatened heritage, to demands that military forces be deployed to guard important sites and expel ISIS fighters from areas rich in tangible heritage (Petrovic 2013; Eakin 2015; Bokova 2016; Bowker, Goodall & Haciski 2016; Cuno 2016; Middle East Institute, Asia Society, & the Antiquities Coalition 2016; Weiss & Connelly 2017).

At the same time, our newspapers and screens were filled with images of dead bodies, devastated cities, and thousands of refugees fleeing conflicts in the Middle East. This juxtaposition caused a backlash against those voicing

---

[1] These claims are contested: for example, a recent RAND report argues that "In the absence of reliable statistical data, journalists, researchers, and policy experts regularly inflate the importance of antiquities trafficking in funding for international terrorism and organized crime. Linking cultural property crimes to these high-profile law enforcement issues offers a means to bring funding and political attention to what has traditionally been an underrecognized issue." See Sargent et al. (2020: 10). See also Losson (2017).

Helen Frowe and Derek Matravers, *Heritage and War: An Introduction* In: *Heritage and War: Ethical Issues.*
Edited by: William Bülow, Helen Frowe, Derek Matravers, and Joshua Lewis Thomas, Oxford University Press.
© Helen Frowe and Derek Matravers 2023. DOI: 10.1093/oso/9780192862648.003.0001

2   HERITAGE AND WAR

their concerns about the destruction of ancient ruins.[2] In the face of so much human suffering, it can seem inappropriate to worry about anything but the urgent, basic needs of people. This debate has been popularly summarised as a dispute about 'stones versus lives'. In reaction to this criticism, advocates for heritage protection are keen to stress that protecting cultural heritage does not undermine the protection of people. Almost invariably, they defend this claim by arguing that people and heritage are inseparable, and thus conflicts between them are impossible (we can call this the *Inseparability Thesis*).[3]

For example, writing in her capacity as Director-General of UNESCO, Irina Bokova made the (now widely cited) claim that, "there is no need to choose between saving lives and preserving cultural heritage: the two are inseparable" (Bokova 2015). Thomas Weiss and Nina Connelly argue that "the protection of people and the protection of heritage are inseparable [...] there is no need for a hierarchy of protection because the choice between the two is false, just as a choice between people and the natural environment is false" (Weiss & Connelly 2017: 6). The protection of people and the protection of heritage are, they argue, "conceptually and operationally inseparable" (Weiss & Connelly 2019: 2). Peter Stone, Chair of the UK Blue Shield, an organisation devoted to the protection of heritage in war, argues that "the line between protecting people and protecting their cultural property and heritage is so fine as to be almost invisible" (Stone 2017: 32). The art historian Nausikaä El-Mecky suggests that heritage and people are sometimes "one and the same thing" (El-Mecky 2016). Amr Al-Azm, the former Director of Scientific and Conservation Laboratories at the General Department of Antiquities and Museums in Syria, rejects the idea that one might need to choose between heritage and people (Al-Azm 2018). Cristina Menegazzi, leader of UNESCO's Emergency Safeguarding of the Syrian Cultural Heritage project, similarly insists that those working in heritage do not recognise any conflict between protecting people and protecting heritage (Menegazzi 2018).

And yet, conflicts between protecting heritage and protecting human life are rife, both within war and without. They arise between heritage and civilians and between heritage and combatants. They are manifest in debates about the distribution of scarce resources, legal conventions pertaining to heritage protection, and calls for military intervention to protect cultural

---

[2] Lynn Meskell notes a similar reaction to UNESCO's funding of the restoration of the Bamiyan Buddhas in Afghanistan in 2003, where "funding was being channeled into preserving monuments at the very moment when living people needed the greatest support" (Meskell 2018).

[3] The thesis is criticised in Hatala Matthes (2018) and Frowe & Matravers (2019). For further relevant criticism, see Meskell (2020).

heritage from attack. Because those working on the protection of heritage in war treat the Inseparability Thesis as a near-orthodoxy, they have paid virtually no attention to these conflicts which raise difficult questions about types of value and how to weigh those values against each other.

This lacuna partially motivates this volume (and, indeed, much of our own interest in the ethics of protecting heritage in war). Such questions concerning value fall squarely within the philosophical domain and Chapters 1 to 7 of this volume directly engage with them. By taking conflicts in heritage protection seriously, these essays contribute to supplying a theoretical basis for protecting heritage in war. But, of course, the scope of ethical issues raised by heritage and war goes far beyond these conflicts. Chapters 8 to 11 shed light on a range of moral questions, such as how we ought to respond to heritage that is damaged in war, the nature of the harm caused by such damage, and the morally appropriate treatment of sites of war and conflict that have themselves become heritage sites.

Our aim is not a comprehensive analysis of the many questions raised by the protection or damaging of heritage in war. Rather, our hope is that the breadth and depth of the essays herein serve as evidence of the role that philosophers must play in developing our understanding of, and responses to, these important issues.

2. Outline of the Book

There is a general consensus that, although not entirely absent, the treatment of cultural heritage has been rather neglected in just war writings, both historical and contemporary. However, as Tuukka Kaikkonen and Cian O'Driscoll show in 'Seeking Sanctuary: The Pre-History of Cultural Heritage in the Ethics of War', the idea of certain spaces as sacred and immune to attack in war has a rich history in ancient and medieval writings on war and, indeed, in historical military practice.

Drawing on a wide variety of historical sources, this chapter develops an account of the parallels between the protection of cultural heritage in war and the historic notion of sanctuary. As Kaikkonen and O'Driscoll argue, such writings and practices seem to be the natural starting point for discussions about the protection of cultural heritage in war, since these too focus, in large part, on how the cultural significance of certain buildings ought to render them inviolable under the rules of war. Kaikkonen and O'Driscoll also identify cases in which the violation of sanctuaries was cited as (partial)

4 HERITAGE AND WAR

justification for war, much as attacks on cultural heritage have been invoked as justifications for military intervention in recent times (Bowker, Goodall & Haciski 2016; Weiss & Connelly 2017; Cuno 2016). Although there are, clearly, significant differences between historical sanctuary practices and the protection of cultural heritage—most notably, that the protection of sanctuaries extended to all those who occupied them—this chapter offers a fascinating exploration of the ways in which wartime protections have been afforded to cultural spaces in the past.

In our own chapter, 'Conflicts in Heritage Protection', we develop the case for rejecting the Inseparability Thesis. We argue, first, that the 1954 Hague Convention on the Protection of Cultural Property in Times of Armed Conflict demands that we not only recognise these conflicts but also come up with some rubric for resolving them. We cannot expect military leaders to make necessity or proportionality judgements about damaging heritage—as required by the Convention—in the absence of any guidance about how the protection of heritage weighs against the other goods at stake in war. Without such guidance, such judgements will be unavoidably *ad hoc*.

We then canvass some of the ways in which protecting heritage can require combatants to incur risk to themselves and impose risks on civilians, along with other examples of how protecting heritage conflicts with protecting civilians' interests in life and limb. Together, these conflicts not only demonstrate the implausibility of the Inseparability Thesis but also the importance of taking conflicts between protecting heritage and protecting people seriously. We suggest that adherence to the Inseparability Thesis seems to be best explained by a fear that granting the possibility of conflict between protecting people and protecting heritage will commit us to the impermissibility of protecting heritage. As we argue, this fear is ill-founded, since committing to value pluralism does not require us to sacrifice all of some good for the sake of other, more important goods.

We noted above the demands that something be done in the face of attacks on cultural heritage, including calls for the use of military force to curtail and prevent such attacks. In 'Killing for Culture', Bashshar Haydar examines the conditions under which it is morally permissible to resort to force for the sake of protecting heritage from deliberate destruction. Haydar argues that such force can be permissible under limited circumstances: namely, when the destruction is part of a policy of cultural cleansing that substantially threatens a group's right to self-determination. He argues that, given its connection to self-determination and its typically irreplaceable nature, our reasons to prevent the destruction of heritage are sometimes weightier than our reasons to protect other types of civilian infrastructure. And, he argues, our reasons to protect heritage can justify both the intentional harming of those who culpably attack heritage and the collateral harming of innocent people.

Haydar then considers the question of what he terms 'cultural intervention' by third party armed forces, exploring how the risks that intervention poses to intervening combatants and local populations might be justified in cases of intervening to protect three types of heritage: (i) heritage of particular value to the local population, (ii) heritage of particular value to the interveners, and (iii) heritage that, while culturally significant, lacks particular value for either the local population or the interveners.

In 'Cultural Icons and Reasons of Culture', Dale Dorsey tackles the question of whether combatants may expose civilians to increased risks of harm in order to decrease the risks of damaging cultural heritage. Dorsey argues that, sometimes, combatants are morally required to avoid damaging heritage even if this foreseeably results in civilian and/or combatant deaths. This requirement is not grounded in, for example, the aesthetic value of heritage, or in the historical significance of some particular heritage site or artefact. Rather, he argues, it is grounded in the moral concern that we owe participants in the relevant culture. It is part of respecting the valuing attitude of those moral agents that we give moral weight to the things they value.

However, as Dorsey argues, the criterion of being a participant in the relevant culture—being a *cultural denizen*—is crucial. Being such a denizen is a normatively significant role that is not shared by those who, while admiring or valuing the heritage, lack a participatory connection to it. The fact that, for example, North Dakotans value Le Thèâtre du Grand Guignol as part of Parisian culture will not justify exposing Parisians to increased risks in order to protect the theatre. Only Parisians occupy the normatively significant role regarding their culture that makes it incumbent upon others to consider their valuing attitudes when deciding the allocation of risk. Insofar as Parisians prefer to decrease risks to their heritage at the cost of increasing risk to themselves, third parties have reason to balance the risks accordingly (although, of course, these reasons need not be decisive).

In 'Cultural Heritage Protection and the Reconciliation Thesis', William Bülow and Joshua Lewis Thomas consider the *Reconciliation Thesis*—that is, the thesis that the goal of securing a lasting peace between belligerents gives combatants reason to preserve heritage in war. They identify three ways in which heritage could make such a contribution: (i) by contributing to the post war economy; (ii) by providing opportunities for cross-cultural education; and (iii) by facilitating the return of displaced populations. The tenor of their

6   HERITAGE AND WAR

discussion is sceptical, for two reasons. First, pursuing heritage protection has opportunity costs—that is, the time and resources spent protecting heritage could otherwise have been directed elsewhere—and, often, those alternatives might be a more effective route to a lasting peace. Second, the Reconciliation Thesis presupposes a number of empirical claims, many of which we have reason to doubt. Bülow and Thomas do not deny the importance of pursuing a lasting peace. However, they conclude that the Reconciliation Thesis provides only limited, and heavily caveated, support for moving heritage protection up the list of military priorities.

In 'Responding to Cultural Wrongs in Palestine and Israel', Victor Tadros addresses the moral obligations of those who participate in the destruction of cultural heritage during war. Tadros focuses on the town of Lydda, a historic town in Palestine that was renamed Lod after the creation of Israel. During the 1948 war, much of the Arab population of the town was forcibly displaced by the Israeli armed forces, and the town was subsequently settled by Jewish immigrants. The old town centre was largely demolished, destroying the buildings and spaces that had structured the cultural life of the Arab population. Arab homes and businesses were commandeered by Jewish settlers. Within a comparatively short space of time, the cultural history of the Arab population was almost entirely erased from the town.

What is owed, by whom, and to whom, following this sort of cultural destruction? Tadros focuses on the Moroccan and Tunisian Jews who arrived in Lydda after the 1948 war and their impact on the living, embedded culture of the now-displaced Palestinian population. He argues that, at least sometimes, citizens ought to combat or compensate for the destruction of cultural heritage, particularly when they are beneficiaries of the destruction. Initially, these settlers had obligations to preserve the town as it was and, insofar as they were able, fight to secure the Palestinians' right to return.

But, Tadros argues, this obligation weakens both as the prospects of return diminish and in light of the settlers' own needs to develop their environment in line with their own cultural practices. Whereas certain types of iconic heritage—grand monuments and so forth—can and should be preserved intact, it is much harder for communities to live in a town without replacing the living, embedded culture (which includes not merely intangible heritage but also unremarkable but central physical spaces, such as marketplaces, coffee shops, bars, parks, gardens and so forth). Moreover, there is, Tadros argues, no valuable sense in which Lod's current occupants could sustain the living, embedded culture of the Palestinians; as he puts it, the value of a living embedded culture cannot be "realised by others aping the conduct that

Palestinians would have engaged in had they not been driven out". But this does not mean that the current occupants of Lod simply lack obligations to the (displaced) Palestinian occupants. Rather, what is called for is genuine engagement with both the Palestinian diaspora and the small number of remaining Arab occupants of Lod aimed at accommodating their cultural practices and values in any further development of the town.

In 'When Damage Becomes Memorial', Carolyn Korsmeyer discusses how war can be memorialised in several ways—most obviously by public art that represents the war in some (usually figurative) way. Drawing upon the notion of 'exemplification', familiar from work by Nelson Goodman and Catharine Elgin, Korsmeyer argues that visible damage surviving from a battle can serve as a memorial by exemplifying that very damage. In contrast to other forms of representation, these memorials deliver a sense of the very presence of war, conveying a palpable sense of what happened at that spot. The direct link they have with the events that shaped them 'put us in touch' with those events (in this, Korsmeyer is drawing on themes which she has explored in earlier work) (Korsmeyer 2019). If Korsmeyer is right, then we have a reason to leave at least some heritage damaged in war in its damaged state. Repairing it, or replacing it, will destroy its capacity to exemplify and thus destroy its status as the kind of memorial that it is.

In 'Architecture and Cultural Memory', Robert Hopkins defends a version of John Ruskin's claim that buildings are somehow an embodiment of our cultural memories. To do this, Hopkins argues that there are cultural memories (that is, the members of a culture can remember its past) that are analogous to personal memories (for example, Hopkins remembers getting his A-level results). Hopkins gives three conditions that must be satisfied in order for something to be a personal memory: for X to remember Y, X has to be able to represent Y (that is, be able to bring Y to mind), to have experienced Y at some time in the past, and X's current ability to represent Y has to directly depend on X's past experience of Y.

The first, and most obvious, difficulty that the first condition raises is that, while persons are able to represent past experiences, it is unclear what it would be for a culture to represent past experiences. Hopkins responds to this difficulty by drawing on Susanne Langer's conception of a 'non-discursive symbol', arguing that buildings represent "the characteristic functional patterns that constitute a culture". This helps Hopkins to show architecture's role in meeting the first condition of something's being a memory. When we experience buildings, we experience them as representations of the past life of the culture, and these experiences constitute the memory of that past life.

8   HERITAGE AND WAR

What of the second and third conditions? Hopkin's task is to show that those conditions, which connect a present self with a past self, have analogues that connect the current life of a culture with its past life. The analogue of the second condition is fairly easily met. A person's bringing to mind an event in the past counts as remembering only if they were the one that, in the past, experienced that event. Analogously, current members of a culture experiencing buildings counts as remembering only if it (the culture) had the experiences that came to be represented in the building—which, Hopkins claims, it did. The third condition is more difficult. Why should the current experience of buildings count as a *memory* of the past, rather than, say, being *a reminder* of the past, or simply *learning about* the past? The answer lies in the current experience's being directly linked to the past that is represented by the building (in a way analogous to that in which current experience can be a memory only if it is directly linked to the experience that caused it). Hopkins focuses on two features of architecture that provide something like this direct link. The first is that the original architect exercises her capacity to represent certain aspects of the culture, and, in experiencing buildings, we inherit that very capacity. The second is that the core of that experience is identical in each case; namely, the very building in question. This second feature plays a role in Hopkins' discussion of the consequences of his view for heritage damaged during war. If buildings are destroyed in war, we lose the opportunities to have experiences that are the memories of our cultural past. If we build replicas, what is lost is the very building in question. Hence, even if the knowledge is in some sense retained, with the loss of directness, its status as a memory is lost.

In 'Heritage Tourism after Conflict: Starting Philosophical Thoughts', Penelope Bernard and Simon Kirchin address the phenomenon of conflict heritage tourism, whereby the sites of past battles, massacres and other horrors of war are turned into tourist destinations, themselves becoming part of a country's heritage. Such sites are both many and popular: think of Auschwitz, Wounded Knee, or the Hastings battlefield (to name but a few). And yet they clearly raise important, if largely neglected, moral questions about the appropriate forms of engagement with sites of such serious suffering. As Bernard and Kirchin argue, there is a seeming moral tension between these sites' histories and their presentation as, often, places of relaxation and enjoyment. Many English castles, for example, hold regular 'family fun days' involving the re-enactment of historic battles as a form of entertainment alongside picnic sites, food stalls and so on.

Bernard and Kirchin consider whether, and why, the creation and sustaining of, and participation in, these heritage sites is morally permissible. As they argue, it is unlikely that we can identify a set of criteria for evaluating all such sites. But, nevertheless, some useful guiding principles emerge from their discussion that can help us to distinguish the impermissible treatment of such sites from their permissible presentation as tourist destinations.

Finally, in 'Stoics on Stuff: Consolations on the Destruction of Cultural Heritage in War', Nancy Sherman turns her long-term investigation of the psychology of war, viewed through the lens of Stoicism, to our attitudes to cultural heritage. The Stoics wrote a great deal about the emotions and about emotional reactions. Sherman argues that the framework they developed provides an illuminating backdrop for thinking about how to react to the rigours of conflict and the destruction of heritage. Although the Stoics held that virtue alone was sufficient for happiness, they nonetheless developed an account of attitudes to external goods, including cultural artefacts and edifices. These they classified as 'indifferents'; those things that have a role in our being in the world, but that are not essential to the good life.

Recognising the importance of heritage, while not making it central to our lives going well, opens up a space that allows us to reflect calmly on our attitudes to these objects. Sherman counterposes the 'official' doctrine of the Stoics, which tends towards a rather harsh asceticism, with a letter from Seneca concerning the grief of a friend at the loss of his home city to fire. In this letter, Seneca reveals a more complex, layered account of the emotions in which there is a time to feel them and a time to master them. The overall message is that we should be vulnerable to feeling emotions, but at the same time not allow ourselves to be undone by that vulnerability. The combination of the assignation of a proper place to external goods, and the mastery of our emotions, allows us, Sherman argues, space to reflect on that heritage which is the source of harm to communities—such as the sacred spaces of Jerusalem which serve as a flashpoint to violence between those of different faiths. In that psychological space that Stoicism encourages, we can "reflect on how and why we value what we do in a good life", guided by Seneca's injunction to "cultivate humanity".

References

Al-Azm, A. (2018) 'Protecting Syria's Cultural Heritage the Local Way', presented at the 'Stones Vs. Lives: Proportionality and Non-Human Value' workshop, American University of Beirut, 19 November. Available at: https://www.youtube.com/watch?v=DA5BmoDD3Cg.

Bokova, I. (2015) 'Culture on the Front Line of New Wars', *Brown Journal of World Affairs* 22/1: 289–296.

Bokova, I. (2016) 'Terrorists Are Destroying Our Cultural Heritage. It's Time to Fight Back', *World Economic Forum*. Available at: https://www.weforum.org/agenda/2016/01/terrorists-are-destroying-our-culture-heritage-it-s-time-to-fight-back/.

Bowker, D.W., Goodall, L., & Haciski, R.A. (2016) 'Confronting ISIS's War on Cultural Property', *ASIL Insights* 20/12.

Cuno, J. (2016) 'The Responsibility to Protect the World's Cultural Heritage', *Brown Journal of World Affairs* 23/1: 97–109.

Eakin, H. (2015) 'Use Force to Stop ISIS' Destruction of Art and History', *The New York Times*, 3 April.

El-Mecky, N. (2016) 'Inside the UNESCO Conference to Save Syria's Heritage', *Apollo Magazine*, 10 June.

Frowe, H., & Matravers, D. (2019) 'Conflict and Cultural Heritage: A Moral Analysis of the Challenges of Heritage Protection', J. Paul Getty Trust Occasional Papers in Cultural Heritage Policy, 3 (Los Angeles, CA: J. Paul Getty Trust).

Hatala Matthes, E. (2018) 'Saving Lives or Saving Stones? The Ethics of Cultural Heritage Protection in War', *Public Affairs Quarterly* 32/1: 67–84.

Korsmeyer, C. (2019) *Things: In Touch with the Past* (Oxford: Oxford University Press).

Losson, P. (2017) 'Does the International Trafficking of Cultural Heritage Really Fuel Military Conflicts?', *Studies in Conflict and Terrorism* 40/6: 484–495.

Menegazzi, C. (2018) 'The Role of UNESCO for the Preservation of Syrian Cultural Heritage', presented at the 'Stones Vs. Lives: Proportionality and Non-Human Value' Workshop, American University of Beirut, 19 November. Available at: https://www.youtube.com/watch?v=790IsxaTQtc.

Meskell, L. (2018) *A Future in Ruins: UNESCO, World Heritage and the Dream of Peace* (New York: Oxford University Press).

Meskell, L. (2020) 'Toilets First, Temples Second: Adopting Heritage in Neoliberal India', *International Journal of Heritage Studies* 27/2: 151–169.

Middle East Institute, Asia Society, & the Antiquities Coalition (2016) 'Culture under Threat: Recommendations for the US Government', April. Available at: http://www.academia.edu/30873427/Culture_Under_Threat_Recommendations_for_the_U.S_Government.

Petrovic, J. (2013) 'What Next for Endangered Cultural Treasures? The Timbuktu Crisis and the Responsibility to Protect', *New Zealand Journal of Public and International Law* 11/2: 381–426.

Sargent, M., Marrone, J.V., Evans, A., Lilly, B., Nemeth, E., & Dalzell, S. (2020) 'Tracking and Disrupting the Illicit Antiquities Trade with Open-Source Data',

RAND Corporation. Available at: https://www.rand.org/pubs/research_reports/RR2706.html.

Stone, P. (2017) 'Cultural Property Protection and the Blue Shield', *In Harm's Way: Aspects of Cultural* Heritage *Protection* (British Council): 30–37. https://www.britishcouncil.org/sites/default/files/in_harms_way_-_second_edition_online_version.pdf.

Watson, A. (2015) 'How Antiquities Are Funding Terrorism', *Financial Times*, 29 June.

Weiss, T.G., & Connelly, N. (2017) 'Cultural Cleansing and Mass Atrocities: Protecting Cultural Heritage in Armed Conflict Zones', J. Paul Getty Trust Occasional Papers in Cultural Heritage Policy, 1 (Los Angeles, CA: J. Paul Getty Trust).

Weiss, T. G., & Connelly, N. (2019) 'Protecting Cultural Heritage in War Zones', *Third World Quarterly* 40/1: 1–17.

2

Seeking Sanctuary

The Pre-History of Cultural Heritage in the Ethics of War

Tuukka Kaikkonen and Cian O'Driscoll

1. Introduction

The focus of this volume is the ethics of cultural heritage. It challenges us to reflect on both what kind of sites and spaces warrant protection from war, and what form that protection should take. These questions are of course topical, speaking, as they do, to outrages committed in recent years by so-called ISIS in Palmyra and, before that, by the Taliban in Bamiyan. Nor were these isolated events: reports suggest that ISIS plundered and destroyed at least 28 historical religious buildings between June 2014 and February 2015.[1] So far, then, as attacks on cultural heritage sites have emerged as a preferred weapon of war, there is urgent need to consider how (if at all) these sites should be protected, and how law and ethics are implicated in this domain. The purpose of this chapter, however, is to zoom out, so to speak, and put these issues in historical perspective. What we discover when we do this is that efforts to safeguard cultural heritage sites in war are part of a much deeper story, a story that pertains to a neglected set of *jus in bello* restraints on the conduct of war.

Jus in bello norms have typically fastened onto, and sought to limit, war by regulating four core aspects of the conduct of war: the persons who wage it and are targeted by it, the weapons and technologies it involves, the span of time allotted to it, and the sites and spaces upon which it may be fought. Contemporary just war theorists have devoted a great deal of attention to the first two of these categories, and there has also been a recent turn in the literature towards analysing the wartime constraints that are temporal in

---

[1] For more details, see al-Taie (2015).

Tuukka Kaikkonen and Cian O'Driscoll, *Seeking Sanctuary: The Pre-History of Cultural Heritage in the Ethics of War*
In: *Heritage and War: Ethical Issues*. Edited by: William Bülow, Helen Frowe, Derek Matravers, and Joshua Lewis Thomas, Oxford University Press. © Tuukka Kaikkonen and Cian O'Driscoll 2023. DOI: 10.1093/oso/9780192862648.003.0002

nature.[2] Very little attention, however, has been paid to attempts to curb the destructiveness of war that are primarily spatial in nature. The discussion of the ethics of cultural heritage protection in armed conflict falls within this neglected category. This alone is enough to render it an interesting avenue of inquiry. The picture becomes even more interesting, however, when one draws the obvious but often overlooked connection between the protection of cultural heritage sites and ancient and medieval sanctuary traditions relating to sacred spaces.[3]

Similar to the claim that cultural heritage sites, many of which also happen to be religious spaces, should be protected from the ravages of war, historical sanctuary practices forbade belligerent parties from extending hostilities into places and buildings that were imbued with sacred meaning. To this day, many such sites continue to be valued as sites of historical, cultural, or religious meaning—not to mention educational or economic value. Consider, for instance, the Parthenon, which functioned as a sanctuary in ancient Greek times and has continued to be claimed (and contested) as a site of religious, military, or cultural value ever since (Pedley 2005, 226–32). The enduring importance of such sites is reflected in international humanitarian law (IHL), which accords special protections to sites, buildings, and objects of cultural, historical, spiritual, scientific, or artistic significance.[4] And yet, despite the efforts that go into protecting former sanctuary *sites*, little is spoken of sanctuary *practices* today, at least in relation to the ethics of war. Indeed, the notion of 'sanctuary' has acquired an archaic ring, and most scholars would presumably regard it as an historical artefact that went the way of the dinosaurs, long before Henri Dunant kickstarted the process that led to the codification of the laws of war. It does not feature in contemporary just war theory in any notable way. That is to say, there is no treatment of it in the current ethics of war literature. Perhaps more surprisingly, nor is there any sustained treatment of it in the historical literature on the just war tradition. It does not appear in the

---

[2] The latter category includes discussion of truce periods, holidays or festive periods during which fighting is prohibited, last resort, ultimatums, and even what is meant by categories such as 'wartime' and 'peacetime' (Dudziak 2012; Thaler 2014; Hom 2020).

[3] One partial exception is Cox (2013), who interrogates the wartime protection and destruction of ecclesiastical property by medieval English armies. Heritage protection in the just war tradition has also received attention from Brunstetter (2019), although without explicit connections being drawn between heritage and sanctuary.

[4] This can be illustrated by Article 1 of the 1954 Hague Convention, which specifies as subject of protection 'movable or immovable property of great importance to the cultural heritage of every people, such as monuments of architecture, art or history, whether religious or secular'. In turn, Article 53 of the 1977 Additional Protocol I to the 1949 Geneva Conventions specifies that 'it is prohibited (a) to commit any acts of hostility directed against the historic monuments, works of art or places of worship which constitute the cultural or spiritual heritage of peoples'.

14   HERITAGE AND WAR

indexes where one might expect to find it: it is conspicuous by its absence from the works of James Turner Johnson (1975, 1981, 1999), Frederick Russell (1977), Philippe Contamine (1984), Stephen Neff (2005), and even from the anthological work of Gregory Reichberg, Henrik Syse, and Endre Begby (2006c).[5] Despite this, the concept of sanctuary has retained a certain resonance. This is true not only in respect of refugees and asylum seekers, but also in relation to armed conflict: it echoes in the language of 'safe havens' and in the proclivity of vulnerable populations to seek shelter in churches, mosques, and sacred spaces more generally. It speaks to a basic folk understanding that there are certain sites, deemed to be sacred, that war must not be enacted upon, and which therefore can provide refuge to anyone within its boundaries.

What is remarkable about this practice for our purpose is that it operates counter to the standard way that wartime protections typically function today. Special protections notwithstanding, in IHL, protection generally stems from, and attaches to, the immunity of certain categories of person and extends only indirectly to the places that they occupy. Consider, for example, how the Israeli Defence Force treats buildings as permissible or impermissible targets depending on whether they house hostile armed forces or non-combatants only (Schmitt and Merriam 2015, 104–10). In such cases, the status of immunity is conferred (or not) upon a building, not because of the properties of the building itself, but because of the characteristics of persons present within it. Sanctuary practices take a very different form. They endow immunity directly upon buildings or sites regarded as sacred, with that cloak of protection then extending to any persons or entities residing within that space. The source of inviolability, in these cases, is the space itself, not the persons who happen to inhabit it. In this respect, there is a strong similarity or even continuity between historical sanctuary practices and current moves to codify the inviolability of cultural heritage sites in the context of warfare.[6] Might the move to endow cultural heritage sites with legal and ethical protections be helpfully understood as a transmutation of historical sanctuary practices?

---

[5] This is not to neglect the occasional in-text mentions of holy sites in Reichberg, Syse, and Begby (2006c) and Reichberg and Syse (2014).

[6] An even closer congruence between sanctuary and IHL can be found in the protections that the latter confers on medical facilities and neutralised zones. The 1949 Geneva Convention IV Articles 14 and 18 prohibit the use of armed force against hospitals and wounded and vulnerable people in those facilities, while Article 15 outlines the protections that can be conferred on neutralised zones. However, as articulated in Article 19, and as is the case with cultural heritage sites, these protections can be temporarily revoked when medical facilities are being used for military purposes (for a recent debate on hospital protections, see Beer 2019; Gordon and Perugini 2019). In this context, we would like to extend our thanks to Rory Cox for pointing out historical connections between medieval hospitals and religious and military institutions and protections (see e.g., Forey 1992). These connections could benefit from a more extensive treatment than can be attempted here.

And, if so, what light might this shine on the ethics of cultural heritage? This chapter considers these questions.

2. Sanctuary in the Ancient Levant and Greece

The entry for *sanctuary* in the Merriam-Webster dictionary comprises two parts: it defines sanctuary as a consecrated place, but also as a place of refuge and protection. This duality is key to understanding how sanctuary has historically operated as a form of wartime constraint. The word 'sanctuary' stems from the Latin word *sanctus*, meaning holy. Any site designated as a sanctuary was understood to be a sacred space, and any protections it conferred derived from this status. What protections were these? Historically, sanctuaries constituted inviolate spaces, such that it was illicit to transgress or harm them in any way, while they also conferred protections on those in their vicinity. Unpacking these characteristics is important if we wish to understand how the institution was administered and contested and how its violations were at times invoked as a cause for war. A brief historical survey of sanctuary will be helpful towards this end.

Biblical cities of refuge provide a convenient starting point for our historical survey, not least because of their enduring relevance for institutions of sanctuary today (Marfleet 2011; Rose 2012; Bagelman 2016; Houston 2016; Rabben 2016; Delgado 2018). Six such cities are mentioned in the Hebrew Bible (Old Testament) (Hassner 2008, 24–26; see also Burnside 2010; Marfleet 2011, 441–42). In these cities, protection was localised in the inner sanctum of a temple, where those who had committed manslaughter could seek shelter and escape from feuding associates. Murderers were exempted from this protection, however, and the decision to confer or withdraw sanctuary protection was ultimately the prerogative of the city's ruler (Hassner 2008, 26).[7] In cities of refuge, then, we see an attempt to articulate a judicial institution, administered by political authority, on the basis of divine sanctions (Siebold 1934, 534)—an articulation of spatial protection norms that were to recur over time in slightly different yet recognisable guises.

Moving into ancient Greece, we find that sanctuaries proliferate in the material and written records. Ritual sites are plentiful in pre-classical times (de Polignac 2009, 427–29; Kindt 2011; Renfrew 2011). However, it is through

---

[7] Note the relatively little discussed act of supplication that attends to sanctuary claims (Bagelman 2016, 78–85).

16 HERITAGE AND WAR

histories, plays, and other commentary that we can develop an appraisal for the norms that governed sanctuary protections (Pedley 2005, 25–26). What we have at hand is less a record of formal laws and rules and more one of shared customs.[8] These illuminate a distinctive stream of norms and practices that would remain influential into the Roman period and beyond.

Some features of Greek sanctuaries remained salient from the Archaic to the Roman period, including during the peak of classical sanctuaries in the eight to fourth centuries BCE (Pedley 2005, 22). Greek sanctuaries, like those in the Eastern Mediterranean, were associated with deities, whose presence pervaded all aspects of life (Mikalson 2009, 31–51).[9] While different *poleis* held different patron gods or goddesses in highest regard (Mikalson 2009, 160), religion united the Greek world and granted a sense of identity that distinguished Greeks from non-Greek barbarians (Cartledge 2002, 169–71). The importance of such shared norms and ideas is reflected in the abundance of sanctuaries throughout the Greek world, some of which developed into prominent temple complexes (Pedley 2005, 29–56; de Polignac 2009). The importance of sanctuaries is also seen in the wide range of functions they served, including as gathering places, boundary markers, and as sites where affiliations and identity were communicated, mediated, and affirmed (Bederman 2001, 251–52; Pedley 2005, 11–12, 29–38; Sekunda 2013, 211). And, most importantly for our purposes here, sanctuaries also served as *asylia*: inviolable places that are protected from seizure and plunder and which extend those protections to those who seek refuge within their boundaries.

Greek sanctuaries were limited in their spatial scope. The sacred sanctuary perimeter (*temenos*) was marked by a physical or notional wall (Pedley 2005, 58–60). Sanctuary operated strictly within these boundaries, and not beyond them. However, within this space, the protections were quite liberal: persons and objects were the property of the deity and protected by divine and public sanctions (Pedley 2005, 97; Mikalson 2009, 172–73). Divine protection was absolute, and protections appear to have been extended to slaves and murderers (Siebold 1934, 534; Pedley 2005, 97–98).[10] This is not to claim that

---

[8] This is familiar terrain to students of Greek war (Ober 1994, 12–13).

[9] 'Religion' and its implied antonym, 'secular', would probably have seemed alien to the ancient Greeks (Cartledge 2002, 167–69; Kindt 2009).

[10] The apparent disregard for the character or deeds of sanctuary-seekers contrasts with the more restricted protections that the biblical cities of refuge and later Roman and medieval sanctuaries provided. Whether non-Greeks were accorded similarly liberal protections is less clear. For example, *xenoi* were denied sanctuary in Delos (Hall 2007, 91). And while non-Greek sanctuaries were sometimes respected (Bederman 2001, 250), at other times they were wantonly destroyed and looted, as shown by the sacking of Etruscan temples by Dionysius I of Syracuse (van Wees 2004, 27). This points

sanctuaries were never violated, but rather, to note the normative scope of the protections they conferred, in times of peace and war. Indeed, the general belief in the inviolability of sanctuary was such that, rather than transgress it, generals and armies often resorted to the dubious practice of trickery and deception in a bid to lure their enemies out of sanctuaries where they received protection to open ground where they might be killed without angering the gods (Herodotus 1998, 379–80).

The connection between sanctuary and war can be further elaborated. The practice of sanctuary is widely referred to in classical Greek historical literature, and it occupied a prominent role in Thucydides' *History of the Peloponnesian War*. Thucydides (2009, 267–68) records that the first two articles of the doomed Peace of Nicias brokered between Athens and Sparta pertained directly to sanctuary temples, effectively guaranteeing their status and proscribing any attempts to inhibit their activities. Elsewhere, he singles out the revolt at Corcyra and the conduct of the Athenians at the Battle of Delion as evidence, not only of improper behaviour, but also of the fraying of standards of decency in Greek affairs. Both cases involved the violation of sanctuary norms. At Corcyra, Thucydides records, people were slain on temple altars (2009, 169), while the Athenians' conduct at Delion was marred by their decision to fortify an Apollonian temple in Boeotian territory (2009, 237–38). The provision of sanctuary, and its violation, was, it seems, a key part of the Greek understanding of warfare—and its limitation.

We therefore see how sanctuaries were governed by widely shared (if contested) norms about their appropriate military use in and outside of war.[11] Sanctuaries served a number of military functions, including the articulation of norms (Nevin 2017), provision of counsel (Bederman 2001, 251–52; Pedley 2005, 90; Rawlings 2007, 180–87), and deposition of booty (Pedley 2005, 11). Sanctuaries also made attractive military campsites and places of shelter in times of war. Consider, for example, Herodotus's (1998, 393–94) description of sanctuary stopovers by Athenian forces *en route* to and from Marathon in 490 BCE (Pedley 2005, 35). Such military use of sanctuaries was controversial (Krentz 2007, 162–63; Sekunda 2013, 211), as were measures taken to remove adversaries taking refuge in sanctuaries. Sanctuaries could therefore both support and frustrate military manoeuvres, and controversy about such uses

---

to a broader question about whose culture, religion, or person counts as worthy of protection—a question that looms large in the ethics of heritage and war (Brunstetter 2019).

[11] For discussion of shared norms of warfare, see Ober (1994), Bederman (2001, 249–50), van Wees (2004), and O'Driscoll (2015).

18   HERITAGE AND WAR

resonates with more recent debates about the permissible military uses and targeting of heritage and places of worship.

That violations of sanctuary received commentary and condemnation points to shared respect for the institution across ancient Greece; that such norms regulated the use of force in the absence of a centralised sovereign authority is notable. Indeed, it was sanctuaries that served as the basis for alliances and arbitration of disputes. Their centrality to the diplomatic and legal regulation of war in the classical Greek world is illustrated by amphictyonies, which were alliances formed around co-custodianship of shared religious sites (Bederman 2001, 168–71; Hall 2007, 99; Singor 2009, 588).[12] This speaks to the function of sanctuaries as places of arbitration, resonating with the more recent concept of neutral zones articulated in IHL.[13] At times, however, the violations of such sites gave grounds for war, as was the case with the so-called First Sacred War that was waged over access to the Delphic lands in 695–586 BCE (Ober 1994, 12; Bederman 2001, 169–70; van Wees 2004, 20).[14] Such instances may well be read as cynical exploitation of sanctuary norms for political purposes. But that such appeals were made at all reinforces the case that sanctuaries mattered greatly in the context of Greek war, and that these norms were founded on a shared understanding of what can and cannot be violated—a salient feature of heritage protections through the ages (Brunstetter 2019).

3. Sanctuary in the Roman World

As the Greek world was overtaken by the expanding Roman polity, Greek customs and beliefs were co-opted into republican and imperial Roman habits and practices.[15] Sanctuary customs were no exception: these were among the

---

[12] Worth noting here is that besides religious sanctuaries, there existed a parallel institution of asylum based in the town of Teos, which prefigures modern-day political asylum (Bederman 2001, 126, fn 233).

[13] See also footnote 5. We thank Rory Cox for this suggestion.

[14] Alleged sacrileges were invoked as causes for war on other occasions as well. Before the onset of the Peloponnesian War (431–404 BCE), Sparta invoked historical sacrilege as one reason for waging war on Athens (van Wees 2004, 20). And in 338 BCE, Philip II of Macedon cited the Persian ravaging of Athena's sanctuary in 480 BCE retrospectively as grounds for an eastern campaign of conquest (Finley 1966, 87–88)—an account that contrasts with the Persians' reputation for restraint and diplomatic acumen (Bederman 2001, 93–94).

[15] The appeal of Greek culture was not limited to Rome (e.g., Rasmussen 2011). Relatedly, the relationship between Roman and other religions was complex (Hingley 2011). Coexistence and syncretism found their counterpoints in the occasional violation and destruction of the holy sites or persons. Examples include Julius Caesar's campaigns in the Gaul in 58–51 BCE (Raaflaub 2021) and the

things that the Greeks 'were thought to know best' (Pedley 2005, 207). Roman literature is replete with references to respect for sanctuaries, with writers from Polybius (2010, 275) to Plutarch (2013, 42–43) acknowledging its force and heaping opprobrium upon anyone who would transgress it. The judgement Polybius reached in the case of the Aetolians is typical in this regard. Charging the Aetolians with the destruction of a sanctuary temple at Dodona, he (Polybius 2010, 275) finds that 'it makes no difference to Aetolians whether it is a time of peace or of war, since in either case they are prepared to violate the canons of normal human behaviour'.

The Romans were not always blameless themselves in this respect. There are several consequential episodes involving Roman violation of sanctuary norms. We might think here of the devastation of Corinth by the forces of Mummius in 146 BCE and the pillaging of temples by Sulla in the first century BCE (Pedley 2005, 206).[16] Livy (2017, 271–73) also furnishes a detailed narration of a particular instance of Roman misconduct towards sanctuary temples in the course of their dispute with the Locrians. Having gained military ascendancy over their foe, he writes, they violated their temples and even went to the extreme of looting their treasures. The men guilty of this misdeed should, Livy continues, have realised the error of their ways and sought to atone for it by making an expiatory offering—as Pyrrhus had once done. The fact that they did not do so would prove costly:

> Those who had violated the temple were subsequently seized by a spirit of madness causing them to turn on each other with the fury of enemies intent upon mutual annihilation. Soldiers and officers alike joined in the bloody riot and were killed or mutilated in large numbers. Such was the punishment which overtook those who exercised their military prerogatives of violence and rapine in places made sacred by religion. (Case 1915, 184)

What is noteworthy here is not just the fact of Rome's violation of sanctuary norms, or even Livy's apparent disapproval of this misdeed, but the belief that anyone who transgressed sacred spaces in this way would subsequently suffer the wrath of the gods. This highlights the extent to which the idea

---

destruction of Jerusalem's Second Temple by the forces of General Titus in 70 CE (Schiffman 2003; Goodman 2007, 7–27).

[16] Sanctuary troubled some Roman politicians. This was probably due to the provision of sanctuary to slaves, who did not enjoy even partial legal protections until the later imperial period (Siebold 1934, 535; Hunt 2018, 204–06).

of sanctuary was not only divinely charged, but also divinely backed and indeed enforced.

Generally speaking, then, Roman culture attached considerable weight to the importance of sanctuary. In some instances, Roman rectitude vis-à-vis sanctuary norms and other wartime constraints were cited as both a source and marker of Roman greatness. Certain Roman leaders even adopted sanctuaries to serve the needs of the imperial cult (Siebold 1934, 535; Bederman 2001, 262; Pedley 2005, 206–07). This continued until Rome converted into Christianity in the fourth century CE and pagan sites either fell into disuse or were destroyed, sometimes to supply material for Christian churches (Pedley 2005, 207–09).[17] But while the material fabric of sanctuaries was transformed, the institution itself continued in many ways unchallenged, and would become further elaborated on in the following centuries.

During this period, Rome's formal Christianisation promoted a persecuted minority religion into an influential social, moral, and political force. It also saw Roman law fused with Christian teachings, and this included laws and customs governing the provision of sanctuary (Marfleet 2011, 445). Church authorities became empowered as arbiters of sanctuary protections, which were now understood as the workings of God's mercy on earth. This was the view articulated by St Augustine (354–430 CE), who, in his *City of God*, reflected on the preservation of churches and sanctuary-seekers during the sack of Rome by the forces of Alaric in 410 CE (Reichberg, Syse, and Begby 2006c, 83–84).[18] This seemingly miraculous outcome Augustine attributed not to civilised restraint by the (Christianised) barbarians, but rather as the sign of God's power (Heather 2007, 227–32)—a sign of a protective power that also compared favourably against the sacking of sites in antiquity (Reichberg, Syse, and Begby 2006c, 83–84).

Augustine's account is not a balanced assessment of how sanctuary protections worked in antiquity. It gives too much weight to past violations and neglects how Christian sanctuaries were a development of the very traditions that he condemns. But for all its biases, Augustine's commentary matters because it demonstrates the considerable weight given to sanctuary as a protective institution that also served as an articulation of faith. And it marks a moment

---

[17] The reuse of sacred sites has many historical parallels (Baer 2014, 34–36), as seen for instance in the case of the Parthenon (Pedley 2005, 225–30).

[18] It is interesting to note the prominence that Augustine afforded sanctuary in his treatment of the sack of Rome, and intriguing that this aspect has not been subjected to any sustained analysis by just war scholars.

where the two streams of sanctuary traditions—biblical and classical—merge. It is this confluence and its flow into medieval Europe that we now examine.

4. Medieval Sanctuary

The Middle Ages might be called a golden age of sanctuary. As a protective institution, sanctuary not only retained but also expanded its status during this period. It did so as an outcome of the Christianisation of Europe and the frequent conflict and unrest.[19] For as Christianity spread, so did the landscape grow thick with Christian holy sites. And many of these served as sanctuaries. This included not only churches and cathedrals but also houses of clergy, monasteries, cemeteries, shrines, hospitals, and other sites associated with relics, miracles, or saints (Rosser 1996, 60–61; Lambert 2009, 121–22; Jordan 2010, 20; Marfleet 2011, 446).[20] Such sites probably numbered in the thousands in England alone (Rosser 1996, 70). Religious and political authorities both had enough to gain from the institution to sustain it even while they sought to regulate it through various means,[21] such as the establishment of chartered sanctuaries from the twelfth century onwards (Rosser 1996; Jordan 2010; Shoemaker 2011, 2013; McSheffrey 2017).[22] Such regulation and contestation over who controlled sanctuary lasted until the Reformation (Rosser 1996, 60; Shoemaker 2013, 24–26; McSheffrey 2017, 23–24). Until then,

---

[19] We do not cover sanctuary norms and practices in the Eastern Roman Empire (Macrides 1988; Iliya 2017), or the Islamic world (Hassner 2007, 2008, 28–29; Zaman 2016). Our focus is on Western Europe, particularly England. For recent historical overviews, see Jordan (2010), Shoemaker (2011, 2013), and McSheffrey (2017). Research on sanctuary elsewhere in Europe has received less attention, but see e.g., Jordan (2010, 18–20).

[20] There was a growing tendency over time to associate sanctuary protections with the sacred space itself, rather than with the persons administering them (Lambert 2009, 36–38; Shoemaker 2011, 17). It is interesting to also note how the very (living) bodies of the clergy were at times regarded as 'walking sanctuaries' (Rosser 1996, 62)—a belief that has some resonance with the use of human shields today.

[21] Sanctuaries allowed the clergy to live up to the ideals of Christian mercy and to administer fines for breaches. They also granted political authorities legitimacy and a means to funnel felons into trial or exile (Rosser 1996, 63–68; Hassner 2008, 27; Lambert 2009, 122; Jordan 2010, 30; Marfleet 2011, 446; Shoemaker 2011, 18–25; 2013, 18–20; McSheffrey 2017, 3). Sanctuary-seekers and local communities also had to gain from the protection that sanctuaries provided against blood feuds and draconian laws (Rosser 1996, 74–75).

[22] In contrast to the 'general' sanctuaries, chartered sanctuaries were few in number, vastly larger, and invariably adjacent to sites of religious, political, and mercantile power (Rosser 1996, 63; Marfleet 2011, 447; McSheffrey 2017, 10–11). And instead of the thirty to forty days of protection that was accorded by general sanctuaries (Lambert 2009, 121; Helmholz 2001, 18, 61), chartered sanctuaries could house fugitives for an unlimited period (Rosser 1996, 70; McSheffrey 2017, 8). But while these protections were enshrined in law, they were not reducible to it; rather, law reinforced and regulated what was, at its root, sacred property.

22 HERITAGE AND WAR

however, sanctuary remained a key institution for the administration of protection, including at times of conflict.

The expansion of sanctuary should not blind us to how its core functions remained stable throughout the Middle Ages. As in antiquity, sanctuaries were spaces of peace and protection from harm, including protection from seizure by political authorities (Helmholz 2001, 25–30; Lambert 2009, 121; McSheffrey 2017, 2). Indeed, sanctuary played a key role in the medieval system of justice, and its scope expanded over time to protect those who were suspected of crimes large and small—including public debtors and those who had committed manslaughter (Rosser 1996, 71–73; Marfleet 2011, 447; Shoemaker 2011, 48, 52).[23]

The long history of sanctuary protections and the political and clerical investment into them resulted in a melange of customs, laws, and proclamations that sought to establish, elaborate, reinforce, and control the institution.[24] Without going into these developments in great detail here, we can note how notions of spatial protection were inherited from Roman law and customary traditions and combined with Christian teachings of mercy (Shoemaker 2011, 29–43; 2013, 16; McSheffrey 2017, 6–7). For example, the fourth-century Theodosian Code declared clerical persons and Christian sites inviolable, a provision that was reinforced by Pope Leo I in the fifth century (Hassner 2008, 27; Marfleet 2011, 455; Shoemaker 2011, 29–55). Over the course of the first millennium, these provisions were further adapted to curb customary blood feuds in the Frankish and Anglo-Saxon kingdoms (Jurasinski 2010; Shoemaker 2011, 54–55, 78–92; Cox 2013, 1381; 2017a, 109). Such regulatory work continued well into the second millennium, often in response to power transitions (e.g., Shoemaker 2011; Jordan 2017; McSheffrey 2017). This enduring engagement with sanctuary suggests that not only were there notable political gains to be had from this institution, but also that protection remained sorely needed in a world of internecine strife.

This takes us to the function of sanctuaries in regulating medieval conflict. In the context of unrest, religious and political authorities—including military commanders—sought to shape and regulate sanctuary provisions to both

---

[23] Sanctuary remained closed off for others, such as heretics, excommuned Christians, and Jews (Hassner 2008, 27; Jordan 2010, 21–22; Shoemaker 2011, 22, 26, 35–37). By no coincidence, such exclusivity is also characteristic of how heritage protections have been administered and denied through history (Brunstetter 2019).

[24] This is nicely illustrated by Shoemaker (2011, 48), who describes an incident involving 'an English-born abbot, a Spanish-born bishop, and the Frankish emperor (through his scribes)…marshal[ling] passages of the Theodosian Code, Irish and Frankish canon law collections, and Visigothic and Salic royal law in a dispute over sanctuary law'.

limit and, at times, permit their infringements.[25] An attempt to do the former is seen in the Peace of God (*Pax Dei*) movement, which church authorities declared at Charroux in 989 to restrain the recurrent violence that was visited on sanctuaries and innocent persons (Contamine 1984, 270–72; Strickland 1996, 70–71; Reichberg, Syse, and Begby 2006a; Cox 2017a, 108–09). Both this movement and its corollary, the Truce of God (*Treuga Dei*), were prompted not least by the unrest that followed the fragmentation of the Frankish kingdom in the ninth century (Strickland 1996, 70–71). And while scholastics such as Gratian viewed the Truce of God as hopelessly idealistic (Shoemaker 2013, 23; Cox 2017a, 110–11; 2017b, 41), the protections accorded to and by sanctuaries continued to expand throughout the following centuries (Lambert 2009, 136–38; Jordan 2010, 29–30; Shoemaker 2013; McSheffrey 2017, 12–15).[26] Thus bolstered, sanctuary endured through the Middle Ages. But as we will see, there also were countervailing forces that sought to limit the protections that sanctuary accorded at times of war.

In light of continued violations, the reinforcement of sanctuary protections is unsurprising. The frequent (if perhaps dramatised) accounts of sanctuary violations we know from the church records show that respect for sanctuary was incomplete and inconsistent (Strickland 1996, 76–80).[27] And while military ordinances from the thirteenth and fourteenth centuries attempted to protect ecclesiastical property, they ultimately left the regulation of force to military commanders' discretion (Cox 2013, 1416). Moreover, some types of property, such as fortified churches, also appear to have been exempted from the protections.[28] More often than not, it was necessity and opportunity, as well as chivalric codes of honour, rather than the threat of eternal damnation

---

[25] Medieval society was a martial world where military codes of honour mattered, often more so than did civil and canon laws (Strickland 1996, 78–79). For if law is understood as requiring compliance and enforcement (Keen 1965; Strickland 1996, 34, 46, 53; Cox 2013, 1384), no 'law of war' is in sight prior to the fourteenth century (Keen 1965, 21; Strickland 1996, 32–33, 53). And while the teachings of the church held some sway over the waging of war (Strickland 1996, 68), the conduct of combatants was shaped more by practical necessity, opportunity for profit, and customary codes of honour and chivalry (Keen 1965, 19–22; Contamine 1984, 290–91; Strickland 1996, 48–51, 97). These also governed the conduct of soldiers towards sanctuaries (Strickland 1996, 76–80). But such codes did by no means provide complete protection, as they never have.

[26] Other examples of political dynamics shaping sanctuary include the growing regulation of sanctuary protections by the Angevin kings in the aftermath of the Norman Conquest (Shoemaker 2013) and royal sanctuary claims during the Wars of the Roses (McSheffrey 2017).

[27] A notable example of such violations includes the execution of Thomas Becket, Archbishop of Canterbury, by Henry II's followers in 1170 (Hassner 2008, 27).

[28] We see this in France, where fortified churches were denied sanctuary provisions (Jordan 2010, 21). Cox (2013, 1393) likewise suggests that churches used for military purposes may have been treated as lay property rather than as sanctified spaces. Given the temptations for militaries to target church property for loot and tactical advantages (Strickland 1996, 84–91), such redesignation of churches as military objects may have been quite frequent.

24 HERITAGE AND WAR

(which, in any case, could always be atoned for!) that weighed more in whether sanctuaries were respected or not (Strickland 1996, 78–91).

Given their vulnerability to ransacking and destruction in war, sanctuaries continued to furnish causes for defensive and offensive campaigns throughout the Middle Ages. Sometimes, past violations supplied justification for wars against fellow Christians, as seen in Henry I's invocation of sanctuary breaches in support of his invasion of Normandy in 1106 (Shoemaker 2013, 19). At other times, violations gave grounds for wars against non-Christians. This was seen at the outset of the Crusades (Contamine 1984, 277–79; Cox 2017a, 113), as is made plain by the speech that Pope Urban II gave at Clermont in 1095, in which he invoked the defence and cleansing of the Holy Land to mobilise Christendom for the First Crusade (Contamine 1984, 278; Reichberg, Syse, and Begby 2006b, 101–02). The Holy Land needed purging, and holy sites were key locations for such cleansing. Such justifications are clearly relevant when we consider the prospect of armed intervention for culture (Weiss and Connelly 2017; Frowe and Matravers 2019 and Chapter 1 in this volume), and describe the blurring of the lines between protection and aggression that reverberates through time into recent history (O'Driscoll 2008).[29]

Moving into the modern period, and after a long and, one might say, illustrious history, the institution of sanctuary began to decline. The notion of a sacred space immune to the reach of temporal rulers became increasingly tested over time. This was both due to growing disenchantment with the abuse of such protections by unscrupulous sanctuary-seekers and because the notion of immunity was increasingly at odds with claims to sovereign territorial authority (Shoemaker 2013, 22–25). These tensions came to a head during the political and religious ferment that characterised the Reformation. Sanctuary was subsequently abolished in England by royal decree in 1624 (Hassner 2008, 27; Marfleet 2011, 440), and the institution declined in Europe over the following centuries (Marfleet 2011, 447–52), ultimately to disappear from even the canon laws of the Catholic church in the 20th century (Shoemaker 2013, 26). Having endured for millennia, sanctuary therefore became all but erased from religious and secular laws in the space of a few centuries. This both explains and is reflected in its absence from the literatures on the law of armed conflict and the ethics of war.

This erasure of sanctuary of course did not, however, lead to its complete disappearance. It remains with us in two distinct but related ways. On the one

---

[29] It deserves mentioning that during these campaigns, holy sites and their occupants were subject to violent force (e.g., France 1994), under the notion of unrestrained or total war (*bellum romanum*) (Cox 2017a, 112–13).

hand, it has endured in a vestigial fashion in the outreach activities of churches and religious organisations. On the other, it went underground, transformed, fragmented, and rearticulated into a variety of protective institutions such as safe havens, political asylum, 'sanctuary cities', and—the focus of this volume—the development of legal and ethical protections for cultural heritage sites.[30] In relation to the latter, and as Frowe and Matravers discuss in their Introduction, IHL offers protections to cultural heritage sites and places of worship against the use of armed force, unless these sites are used for military functions. However, in contrast to how sanctuaries operated historically, these protections are solely focused on the property; its occupants are not accorded legal protection. In this regard, the legal protections granted to heritage sites are less elaborate than those that sanctuaries used to provide.[31] Despite this important difference between heritage laws and sanctuary norms and practices, however, the continuities and similarities are worth emphasising. It is revealing, in our view, that places of worship and of cultural heritage are both covered by the same legal provisions in IHL. This, to us, suggests conceptual and historical similarities and connections between sanctuary norms and practices, cultural heritage laws, and notions of spaces that deserve special protections, whether on religious or secular grounds. While the time of sanctuaries may have passed, key norms that governed sanctuaries historically have been transmitted to, and reproduced in, humanitarian laws, albeit in amended form.

5. Conclusion

In this chapter, we have raised the possibility that the contemporary legal protections granted to cultural heritage sites are a recent iteration of spatial protections with a deep history. Specifically, we have suggested that the contemporary move to grant legal and ethical protections to cultural heritage sites has a great deal in common with, and may even be partly traceable to, historical sanctuary practices. While our claim that there appears to be a connection between historical sanctuary practices and the current move to establish protections for cultural heritage sites requires more fine-grained

---

[30] Pioneering authorities on international law, such as Emer de Vattel (2008, 571–72; see also Christov 2017, 161), continued to call for the protection of holy sites from war. Vattel also called for the protection of monuments, palaces, and other sites of value, showing a broadening recognition for cultural heritage (Brunstetter 2019).

[31] As mentioned in footnote 6, the protections given to hospitals and those within them are more like historical sanctuary protections than those granted to cultural heritage sites.

26 HERITAGE AND WAR

empirical and contextual examination, certain areas of overlap are apparent. Most obviously, both trade in the idea that sites of cultural and/or religious significance, typically churches and temples, should be regarded as inviolable, and both proceed by endowing the places themselves, rather than the persons that inhabit them, with immunity from direct armed attack. Where, however, the legal protections accorded to heritage sites and objects are contingent on how the sites are being used, and by whom, these limitations did not consistently apply to sanctuary. Sanctuary was a sacred space and not to be marred by mortal conflict; to interfere with sanctuary was to commit sacrilege and invite public condemnation and divine retribution. Protecting the integrity of the space was paramount; it was often less important who the occupants were or what they did, as long as they did not breach this primary protection. The conclusion we draw from this is that sanctuary was a key institution whose role in granting spatial protections prefigured but also exceeded the scope of protections that are accorded to heritage sites and objects in IHL and just war theory today.

This leads to further questions. What, if any, direct points of contact are there between historical sanctuary practices and the advent of the idea that sites of cultural value should be protected in wartime? What form did sanctuary practices take in non-Western European contexts? Did they follow the same trajectories as the story essayed in this chapter, or do they tell a different tale? How was the practice of sanctuary engaged by the classic thinkers of the just war tradition, from Augustine to Francisco de Vitoria to Hugo Grotius to Michael Walzer? Why has the practice of sanctuary (and, more generally, spatial restrictions on the conduct of war) hitherto been overlooked by scholars of the law and ethics of war? What might be illuminated by factoring it into our accounts of the evolution of the just war tradition and the law of armed conflict? And would it be productive to devote some time and attention to thinking about how sanctuary practices might be re-calibrated and deployed to curb the destructiveness of contemporary warfare? These questions merit further elucidation and analysis. We hope they will attract some attention from scholars in the field in the coming years.

References

Baer, Marc David. 2014. 'History and Religious Conversion'. In *The Oxford Handbook of Religious Conversion*, edited by Lewis R. Rambo and Charles E. Farhadian, 26–47. New York: Oxford University Press. https://doi.org/10.1093/oxfordhb/9780195338522.001.0001.

Bagelman, Jennifer. 2016. *Sanctuary City: A Suspended State*. London: Palgrave Pivot. https://doi.org/10.1057/9781137480385.

Bederman, David J. 2001. *International Law in Antiquity*. Cambridge: Cambridge University Press. https://doi.org/10.1017/CBO9780511494130.

Beer, Yishai. 2019. 'Save the Injured—Don't Kill IHL: Rejecting Absolute Immunity for "Shielding Hospitals"'. *European Journal of International Law* 30 (2): 465–80. https://doi.org/10.1093/ejil/chz037.

Brunstetter, Daniel R. 2019. 'A Tale of Two Cities: The Just War Tradition and Cultural Heritage in Times of War'. *Global Intellectual History* 4 (4): 369–88. https://doi.org/10.1080/23801883.2018.1461024.

Burnside, Jonathan P. 2010. 'Exodus and Asylum: Uncovering the Relationship between Biblical Law and Narrative'. *Journal for the Study of the Old Testament* 34 (3): 243–66. https://doi.org/10.1177/0309089210363028.

Cartledge, Paul. 2002. *The Greeks: A Portrait of Self and Others*. Oxford: Oxford University Press.

Case, Shirley Jackson. 1915. 'Religion and War in the Graeco-Roman World'. *The American Journal of Theology* 19 (2): 179–99.

Christov, Theodore. 2017. 'Emer de Vattel (1714–1767)'. In *Just War Thinkers: From Cicero to the 21st Century*, edited by Daniel R. Brunstetter and Cian O'Driscoll, 156–67. Abingdon: Routledge. https://doi.org/10.4324/9781315650470.

Contamine, Philippe. 1984. *War in the Middle Ages*. Translated by Michael Jones. New York: Blackwell.

Cox, Rory. 2013. 'A Law of War? English Protection and Destruction of Ecclesiastical Property during the Fourteenth Century'. *The English Historical Review* 128 (535): 1381–417.

Cox, Rory. 2017a. 'The Ethics of War Up to Thomas Aquinas'. In *The Oxford Handbook of Ethics of War*, edited by Seth Lazar and Helen Frowe, 99–116. New York: Oxford University Press. https://doi.org/10.1093/oxfordhb/9780199943418.013.19.

Cox, Rory. 2017b. 'Gratian (circa 12th Century)'. In *Just War Thinkers: From Cicero to the 21st Century*, edited by Daniel R. Brunstetter and Cian O'Driscoll, 34–49. Abingdon: Routledge. https://doi.org/10.4324/9781315650470.

Delgado, Melvin. 2018. *Sanctuary Cities, Communities, and Organizations: A Nation at a Crossroads*. Oxford: Oxford University Press. http://ebookcentral.proquest.com/lib/anu/detail.action?docID=5493815.

Dudziak, Mary. 2012. *War Time: An Idea, Its History, Its Consequences*. Oxford: Oxford University Press.

Finley, Moses I. 1966. *The Ancient Greeks*. Harmondsworth: Penguin in association with Chatto & Windus.

Forey, Alan. 1992. *The Military Orders: From the Twelfth to the Early Fourteenth Centuries. New Studies in Medieval History*. Basingstoke: Macmillan.

France, John. 1994. *Victory in the East: A Military History of the First Crusade.* Cambridge: Cambridge University Press.

Frowe, Helen, and Derek Matravers. 2019. 'Conflict and Cultural Heritage: A Moral Analysis of the Challenges of Heritage Protection', J. Paul Getty Trust Occasional Papers in Cultural Heritage Policy, 3. Los Angeles, CA: Getty Publications. https://www.getty.edu/publications/occasional-papers-3/.

Goodman, Martin. 2007. *Rome and Jerusalem: The Clash of Ancient Civilizations.* New York: Alfred A. Knopf.

Gordon, Neve, and Nicola Perugini. 2019. ' "Hospital Shields" and the Limits of International Law'. *European Journal of International Law* 30 (2): 439–63. https://doi.org/10.1093/ejil/chz029.

Hall, Jonathan M. 2007. 'International Relations'. In *The Cambridge History of Greek and Roman Warfare: Volume 1: Greece, the Hellenistic World and the Rise of Rome*, edited by Philip Sabin, Hans van Wees, and Michael Whitby, 85–107. Cambridge: Cambridge University Press. https://doi.org/10.1017/CHOL9780521782739.

Hassner, Ron E. 2007. 'Islamic Just War Theory and the Challenge of Sacred Space in Iraq'. *Journal of International Affairs* 61 (1): 131–52.

Hassner, Ron E. 2008. ' "At the Horns of the Altar": Counterinsurgency and the Religious Roots of the Sanctuary Practice'. *Civil Wars* 10 (1): 22–39. https://doi.org/10.1080/13698240701835441.

Heather, Peter. 2007. 'The City of God'. In *The Fall of the Roman Empire: A New History of Rome and the Barbarians*, 192–250. New York: Oxford University Press. https://ebookcentral.proquest.com/lib/anu/detail.action?docID=991962.

Helmholz, Richard H. 2001. *The Ius Commune in England: Four Studies.* Oxford: Oxford University Press. http://ebookcentral.proquest.com/lib/anu/detail.action?docID=281397.

Herodotus. 1998. *The Histories.* Translated by Robin Waterfield. Oxford: Oxford University Press.

Hingley, Richard. 2011. 'Rome: Imperial and Local Religions'. In *The Oxford Handbook of the Archaeology of Ritual and Religion*, edited by Timothy Insoll, 745–57. Oxford: Oxford University Press.

Hom, Andrew R. 2020. *International Relations and the Problem of Time.* Oxford: Oxford University Press. https://global.oup.com/academic/product/international-relations-and-the-problem-of-time-9780198850014?cc=au&lang=en&#.

Houston, Serin D. 2016. 'Sacred Squatting: Seeking Sanctuary in Religious Spaces'. In *Migration, Squatting and Radical Autonomy*, edited by Pierpaolo Mudu and Sutapa Chattopadhyay, 183–88. London: Routledge.

Hunt, Peter. 2018. *Ancient Greek and Roman Slavery.* Hoboken: Wiley-Blackwell. https://ebookcentral.proquest.com/lib/anu/detail.action?docID=5047922.

Iliya, Nazarov. 2017. 'Foundations Right of Church Asylum in the Context of the Court of Patriarch in Byzantium'. *The Lawyer Quarterly* 7 (7): 60–64.

Johnson, James Turner. 1975. *Ideology, Reason, and the Limitation of War*. Princeton, NJ: Princeton University Press. https://press.princeton.edu/books/hardcover/9780691645018/ideology-reason-and-the-limitation-of-war.

Johnson, James Turner. 1981. *Just War Tradition and the Restraint of War*. Princeton, NJ: Princeton University Press. https://press.princeton.edu/books/paperback/9780691612225/just-war-tradition-and-the-restraint-of-war.

Johnson, James Turner. 1999. *Morality and Contemporary Warfare*. New Haven, CT: Yale University Press.

Jordan, William Chester. 2010. 'A Fresh Look at Medieval Sanctuary'. In *Law and the Illicit in Medieval Europe*, 17–32. Philadelphia, PA: University of Pennsylvania Press. https://doi.org/10.9783/9780812208856.17.

Jordan, William Chester. 2017. *From England to France: Felony and Exile in the High Middle Ages*. Princeton, NJ: Princeton University Press. https://doi.org/10.23943/princeton/9780691164953.001.0001.

Jurasinski, Stefan. 2010. 'Sanctuary, House-Peace, and the Traditionalism of Alfred's Laws'. *The Journal of Legal History* 31 (2): 129–47. https://doi.org/10.1080/01440365.2010.496928.

Keen, Maurice Hugh. 1965. *The Laws of War in the Late Middle Ages*. London: Routledge & K. Paul.

Kindt, Julia. 2009. 'Polis Religion—a Critical Appreciation'. *Kernos. Revue Internationale et Pluridisciplinaire de Religion Grecque Antique*, 22 (January): 9–34. https://doi.org/10.4000/kernos.1765.

Kindt, Julia. 2011. 'Ancient Greece'. In *The Oxford Handbook of the Archaeology of Ritual and Religion*, edited by Timothy Insoll, 696–709. Oxford: Oxford University Press.

Krentz, Peter. 2007. 'War'. In *The Cambridge History of Greek and Roman Warfare: Volume 1: Greece, the Hellenistic World and the Rise of Rome*, edited by Philip Sabin, Hans van Wees, and Michael Whitby, 147–85. Cambridge: Cambridge University Press. https://doi.org/10.1017/CHOL9780521782739.

Lambert, T. B. 2009. 'Spiritual Protection and Secular Power: The Evolution of Sanctuary and Legal Privilege in Ripon and Beverley, 900–1300'. In *Peace and Protection in the Middle Ages*, edited by T. B. Lambert and D. W. Rollason, 121–40. Toronto: Pontifical Institute of Medieval Studies.

Livy. 2017. *History of Rome*. Electronic resource. Translated by John Yardley. Cambridge, MA: Harvard University Press. https://virtual.anu.edu.au/login/?url=https://www.loebclassics.com/view/LCL233/2019/volume.xml.

Macrides, R. J. 1988. 'Killing, Asylum, and the Law in Byzantium'. *Speculum* 63 (3): 509–38. https://doi.org/10.2307/2852633.

Marfleet, Philip. 2011. 'Understanding "Sanctuary": Faith and Traditions of Asylum'. *Journal of Refugee Studies* 24 (3): 440–55. https://doi.org/10.1093/jrs/fer040.

McSheffrey, Shannon. 2017. *Seeking Sanctuary: Crime, Mercy, and Politics in English Courts, 1400–1550.* Oxford: Oxford University Press. https://doi.org/10.1093/oso/9780198798149.001.0001.

Mikalson, Jon D. 2009. *Ancient Greek Religion.* Chichester: Wiley-Blackwell. http://ebookcentral.proquest.com/lib/anu/detail.action?docID=819395.

Neff, Stephen C. 2005. *War and the Law of Nations: A General History.* Cambridge: Cambridge University Press.

Nevin, Sonya. 2017. *Military Leaders and Sacred Space in Classical Greek Warfare: Temples, Sanctuaries and Conflict in Antiquity.* London: I. B. Tauris. https://doi.org/10.5040/9781350987197.

Ober, Josiah. 1994. 'Classical Greek Times'. In *The Laws of War: Constraints on Warfare in the Western World,* edited by Michael Howard, George J. Andreopoulos, and Mark R. Shulman, 12–26. New Haven, CT: Yale University Press.

O'Driscoll, Cian. 2008. *The Renegotiation of the Just War Tradition and the Right to War in the Twenty-First Century.* New York: Palgrave Macmillan. https://doi.org/10.1057/9780230612037.

O'Driscoll, Cian. 2015. 'Rewriting the Just War Tradition: Just War in Classical Greek Political Thought and Practice'. *International Studies Quarterly* 59 (1): 1–10. https://doi.org/10.1111/isqu.12187.

Pedley, John Griffiths. 2005. *Sanctuaries and the Sacred in the Ancient Greek World.* Cambridge: Cambridge University Press.

Plutarch. 2013. *Plutarch: Demosthenes and Cicero.* Translated by Andrew Lintott. Oxford: Oxford University Press. https://doi.org/10.1093/acprof:oso/9780199699711.001.0001.

Polignac, François de. 2009. 'Sanctuaries and Festivals'. In *A Companion to Archaic Greece,* edited by Kurt A. Raaflaub and Hans van Wees, 427–43. Chichester: Wiley-Blackwell.

Polybius. 2010. *The Histories.* Translated by Robin Waterfield. Oxford: Oxford University Press.

Raaflaub, Kurt. 2021. 'Caesar and Genocide: Confronting the Dark Side of Caesar's Gallic Wars'. *New England Classical Journal* 48 (1): 54–80. https://doi.org/10.52284/NECJ/48.1/article/raaflaub.

Rabben, Linda. 2016. *Sanctuary and Asylum: A Social and Political History.* Seattle, WA: University of Washington Press.

Rasmussen, Tom. 2011. 'Etruscan Ritual and Religion'. In *The Oxford Handbook of the Archaeology of Ritual and Religion,* edited by Timothy Insoll, 710–20. Oxford: Oxford University Press.

Rawlings, Louis. 2007. *The Ancient Greeks at War*. Manchester: Manchester University Press. http://ebookcentral.proquest.com/lib/anu/detail.action?docID=1069474.

Reichberg, Gregory M., and Henrik Syse, eds. 2014. *Religion, War, and Ethics: A Sourcebook of Textual Traditions*. With the assistance of Nicole M. Hartwell. Cambridge: Cambridge University Press. https://doi.org/10.1017/CBO9780511979651.

Reichberg, Gregory M., Henrik Syse, and Endre Begby, eds. 2006a. 'Medieval Peace Movements (975–1123): Religious Limitations on Warfare'. In *The Ethics of War: Classic and Contemporary Readings*, 93–97. London: Blackwell.

Reichberg, Gregory M., Henrik Syse, and Endre Begby, eds. 2006b. 'Speech at Clermont, 27 November 1095 AD'. In *The Ethics of War: Classic and Contemporary Readings*, 101–2. London: Blackwell.

Reichberg, Gregory M., Henrik Syse, and Endre Begby, eds. 2006c. *The Ethics of War: Classic and Contemporary Readings*. London: Blackwell.

Renfrew, Colin. 2011. 'Prehistoric Religions in the Aegean'. In *The Oxford Handbook of the Archaeology of Ritual and Religion*, edited by Timothy Insoll, 681–94. Oxford: Oxford University Press.

Rose, Ananda. 2012. 'Sanctuary Old and New: The Biblical Tradition of Radical Hospitality'. In *Showdown in the Sonoran Desert*. New York: Oxford University Press. https://doi.org/10.1093/acprof:oso/9780199890934.003.0003.

Rosser, Gervase. 1996. 'Sanctuary and Social Negotiation in Medieval England'. In *The Cloister and the World*, edited by John Blair and Brian Golding, 57–82. Oxford: Oxford University Press. https://oxford.universitypressscholarship.com/10.1093/acprof:oso/9780198204404.001.0001/acprof-9780198204404-chapter-4.

Russell, Frederick Hooker. 1977. *The Just War in the Middle Ages*. Cambridge: Cambridge University Press.

Schiffman, Lawrence H. 2003. 'Jerusalem: Twice Destroyed, Twice Rebuilt'. *The Classical World* 97 (1): 31–40. https://doi.org/10.2307/4352823.

Schmitt, Michael N., and John J. Merriam. 2015. 'The Tyranny of Context: Israeli Targeting Practices in Legal Perspective'. *University of Pennsylvania Journal of International Law* 37 (1): 53–139.

Sekunda, Nicholas V. 2013. 'War and Society in Greece'. In *The Oxford Handbook of Warfare in the Classical World*, edited by Brian Campbell and Lawrence A. Tritle, 198–215. Oxford: Oxford University Press. https://doi.org/10.1093/oxfordhb/9780195304657.013.0010.

Shoemaker, Karl. 2011. *Sanctuary and Crime in the Middle Ages, 400–1500*. Bronx: Fordham University Press. http://ebookcentral.proquest.com/lib/anu/detail.action?docID=3239565.

Shoemaker, Karl. 2013. 'Sanctuary for Crime in the Early Common Law'. In *Sanctuary Practices in International Perspectives: Migration, Citizenship, and Social Movements*, edited by Randy K. Lippert and Sean Rehaag, 15–27. Abingdon: Routledge. https://ebookcentral.proquest.com/lib/anu/detail.action?docID=1047031.

Siebold, Martin. 1934. 'Sanctuary'. In *Encyclopaedia of the Social Sciences, Vol XIII*, edited by Edwin R. Seligman and Alvin Johnson, 534–37. New York: Macmillan. http://archive.org/details/encyclopaediaoft030465mbp.

Singor, Henk. 2009. 'War and International Relations'. In *A Companion to Archaic Greece*, edited by Kurt A. Raaflaub and Hans van Wees, 587–603. Chichester: Wiley-Blackwell.

Strickland, Matthew. 1996. *War and Chivalry: The Conduct and Perception of War in England and Normandy, 1066–1217*. Cambridge: Cambridge University Press.

Taie, Khalid al-. 2015. 'Iraq Churches, Mosques under ISIL Attack'. *Mawtani*. 13 February 2015. https://web.archive.org/web/20150219092526/http:/mawtani.al-shorfa.com/en_GB/articles/iii/features/2015/02/13/feature-01#.

Thaler, Mathias. 2014. 'On Time in Just War Theory: From "Chronos" to "Kairos"'. *Polity* 46 (4): 520–46.

Thucydides. 2009. *The Peloponnesian War*. Translated by Martin Hammond. Oxford: Oxford University Press.

Vattel, Emer de. 2008. 'Book III: Of War'. In *The Law of Nations*, edited by Béla Kapossy and Richard Whatmore, 469–649. Indianapolis, IN: Liberty Fund. http://ebookcentral.proquest.com/lib/anu/detail.action?docID=3327319.

Wees, Hans van. 2004. *Greek Warfare: Myths and Realities*. London: Duckworth.

Weiss, Thomas G., and Nina Connelly. 2017. 'Cultural Cleansing and Mass Atrocities', J. Paul Getty Trust Occasional Papers in Cultural Heritage Policy, 1. Los Angeles, CA: Getty Publications. https://www.getty.edu/publications/pdfs/CulturalCleansing_Weiss_Connelly.pdf.

Zaman, Tahir. 2016. 'The Noble Sanctuary: Islamic Traditions of Refuge and Sanctuary'. In *Islamic Traditions of Refuge in the Crises of Iraq and Syria. Religion and Global Migrations*, 19–42. New York: Palgrave Macmillan. https://doi.org/10.1057/9781137550064_2.

3
Conflicts in Heritage Protection

Helen Frowe and Derek Matravers

1. Introduction

In our Introduction to this volume, we described the Inseparability Thesis. According to this thesis, heritage and people are inseparable, such that conflicts between protecting heritage and protecting people are impossible. In this chapter, we canvass some of the ways in which, contrary to the Inseparability Thesis, protecting heritage can conflict with protecting people, including protecting them from threats to life and limb. We do not argue here for a particular resolution of these conflicts; our goal is to make the case that the Inseparability Thesis, and its sway over the protection of heritage in war, must be rejected if we are to make progress on these difficult ethical issues. We also aim to motivate the case for greater philosophical engagement with these issues by identifying some of the difficult philosophical questions raised by the moral status of heritage.

Conflicts between protecting heritage and protecting people most obviously arise when there is a scarcity of relevant resources. In these cases, using resources (such as money, equipment, time, space, or personnel) to protect heritage can mean failing to protect something else of value, including people's lives. For example, some US military commanders argued that they failed to protect the Iraq Museum from looters in 2003 because they could not spare the personnel from other missions (Bowker, Goodall, & Haciski 2016; Peterson 2007: 182). This scarce-resources type of conflict has been the near-exclusive focus of the 'stones versus lives' debate described in the Introduction. Clearly, it raises important philosophical questions, some of which are familiar from debates about the value and distribution of public goods (Cullity 2008; Munoz-Darde 2013).

Less obviously, but no less importantly, conflicts between people and heritage also arise when we cannot protect heritage without harming, or risking harming, people. Protecting heritage in war can require ordering combatants

---

Helen Frowe and Derek Matravers, *Conflicts in Heritage Protection* In: *Heritage and War: Ethical Issues.*
Edited by: William Bülow, Helen Frowe, Derek Matravers, and Joshua Lewis Thomas, Oxford University Press.
© Helen Frowe and Derek Matravers 2023. DOI: 10.1093/oso/9780192862648.003.0003

34 HERITAGE AND WAR

to both incur risks of serious harm to themselves and impose risks of serious harm on others. Because the Inseparability Thesis dominates the discourse in heritage protection and has, in particular, shaped the narrative around protecting heritage in war, scant attention has been paid to these conflicts. It is these that are our focus here.

We begin, in Section 2, with a brief summary of current legal obligations with respect to the treatment of heritage in war zones, which reveals some important theoretical lacunae. As we argue, the most important legal convention on protecting heritage in war—the 1954 Hague Convention on the Protection of Cultural Property in Times of Armed Conflict (henceforth, the Hague Convention)—both acknowledges conflicts between people and heritage and requires that military leaders navigate these conflicts. In Section 3, we identify some ways in which protecting heritage can require combatants to incur risks of harm to themselves. In Section 4, we identify some ways in which protecting heritage can require imposing risks of harm on civilians. In Section 5, we consider what might motivate the popularity of the Inseparability Thesis. We suggest that adopting a value pluralist approach can allow us to acknowledge conflicts between people and heritage without thereby committing us to the view that heritage protection is impermissible. In Section 6, we reject what might seem like some easy ways to avoid these conflicts—namely, by deeming it generally impermissible to impose risks on persons for the sake of heritage, or pointing to existing legal frameworks about protecting civilians in war. Section 7 concludes.

2. The Hague Convention

The Hague Convention, along with its two Additional Protocols, sets out the obligations of state parties with respect to (tangible) cultural heritage in war. The Convention defines cultural heritage as encompassing,

> movable or immovable property of great importance to the cultural heritage of every people, such as monuments of architecture, art or history, whether religious or secular; archaeological sites; groups of buildings which, as a whole, are of historical or artistic interest; works of art; manuscripts, books and other objects of artistic, historical or archaeological interest; as well as scientific collections and important collections of books or archives or of reproductions of the property defined above.
>
> (1954 HC: Art. 1.a)

The obligations conferred on states include taking protective measures towards their own heritage sites and artefacts, protecting heritage in occupied territory, and limiting the use and damaging of heritage sites by their combatants. Combatants may *intentionally damage* cultural heritage on the grounds of imperative military necessity—that is, in pursuit of military advantage— only when the heritage has, by its function, been turned into a military objective, and there is no feasible alternative for obtaining a similar military advantage (1954 HC 2nd Prot., Art. 6.a). So, for example, it is permissible to target an ancient fort that is currently being used as a military base if there is no feasible alternative.

Combatants may *make use of* heritage, in ways likely to expose it to damage, again on the grounds of imperative military necessity, only when there is no feasible alternative for obtaining a similar military advantage, and only if the site has not been awarded 'enhanced protection' under the Convention (1954 HC 2nd Prot., Art. 6.b). So, for example, it is permissible to use an ancient fort as a military base, even if this is likely to result in its being damaged, if these conditions are met.

Finally, combatants must take all feasible precautions to avoid *collaterally damaging* cultural property, and any collateral damage caused must not be excessive to the concrete and direct military advantage anticipated (1954 HC 2nd Prot., Art. 7.c). They must also, to the maximum extent feasible, refrain from placing military objectives near cultural property (1954 HC 2nd Prot., Art. 8.b).

In the Hague Convention, then, *military necessity* refers to military advantage—that is, to the contribution that an offensive is expected to make to winning the war.[1] An offensive is a matter of imperative military necessity if its success will substantially increase the chances of victory. Somewhat confusingly, the use of *feasibility* in the Convention refers to what philosophers who work on the ethics of war usually call 'necessity'. A course of action satisfies the necessity (or feasibility) condition when there is no less harmful means of achieving the relevant good. This notion of necessity (or feasibility), then, is essentially comparative. It requires ranking available means of achieving a goal in terms of the goods and harms that are expected to result from each course of action.

---

[1] In international law more generally, 'military necessity' is used to refer both to securing a military advantage and to constraints on the means of waging war. For discussion of this, and a reading of the Hague Convention supportive of our interpretation here, see Forrest (2007: 212–213).

36   HERITAGE AND WAR

By way of illustration, imagine that two courses of action, Offensive A and Offensive B, have roughly equal chances of achieving the same military advantage, and that there are no other courses of action that can achieve that advantage. Offensive A is very likely to kill two civilians, and Offensive B is very likely to kill one civilian. Assessing necessity in this case is straightforward, because the death of two civilians is clearly morally worse than the death of one. Taking the risk of killing the additional civilian is thus unnecessary, given the availability of Offensive B. This is true even if killing two civilians is not excessive, given the anticipated military advantage. And, since A and B are the only available means of achieving the advantage, and B is the least harmful of those means, then there is no feasible alternative to B for achieving the advantage. Risking the one civilian's life thus satisfies the necessity condition.

It is much less obvious how one ought to incorporate damage to heritage sites into necessity (or feasibility) calculations. Imagine that Offensive B is very likely not only to kill one civilian but also to damage some beautiful ancient ruins, whereas Offensive A avoids the ruins entirely but, recall, is very likely to kill two civilians. Is risking the death of the additional civilian necessary? Is Offensive A a feasible alternative to Offensive B? What if the increased harm is not to civilians, but rather to one's combatants? How much costlier or riskier must the alternatives be, in order to render those alternatives infeasible and the damage to heritage necessary? The Hague Convention provides no guidance on these matters.[2]

Similar problems arise with respect to the notion of excessive damage (or *proportionality*, as it is more widely known). The Convention requires that combatants refrain from collaterally damaging protected cultural heritage only if that damage "would be excessive in relation to the concrete and direct military advantage anticipated" (1954 HC 2nd Prot., Art. 7.c). But how are combatants to judge whether damage to heritage is excessive compared to a military advantage? The UNESCO Military Manual suggests that "the measure of incidental damage to be caused to cultural property is a question not just of cubic metres but also, crucially, of the cultural value of the object, building or site likely to be harmed" (UNESCO Military Manual: 34). This is surely right. But knowing how to evaluate damage to heritage—itself no easy task—is only half of the problem. The other half is knowing how that damage compares to (a) the value of the military advantage, and (b) the harms of alternative means of achieving that advantage. In our scenario above, for

---

[2] For legal discussion of this and other shortcomings, see Hladík (1999).

example, knowing that the ruins have very significant cultural value does not, in itself, tell us whether we ought to choose Offensive A or Offensive B, or abandon the advantage altogether.[3]

To answer that question, we need both an account of the value of heritage and an account of when we may risk harm to other things of value, including human beings, in order to protect heritage. Answering these questions is a task for philosophers. Yet, surprisingly little philosophical work has been done on the value of heritage, particularly on the questions of its comparative value.[4] And, despite the significant philosophical interest in the ethics of war in recent years, the status of heritage in war has attracted little attention.[5]

3. Risks to Combatants

Combatants can incur risk to themselves in the course of trying to save heritage from some other threat. For example, the Hague Convention requires occupying states to preserve cultural heritage in territory they control, should national authorities be unable to do so (1954 HC: Art. 5.3). The retrieval of Jewish archival material from the basement of the Iraqi Intelligence headquarters by US combatants in 2003 exemplifies combatants incurring this kind of risk. The headquarters was located next to unexploded artillery and was unstable after being bombed. The bombing also damaged the building's water system, causing the basement to flood with raw sewage.[6] Retrieving the material thus exposed the combatants to a range of threats; one later described

---

[3] In *The Thieves of Baghdad*, Matthew Bogdanos describes how, when some American combatants came under fire from Iraqi combatants stationed with the Children's Museum in Baghdad in 2003, a commanding officer "made the tactically wrong but culturally brilliant decision to pull back those tanks from endangering the museum. This was the only way to avoid the [...] choice between endangering his men and destroying the institution." (See Bogdanos 2005: 205–206.)

[4] Although see Hatala Matthes (2013: 61), Korsmeyer (2019), and Munoz-Darde (2013). For economic analysis of the value of heritage, see Serageldin (1999).

[5] Exceptions include Bülow (2020), Frowe and Matravers (2019), Frowe and Matravers (in progress), Hatala Matthes (2018), and Thompson (2007). There is also some discussion in the historical canon of just war literature (e.g. de Vattel's *Law of Nations* 2015, Book 3, ch.9 and Grotius's 2005 *Rights of War and Peace*).

[6] For a detailed account of the retrieval, see Rich Tenorio, 'Who should keep Iraqi Jewry's archives, saved from Saddam, now on tour in US?' *Times of Israel* 6 January 2016, available at https://www.timesofisrael.com/who-should-keep-iraqi-jewrys-archives-saved-from-saddam-now-on-tour-in-us/. See also e.g. Daniel Sugarman, 'How I became an artefact: the story of Iraq's Jewish Archive and its restoration,' *The Jewish Chronicle*, 4 January 2019, available at https://www.thejc.com/news/news-features/how-i-became-an-artefact-the-story-of-iraq-s-jewish-archive-and-its-restoration-1.478080. Note that in 2003 the United States was not a party to the Hague Convention (although, arguably, obligations to protect cultural property have achieved the status of customary law). See Sandholtz (2005: 222).

becoming "as sick as I've ever been in my life" after being splashed by the contaminated water during the operation.[7]

Combatants can also be required to guard cultural buildings and archaeological sites against looting or attack as part of their obligation to "prohibit, prevent, and, if necessary, put a stop to any form of theft, pillage or misappropriation of, and any acts of vandalism directed against, cultural property" (1954 HC: Art. 4.3; 1954 HC 2nd Prot., Art. 9). As others have pointed out, it is unclear precisely what this obligation to protect cultural heritage entails, including what combatants are permitted to do to those threatening heritage sites (Bowker, Goodall, & Haciski 2016; Peterson 2007: 181–182). Moreover, these obligations are not subject to exemptions on the basis of military necessity.[8]

Combatants can also incur risk to themselves in order to refrain from damaging heritage. As we outlined above, the Hague Convention requires that combatants take "all feasible precautions in the choice of means and methods of attack with a view to avoiding, and in any event minimising, incidental damage to cultural property" (1954 HC 2nd Prot., Art. 7.b). The targeting of an insurgency headquarters in Mali in 2013 exemplifies combatants' incurring this kind of risk. The insurgents had set up their headquarters in a house adjacent to the Mosque of Djinguereber, a world heritage site in Timbuktu. Government forces initially planned to use an airstrike to target the insurgents, but decided that this posed too high a risk of collaterally damaging the mosque. By employing ground artillery instead, they destroyed the house without damaging the mosque.

The case is lauded as an exemplar of cultural property protection in action. UNESCO describe it as an instance of 'best practice' (O'Keefe, Péron, Musayev, & Ferrari 2016: 36). But, as Laurie Rush points out, "clearly this success placed the artillery crew at much greater risk" (Rush 2017: 32). In general, Rush notes, combatants "may need to assume additional risk in order to remove a target that has been deliberately placed near a cultural site or feature" (Rush 2017: 32). As we saw above, the Hague Convention is vague about when the risks of a course of action render it infeasible. But the Convention is clearly intended to compel states to protect heritage even when doing so is somewhat costly to their mission or their troops, or both. A Convention that required states to protect heritage only when doing so imposes no such costs would be toothless.

---

[7] Richard Gonzales, cited in Rich Tenorio, 'Who should keep Iraqi Jewry's archives'.
[8] See https://en.unesco.org/protecting-heritage/faq, Q. 4.

The expectation that combatants should incur these increased risks is iterated in the UNESCO Field Manual, which enjoins combatants to avoid damaging heritage by employing "low-altitude aerial raids by daylight, assault at close quarters instead of bombardment, the use of snipers rather than explosives or automatic-weapon fire to neutralise enemy combatants, and so on, where this does not pose an *unacceptable* risk of military casualties" (UNESCO Military Manual: 35–36, emphasis added). The wording—and indeed the instruction—grants that *some* increased risk to combatants' safety is acceptable for the sake of decreasing the risk of damaging heritage (and, again, nothing is said about how much risk is unacceptable).

These demands are a striking contrast to the view expressed in President Eisenhower's *Letter on Historical Monuments*, which not only explicitly recognises wartime conflicts between people and heritage but also orders that in cases of forced choices between destroying famous buildings and sacrificing combatants, "our men's lives count infinitely more, and the buildings must go" (Eisenhower 1943). David Brown and Andrew Shortland cite an operational Army commander as asking how many lives he is expected to risk to guard "a pile of stones" (Brown and Shortland 2019: 15). As Brown and Shortland emphasise, "this is not a casual statement; it is a very real problem that the Armed Forces must face. The ratification of the Hague Convention by the UK will result in the military being put into harm's way to protect sites" (Brown and Shortland 2019: 15).

The closest the Convention comes to acknowledging these concerns is a requirement that certain decisions to damage cultural heritage may be taken only by senior officers.[9] But this problem is not solved by pushing the judgement up the ranks. Emma Cunliffe, Paul Fox, and Peter Stone emphasise that combatants are unable to make decisions about the value of heritage, hence the provision of lists of prioritised heritage sites by organisations such as the Blue Shield, Heritage For Peace, and UNESCO (Cunliffe, Fox, & Stone 2018: 13; Stone 2013). But although archaeologists and other heritage professionals are able to rank heritage sites against each other, along at least some dimensions of importance, they are not in a position to rank heritage sites against risks to human life and other values at stake in war. Yet this is the comparison demanded by both necessity and proportionality judgements concerning the use of force.

---

[9] The Hague Convention stipulates that the decisions to damage a cultural site under special protection may be taken only by a division commander, or higher (1954 HC: Art. 11.2). Decisions to damage sites under enhanced protection must, if time permits, be taken 'at the highest level of command' (1954 HC 2nd Prot., Art. 13.c.ii).

40 HERITAGE AND WAR

Perhaps one of the starkest illustrations of how protecting heritage can conflict with protecting life comes, ironically, from two staunch proponents of the Inseparability Thesis. Weiss and Connelly argue that states ought to deploy combatants to defend heritage sites from attack, including waging interventionist wars solely for the protection of heritage. They argue that the Responsibility to Protect (R2P) legislation—the political framework outlining states' responsibilities to prevent genocide and crimes against humanity—should be extended to include a responsibility to militarily defend heritage "for its own sake" (Weiss and Connelly 2019. See also Cuno 2016; Bowker, Goodall, & Haciski 2016; Lamb 2016).

Such interventions would involve combatants incurring risks of harm to themselves in order to protect heritage. They would also impose risks of harm on civilians. As Paolo Foradori and Paolo Rosa argue, such intervention should not be regarded as "an easy, minor military operation of 'light peacekeeping' […] on the contrary, it will require very robust, properly trained and substantial forces with heavy arms and equipment" (Foradori & Rosa 2017: 157). Intervention on such a scale almost inevitably poses risks of collateral harm to civilians, both directly and by risking escalation to a wider war. Weiss and Connelly's interventionist proposal also directly pits the lives of the enemy fighters against the value of the heritage, recommending that these fighters be intentionally harmed—most likely killed—in order to save the heritage. And yet they insist that the choice between heritage and human life is a "false choice" (Weiss & Connelly 2017: 6; see also Weiss & Connelly 2019: 13), and that any attempt to distinguish between protecting people and protecting heritage is "a fool's errand" (Weiss & Connelly 2019: 13; see also Weiss 2020).

No modern war has (as far as we know) been fought solely in order to protect tangible heritage. Given states' general reluctance to wage interventionist wars, it seems unlikely that there will be much enthusiasm for the proposed expansion of R2P, or at least for the idea of heritage protection as a just cause for war. But this does not mean that we can set aside the permissibility of forcefully defending heritage. Turkey threatened to use force in defence of the tomb of Suleyman Shah in Syria in 2015 before sending almost six hundred troops to retrieve his remains. Combatants guarding the tomb were besieged by ISIS fighters for several months before the retrieval operation; one Turkish soldier was accidentally killed during the retrieval mission itself (Arsu 2015). The United Nations resolution regarding peacekeeping forces in Mali in 2013 seemingly sanctioned the use of deadly force in defence of heritage as part of a broader peacekeeping mandate.[10] And, as above, there is currently little guidance on whether combatants guarding heritage, such as museums or archaeological sites, in occupied territory are legally permitted to use force (other than in self-defence) as part of discharging these duties. Clearly, using force against people to defend heritage constitutes a conflict between protecting people and protecting heritage.

4. Risks to Civilians

These cases primarily exemplify conflicts between combatants and heritage. Although the Inseparability Thesis ostensibly makes a general claim about the inseparability of persons and heritage, its proponents' writings often imply that only civilians are (relevant) persons. For example, the UK Blue Shield insists that the Hague Convention, "does not place cultural property above *people*, as it exists within a wider framework of laws designed to protect *civilians* and their property in a conflict situation."[11] Weiss and Connelly similarly assume that a hierarchy between persons and heritage would be a hierarchy of "civilians versus culture" (Weiss & Connelly 2019: 13).

As our argument in Section 3 attests, conflicts between combatants and heritage are morally significant, and demand proper moral analysis. But even restricted to civilians, the Inseparability Thesis is false, as shown by our imagined scenario above. In our scenario, one can avoid harm to the ruins by increasing the risks of harm to civilians. And, as we also saw above, waging a military intervention to defend heritage would endanger both combatants' and civilians' lives. Such conflicts are very far from the conceptual or operational impossibilities that proponents of the Inseparability Thesis allege (Weiss and Connelly 2019: 2).

Civilians also cause damage to heritage sites in bids to secure safety, shelter, and income. Syria's city of Serjilla, for example, has been adapted, and in part

---

[10] 'Seemingly,' because it is not entirely clear whether the resolution's sanctioning of 'all necessary means' in fact extends to the protection of heritage. Laurie Rush, for example, cites this as the first instance of the UN's sanctioning lethal force in defence of heritage (Rush 2017: 32). The UN Report on the mission in Mali in December 2014 says that combatants may use deadly force in self-defence, both to protect civilians from physical harm and whilst implementing 'stabilization' tasks (United Nations Security Council 2016). Since the entire mission is described as a stabilisation mission, this implies that it sanctions force to defend heritage. Kirsten Schmalenbach concurs, but also notes that the rules of engagement for the mission are not publicly available (Schmalenbach 2016: 32).

[11] See https://ukblueshield.org.uk (emphasis added).

42   HERITAGE AND WAR

demolished, by refugees looking for homes and farmland, a process described by one news outlet as "salvation [...] at the expense of Syria's cultural legacy" (al-Ibrahim & Fayyad 2015). Emma Cunliffe, Nibal Muhesen, and Marina Lostal describe how civilians "desperate for shelter... have reoccupied ancient sites and even underground tombs and adapted them to their life. This has resulted in new buildings that violate the integrity of the site, the removal of archaeological material for new buildings, rubbish dumps, looting, and the targeting of sites" (Cunliffe, Muhesen, & Lostal 2016).[12] And, of course, there is widespread excavating of archaeological sites by civilians deprived, often by war, of other sources of income to meet their basic needs (these people are often described as 'subsistence diggers') (see Heath 1973; Lange 1976; Matsuda 1998; O'Reilly 2007: 14). At least some such excavations are harmful to the extracted artefacts themselves, damage the wider site, and compromise the site's integrity and value (and, moreover, some such excavations are themselves part of a group's heritage) (see Hart & Chilton 2015). Again, protecting people, including people's lives, conflicts with protecting heritage in these cases. If someone is looting to survive, preventing that looting threatens her survival.

The reconstruction of the Nahr al-Bared refugee camp in Lebanon in 2009 also threw the possibility of conflict between civilians and heritage into stark relief. The original camp, constructed in 1949 for Palestinian refugees, had inadvertently been built on the undiscovered remains of what is now thought to be the Roman town of Orthosia. The refugee camp was destroyed in fighting between the Lebanese army and Fatah al-Islam in 2007. The remains of Orthosia, which is thought to date from the 3rd millennium BC, were discovered when the rubble of the site began to be cleared to facilitate the camp's reconstruction. Joanne Farchack Bajjaly describes how, upon the discovery of the ruins, archaeologists demanded "the immediate cessation of construction work and camp clearances [and] suggested that the authorities change the camp's location, moving it away from the archaeological tell, instead rebuilding the houses in nearby agricultural fields" (Farchack Bajjaly 2011: 186). Residents of the camp were strongly opposed to being relocated; media reports pointed to the archaeologists' suggestion of moving the camp as evidence of "the precedence shards of pottery take over human rights" (Farchack Bajjaly 2011: 187). The Lebanese Council of Ministers eventually rejected a

---

[12] The authors claim that "the damage caused by the re-occupation of such sites by civilians... are crimes" but that it is "questionable" whether they should be prosecuted (Cunliffe, Muhesen, & Lostal 2016: 16).

legal challenge to the decision to rebuild the camp in its original position, citing the priority of the refugees' rights, and the ruins were filled with concrete so that the camp could be rebuilt.

5. Inseparability, Revisited

Given the ubiquity of conflicts between protecting people and protecting heritage, why is the Inseparability Thesis so widely endorsed by heritage organisations and professionals? At the very least, the conflicts arising from scarce resources seem to be obvious. Indeed, these conflicts are a familiar part of both private and public life. They are an inevitable result of the fact that human beings have finite resources, including money, time, energy and space, and a plurality of interests—that is, that a range of goods, such as education, shelter, healthcare, culture, community, creativity, and security are a valuable part of living a good life. These goods are not simply interchangeable: one cannot, for example (fully) compensate for poor healthcare with excellent education. Rather, each contributes to a good life in a distinctive way. Living a good life is not about maximising any particular value, but rather having access to an adequate amount of each.

Since promoting and protecting each of these values makes demands on finite resources, we, and our governments, routinely trade them off against each other. Heritage is no exception; on the contrary, it is just another good in the mix. When protecting heritage demands a scarce resource, choosing to protect the heritage can mean failing to protect some other good, including allowing people to die. If we spend ten million dollars on an art gallery, or restoring a shipwreck, or funding public statues, then we cannot spend that money on cancer treatments that would save lives. It is hard to see how anyone could deny the existence of these conflicts. They are what motivate the complaints about, for example, spending money on restoring the Bamiyan Buddhas instead of providing food and shelter for people fleeing conflict (Meskell 2018: 210). And yet, as we have seen, the choice between protecting heritage and protecting people's lives is routinely dismissed as a false dichotomy by heritage professionals.

We suspect that the popularity of the Inseparability Thesis (largely) rests on a fear that acknowledging conflicts between heritage and other goods will make it impossible to justify the protection of heritage. One might think that these conflicts force us into a dilemma: either we must argue for the permissibility of protecting heritage by claiming that heritage is more important

44   HERITAGE AND WAR

than people's lives, or we must concede that heritage protection is impermissible, given the available alternative of saving lives. Clearly, groups such as UNESCO do not want to defend the first view, given its likely political ramifications. But nor do they want to give up on the protection of heritage. Embracing the Inseparability Thesis is a way of avoiding this dilemma, albeit an implausible one. If one simply denies that protecting heritage can ever conflict with saving lives, then there is no need to justify protecting heritage instead of saving lives.

But this fear is ill-founded. Recognising value pluralism—that is, recognising a range of morally valuable goods—does not force us into this dilemma. As we suggested above, a good life requires access to a range of goods. Even if, for example, hospitals are more important than recreational spaces, we still, plausibly, need some recreational spaces in order to have good lives. Value pluralism forces us to trade goods against each other, but not to sacrifice all of some lesser good for the sake of (any amount of) a more important good.

It is compatible with this pluralist view that protecting heritage sometimes promotes people's other interests besides their interest in heritage, including their interests in life and limb. Proponents of the Inseparability Thesis frequently support their view by pointing to, for example, the economic value of heritage and its role as a source of income for local people. Protecting heritage can indeed protect people's incomes and hence, at least in poorer countries, protect lives. But it is a mistake to infer from this that protecting heritage *always* or *necessarily* protects lives, or that it always *best* protects lives compared to available alternatives. On the contrary, and as the conflicts identified above testify, protecting heritage can increase risks to people's lives and damaging heritage can decrease risks to people's lives. We might save some lives by protecting heritage, but it is, in general, very likely that we can save more lives by using our resources in other ways.

Another possible explanation of the popularity of the Inseparability Thesis lies in its proponents' tendency to conflate *persons* with *peoples*. Those raising the 'stone versus lives' challenge are concerned with the survival of persons—that is, individuals currently in need of life-saving resources, such as water and shelter. In contrast, the defences of the Inseparability Thesis often invoke the importance of heritage for the survival of peoples—that is, communities with distinctive values, beliefs, and ways of life.

For example, James Cuno claims that there is no choice between saving lives and saving heritage because "heritage is completely intertwined with the survival of a people" (Cuno 2017). Even if we were to grant that peoples cannot survive without their (tangible) heritage, it is clearly false that individuals cannot survive without tangible heritage. Cuno's reply is thus no reply at all to those voicing concerns about the survival of persons. In a similar vein, Weiss and Connelly's claim that "air, water and culture are essential for life" elides biological life and biographical life (Weiss & Connelly 2017: 6). Culture might help a person to live a *good* life, but it does not enable her to *live*, as air and water do. These sleights of hand make the false dichotomy retort, and hence the Inseparability Thesis, seem more plausible than it is, although it is still not very plausible. There are many examples of diasporas and migrant communities that, despite a lack of access to their tangible heritage, retain a clear sense of cultural identity through their intangible heritage. Many also build new tangible heritage in their new homelands. This is not to say that destroying tangible heritage cannot sometimes destroy communities: clearly, there are examples of this kind of erosion of peoples. The point is merely the implausibility of the claim that communities cannot survive the loss of their tangible heritage.

6. Taking Conflicts Seriously

The conflicts outlined above straightforwardly falsify the Inseparability Thesis. The failure to recognise such conflicts, and their moral and legal significance, comprehensively undermines the heritage community's response to the 'stones versus lives' challenge. Note that the question of how one ought to respond to these conflicts between people and heritage is quite separate from the fact of the conflicts themselves. One might argue, for example, that one may never knowingly risk harm to persons, or at least to civilians, for the sake of protecting heritage. But this is simply to propose one way of responding to the conflicts, not to show that the conflicts are illusory.

It is, furthermore, an implausible response. We routinely impose risks of serious harm on each other for the sake of securing even trivial goods. Driving to buy ice cream, for example, or kicking a ball about in the park, or riding a horse on a public bridleway, imposes a very small risk of serious harm on others. If imposing these risks is morally permissible, it is surely morally permissible to impose some risks on people, including civilians, for the sake of protecting a non-trivial good such as a cultural heritage site or artefact. An adequate response to these conflicts consists not in ignoring or denying them, but in thinking seriously about the morality of imposing risks on people for the sake of heritage.

Note, further, that wider international humanitarian law does not settle combatants' legal permissions and duties in the face of these conflicts. The

46 HERITAGE AND WAR

Hague Convention stipulates that its obligations are "without prejudice to other precautions required by international humanitarian law in the conduct of military operations" (1954 HC 2nd Prot., Art. 7). But international law does not, for example, prohibit collaterally harming civilians. Rather, it requires that combatants "take all feasible precautions" to limit harms to civilians and their property, and avoid inflicting harm "excessive in relation to the concrete and direct military advantage anticipated" (ICRC 1977: Art. 57.2.a.i and 51.5.b).

The law is notoriously unclear about how combatants should judge these notions of feasibility and excess when weighing military advantage against harms to persons, and harms to combatants against harms to civilians.[13] These are, as is often noted, "value judgements" (ICRC 2018: 52). There is even less clarity when it comes to assessing and weighing damage to cultural heritage, due, in no small part, to the widespread adherence to the Inseparability Thesis amongst those involved with wartime heritage protection and their concomitant refusal to engage with these issues.[14] As we have seen, many heritage professionals erroneously dismiss these conflicts as a false dichotomy or confusion. Weiss and Connelly, for example, describe concerns about saving heritage instead of human lives as a matter of "optics" (Weiss & Connelly 2017: 38). Even those who ostensibly recognise the conflicts tend to respond by way of metaphors. For example, the UN Report of the Special Rapporteur in the Field of Cultural Rights notes that "in the face of large-scale killings or assaults on the security of persons, attacks on cultural heritage may seem less important, and, understandably, there may be conflicting priorities." By way of response to this concern, she continues: "But, as a Haitian sculptor asserted, 'the dead are dead. We know that. But if you don't have the memory of the past, the rest of us can't continue living'" (Bennoune 2016: 18–19). Such cursory treatment is astonishing. These challenges cannot be met with metaphors; they demand genuine engagement with the difficult moral questions concerning heritage protection.

---

[13] For a detailed description and discussion of the range of views on proportionality, see the 2018 report by the International Committee of the Red Cross.

[14] The ICRC report cited above notes only that "the experts disagreed on whether, exceptionally, property damage could be so serious as to 'weigh' more in terms of incidental civilian harm than a single life. One expert considered it could be the case depending on the circumstances, while another discarded the idea even for specially protected or significant property, such as cultural property" (ICRC 2018: 63).

7. Conclusion

As we have argued, current legal obligations for the protection of cultural property in war run far ahead of the theoretical bases for those obligations. Without a better understanding of the comparative value of heritage, and the implications of its destruction, the notions of 'feasible alternatives' and 'excessive damage'—so integral to the provisions of the Hague Convention—remain opaque.

This opacity inevitably bears on combatants' ability to implement those provisions. Moreover, without further clarification of what these obligations demand, it is impossible to know if they are morally binding on combatants. It seems implausible that, for example, a combatant might be morally obliged to incur very high risks to her own life for the sake of saving a cultural artefact, even if she is ordered to do so. Addressing these questions requires us to reflect not only on the value of heritage but also on the scope of combatant consent with respect to the ends for which they may be put at risk.

Likewise, without some clarification of the circumstances under which the Convention might require combatants to decrease risks to heritage at the expense of increasing risks to civilians, we cannot judge whether its provision, that heritage be damaged only when there are no feasible alternatives, provides appropriate levels of protection for civilians. It seems unlikely that one may not impose *any* risk of harm upon a person for the sake of protecting heritage. But it also seems intuitively implausible that combatants are permitted to undertake offensives that impose significant risks of harm on persons for the sake of protecting heritage. And if this is true, we must also think carefully about the permissibility of intentionally harming those who are engaged in damaging cultural heritage. If the protection of heritage does not, ordinarily, warrant the imposition of serious harms on persons, those arguing for the lethal defence of heritage must explain why such defence is proportionate. Again, we cannot shy away from these questions if we want to develop comprehensive and compelling accounts of the ethics of heritage protection.[15]

---

[15] Work related to this chapter was presented at the International Society for Military Ethics Conference at the University of New South Wales, the Morris Colloquium at the University of Colorado at Boulder, the Cultural Heritage Under Siege conference at the J. Paul Getty Trust, Los Angeles, the Lauterpacht Centre for International Law at the University of Cambridge, and the Humanitarian Ethics and Action conference at the Centre for Global Ethics, University of Birmingham. We are very grateful to audiences at these events.

References

1954 Hague Convention on the Protection of Property in the Event of Armed Conflict and its Additional Protocols.

al-Ibrahim, A., & Fayyad, F. (2015), 'Roman Ruins Become Home for Syrian Refugees,' *The New Arab*, 9 February. https://www.alaraby.co.uk/english/features/2015/2/10/roman-ruins-become-home-for-syrian-refugees.

Arsu, S. (2015), 'Turkish Military Evacuates Soldiers Guarding Tomb in Syria,' *The New York Times*, 22 February.

Bennoune, K. (2016), 'Report of the Special Rapporteur in the Field of Cultural Rights,' A/HRC/31/59.

Bogdanos, M. (2005), *The Thieves of Baghdad: One Marine's Passion to Recover the World's Greatest Stolen Treasures* (New York: Bloomsbury).

Bowker, D. W., Goodall, L., & Haciski, R. A. (2016), 'Confronting ISIS's War on Cultural Property,' *ASIL Insights* 20/12. https://www.asil.org/insights/volume/20/issue/12/confronting-isis-war-cultural-property.

Brown, D. and Shortland, A. (2019), 'Two letters from Ike: Military Necessity and Cultural Property Protection,' *British Army Review: Special Report on Culture in Conflict*: 6–17.

Bülow, W. (2020), 'Risking Civilian Lives to Avoid Harm to Cultural Heritage,' *Journal of Ethics and Social Philosophy* 18/3: 266–288.

Cullity, G. (2008), 'Public Goods and Fairness,' *Australasian Journal of Philosophy* 86/1: 1–21.

Cunliffe, E., Fox, P., & Stone, P. (2018), 'The Protection of Cultural Property in the Event of Armed Conflict: Unnecessary Distraction or Mission-Relevant Priority?' *NATO Open Publications* 4/2.

Cunliffe, E., Muhesen, N., & Lostal, M. (2016), 'The Destruction of Cultural Property in the Syrian Conflict: Legal Implications and Obligations,' *International Journal of Cultural Property* 23: 1–31.

Cuno, J. (2016), 'The Responsibility to Protect the World's Cultural Heritage,' *Brown Journal of World Affairs* 23/1: 97–109.

Cuno, J. (2017), 'Remarks at the Program on Protecting Cultural Heritage from Terrorism and Mass Atrocities: Links and Common Responsibilities,' United Nations Headquarters, 21 September 2017.

de Vattel E. (2015), *Law of Nations* (Cambridge: Cambridge University Press).

Eisenhower, D. D. (1943), *Letter on Historical Monuments*, 29 December. Available at http://ochsmrsg.weebly.com/uploads/1/4/9/4/14949746/eisenhower_letter.pdf.

Farchack Bajjaly, J. (2011), 'Politicians: Assassins of Lebanese Heritage? Archaeology in Lebanon in Times of Armed Conflict,' in P. G. Stone (ed.)

Cultural Heritage, Ethics and the Military (Woodbridge, Suffolk: Boydell & Brewer Press): 182–191.

Foradori, P., & Rosa, P. (2017), 'Expanding the Peacekeeping Agenda: The Protection of Cultural Heritage in War-Torn Societies,' *Global Change, Peace and Security* 29/2: 145–160.

Forrest, C. J. S. (2007), 'The Doctrine of Military Necessity and the Protection of Cultural Property during Armed Conflict,' *Case Western International Law Journal* 37/2: 177–219.

Frowe, H., & Matravers, D. (2019), 'Conflict and Cultural Heritage: A Moral Analysis of the Challenges of Heritage Protection,' J. Paul Getty Trust Occasional Papers in Cultural Heritage Policy, 3 (Los Angeles, CA: J. Paul Getty Trust).

Frowe, H., & Matravers, D. (in progress), *Stones and Lives: The Ethics of Protecting Heritage in War*, draft manuscript.

Grotius, H. (2005), *Rights of War and Peace*, R. Tuck (ed.) (Carmel, IN: Liberty Fund Inc.).

Hart, S., & Chilton, E. (2015), 'Digging and Destruction: Artifact Collection as Meaningful Social Practice,' *International Journal of Heritage Studies* 21/4: 318–335.

Hatala Matthes, E. (2013), 'History, Value, and Irreplaceability,' *Ethics* 124/1: 35–64.

Hatala Matthes, E. (2018), 'Saving Stones or Saving Lives? The Ethics of Cultural Heritage Protection in War,' *Public Affairs Quarterly* 32/1: 67–84.

Heath, D. B. (1973), 'Economic Aspects of Commercial Archaeology in Costa Rica,' *American Antiquity* 38, 259–265.

Hladík, J. (1999), 'The 1954 Hague Convention for the Protection of Cultural Property in the Event of Armed Conflict and the Notion of Military Necessity,' *International Review of the Red Cross* 81/835: 621–635.

ICRC (International Committee of the Red Cross) (1977), *Protocol Additional to the Geneva Conventions of 12 August 1949, and relating to the Protection of Victims of International Armed Conflicts (Protocol I)* (Geneva: ICRC).

ICRC (International Committee of the Red Cross) (2018), *The Principle of Proportionality in the Rules Governing the Conduct of Hostilities under International Humanitarian Law* (Geneva: ICRC).

Korsmeyer, C. (2019), *Things: In Touch with the Past* (Oxford: Oxford University Press).

Lamb, F. (2016), 'Can Responsibility to Protect (R2P) Preserve Our Cultural Heritage in Syria?' *Counter Currents*, 28 April.

Lange, F. W. (1976), 'Costa Rica and the "Subsistence Archaeologist",' *Current Anthropology* 17, 305–307.

Matsuda, D. (1998), 'The Ethics of Archaeology: Subsistence Digging, and Artefact Looting in Latin America: Point, Muted Counterpoint,' *Journal of Cultural Property* 7/1: 87–97.

Meskell, L. (2018), *A Future in Ruins: UNESCO, World Heritage, and the Dream of Peace* (New York: Oxford University Press).

Munoz-Darde, V. (2013), 'In the Face of Austerity: The Puzzle of Museums and Universities,' *Journal of Political Philosophy* 21/2: 221–242.

O'Keefe, R., Péron, C., Musayev, T., & Ferrari, G. (2016), *Protection of Cultural Property: Military Manual* (Paris and San Remo: UNESCO and the International Institute of Humanitarian Law).

O'Reilly, D. (2007), 'Shifting Trends of Heritage Destruction in Cambodia: From Temples to Tombs,' *Historical Environment* 20/2: 12–16.

Peterson, K. E. (2007), 'Cultural Apocalypse Now: The Loss of the Iraq Museum and a New Proposal for the Wartime Protection of Museums,' *Minnesota Journal of International Law* 16/55: 163–191.

Rush, L. W. (2017), 'Finding Common Ground: Cultural Property Protection in Modern Conflict,' *Future Anterior: Journal of Historic Preservation, History, Theory and Criticism* 14/1: 25–35.

Sandholtz, W. (2005), 'The Iraqi National Museum and International Law: A Duty to Protect,' *Columbia Journal of Transnational Law* 44: 185–240.

Schmalenbach, K. (2016), 'Ideological Warfare against Cultural Property: UN Strategies and Dilemmas,' *Max Planck Yearbook of International Law* 19/1: 1–38.

Serageldin, I. (1999), 'Cultural Heritage as Public Good: Economic Analysis Applied to Historic Cities,' in I. Kaul, I. Grunberg, & M. A. Stern (eds.) *Global Public Goods: International Cooperation in the Twenty-First Century* (New York: Oxford University Press): 240–263.

Stone, P. (2013), 'War and Heritage: Using Inventories to Protect Cultural Property,' *Conservation Perspectives* 28/2: 13–15.

Thompson, J. (2007), 'War and the Protection of Property,' in I. Primoratz (ed.) *Civilian Immunity in War* (Oxford: Oxford University Press): 239–256.

UK Blue Shield website at https://ukblueshield.org.uk.

United Nations Security Council (2016), 'Report of the Secretary-General on the Situation in Mali,' 23 December.

Weiss, T. G. (2020), 'Heritage and People: A False Choice,' Institute for Advanced Studies, Princeton University, 27 January. Available at https://www.youtube.com/watch?v=l4XA_ZrO1WE.

Weiss, T. G., & Connelly, N. (2017), 'Cultural Cleansing and Mass Atrocities: Protecting Cultural Heritage in Armed Conflict Zones,' J. Paul Getty Trust Occasional Papers in Cultural Heritage Policy, 1 (Los Angeles, CA: J. Paul Getty Trust).

Weiss, T. G., & Connelly, N. (2019), 'Protecting Cultural Heritage in War Zones,' *Third World Quarterly* 40/1: 1–17.

4

Killing for Culture

Bashshar Haydar

1. Introduction

It is not uncommon for historical sites, monuments, art objects, and various other items of what might be described as cultural property or heritage to suffer serious damage.[1] The passage of time, along with various natural calamities, can take its toll in this regard. In addition to natural causes, human factors such as wars, vandalism, looting, and neglect often contribute to the damage and destruction. Regardless of the source or cause of harm to cultural heritage or property, a question arises as to what we ought, or are morally permitted, to do in order to prevent or alleviate such damage.

Most people, I presume, would think it is morally permissible, and perhaps sometimes required, to devote significant resources, such as time, money, and effort, to the protection of cultural heritage. The practices of governments and international organizations, such as UNESCO, confirm this view. A question thus arises as to the extent and manner in which it is morally permissible to devote efforts or resources to the protection of cultural heritage, especially when these resources could be deployed instead to protect human lives from extreme poverty or other life-threatening circumstances or emergencies.

A related, yet separate, question arises as to the extent and manner in which it is morally permissible to *inflict* serious harm on human lives for the sake of protecting cultural heritage. In what follows, I address this question. More specifically, I ask how we should weigh the value of cultural heritage against these other values in the context of armed conflict. I examine the permissibility of resorting to military action for the sake of protecting cultural heritage, when such military action is likely to inflict serious harm on human lives. In this regard, I distinguish three groups of people who might be harmed by

[1] For a definition of cultural heritage or cultural property, see the 1954 Hague Convention for the Protection of Cultural Property in the Event of Armed Conflict (UNESCO 1954), and the 1970 UNESCO Convention on the Means of Prohibiting and Preserving the Illicit Import, Export and Transfer of Ownership of Cultural Property (UNESCO 1970).

Bashshar Haydar, *Killing for Culture* In: *Heritage and War: Ethical Issues*. Edited by: William Bülow, Helen Frowe, Derek Matravers, and Joshua Lewis Thomas, Oxford University Press. © Bashshar Haydar 2023.
DOI: 10.1093/oso/9780192862648.003.0004

such military endeavor: culpable aggressors, non-culpable civilians, and cultural interveners, that is, combatants who are engaged in the military effort of protecting cultural heritage. I examine the permissibility of exposing each of these three groups to harm in order to defend cultural heritage.

Before proceeding to address the above question, it might be worth addressing the view that there is no real conflict between protecting cultural heritage and protecting human lives, on the grounds that whatever is good for the former must also be good for the latter. After all, we value cultural heritage because of its importance for human flourishing. Thus, it might be argued that the only way in which a conflict might arise between the protection of cultural heritage and human lives is if we assign value to cultural heritage that is independent of, or goes beyond, its impact on human lives. The claim that cultural heritage has such a human-independent value is a controversial one. But, even if we dismiss the view that cultural heritage can be valued independently of its impact on human lives, a question remains as to how we should compare the goods that cultural heritage brings to human lives with other goods such as safety, health, and longevity. It is this comparison that one attempts when one asks whether it is morally permissible to inflict harm on human lives for the sake of protecting cultural heritage.

2. Defending Cultural Heritage

Recently, the Notre-Dame Cathedral in Paris suffered significant fire damage. People around the world, not least in France of course, were struck by the news that fire was eating into the cathedral, destroying its tower and threatening to burn the whole thing to ashes. French firefighters were able to prevent a total destruction of the cathedral, but only after considerable damage had already been done. Within a few days of the fire, significant financial resources, reaching up to US$1 billion, were pledged by various individuals and corporations for the restoration of the cathedral.[2]

Notwithstanding some concerns, responses to the generous Notre-Dame donations were overall positive.[3] Yet, many people would be inclined to think differently had the choice between saving human lives and saving the cathedral been of a different kind. Suppose, for example, that the firefighters had

---

[2] See, for example, Stoilas (2019). It is worth noting that much of this promised money was never actually donated (see Chakrabortty 2019).

[3] For some of such concerns, see McNicoll (2019).

to make a choice between either saving the cathedral or rescuing a group of 10 trapped children who happened to be visiting the site on that day. One can be pretty sure that most people would be less comfortable opting to save the cathedral and thus letting the 10 children die, or be seriously harmed, than they would be with opting to allocate resources to restore the damaged cathedral instead of allocating them to saving children living in life-threatening poverty.

In this chapter, I will proceed on the assumption that it is morally permissible to allocate significant resources for the restoration of cultural heritage sites like Notre-Dame Cathedral, even when these resources can be used to save many lives had they been allocated to poverty alleviation. Moreover, I will also assume that we are morally required to save 10 children instead of preventing the fire from significantly damaging the cathedral.[4] These two assumptions might not be consistent.[5] I will not argue against this claim. However, since the above two assumptions enjoy strong intuitive appeal and widespread acceptance, it is worth exploring the moral status of cultural heritage in war while accepting them.

Although wars and other forms of military conflicts do often aim at preventing harm, they almost always involve inflicting harm as well. This is true even of defensive wars. While such wars aim at protecting lives, rights, and property from harm and aggression, they accomplish this by means that inflict harm on others. Hence, the central question concerning the moral status of cultural heritage in the context of war is not whether it is morally permissible to prevent harm from befalling cultural heritage instead of preventing harm from befalling human lives. Rather, the moral central question is whether it is morally permissible to impose substantial risks of serious harm on humans in order to protect cultural heritage.

It is widely accepted that, other things being equal, inflicting harm is morally worse than failing to prevent harm. Or, put in other terms, negative moral duties (duties not to do harm) are stronger than positive duties (duties to prevent harm). Hence, if it is morally wrong to save Notre-Dame Cathedral instead of saving the 10 children, then it would be even worse to either intentionally or collaterally kill 10 children in trying to save the cathedral. This makes the case for resorting to military action in order to protect cultural heritage a rather difficult one to make. This is the case whether we are

---

[4] Note that this leaves open the question of whether the saving of Notre-Dame Cathedral, or other cultural heritage sites, may outweigh the saving, say, of a single innocent human life.
[5] Of course, some have argued that such different attitudes are unjustified. Peter Singer (1972, 2009) and Peter Unger (1996) argue for such a view.

considering attacks on cultural heritage as just cause for war, or something that we might be called upon within a war fought for other reasons.

Before addressing the question of the permissibility of resorting to military action in order to protect cultural heritage, it might be useful to identify the various ways in which cultural heritage may come to be in need of military protection. In this regard, we can distinguish two broad ways in which cultural heritage may be threatened, such that a military defensive response might be called for. First, military action may be called upon in order to prevent acts or policies, violent or otherwise, which intentionally aim at the destruction of cultural heritage. Second, military action may be called upon to prevent the collateral destruction of cultural heritage, which usually takes place in the context of military conflicts. In what follows, I deal only with the first type of situation, that is, when cultural heritage is intentionally targeted. I think what is said about intentional destruction would be of relevance to the case where cultural heritage is harmed only as a side effect.

The intentional targeting of cultural heritage could take place for various reasons. First, it could be part of a campaign of ethnic cleansing. To a certain extent, this was part of the motive behind the destruction of mosques, churches, and other sites during the Lebanese and Bosnian civil wars (Committee on Culture and Education 1995). Second, cultural heritage might be targeted in acts of revenge or punishment. Such a motive can explain many of the attacks on cultural heritage sites in the aforementioned civil wars. The revenge/punishment motive also explains some episodes in WW II. The so-called 'Baedeker Raids', in which the German bombers targeted tourist attraction sites in Britain, belongs to this category (Gore-Langton 2012). Another is the Allied forces' massive bombing campaign of German cities, such as Dresden, towards the end of the war. Third, the targeting of cultural heritage might be ideologically motivated. The Taliban's destruction of the Buddhas of Bamiyan in Afghanistan and ISIS's attacks on Palmyra belong to this category (Crossette 2001). Regardless of the motive, military attacks that aim at damaging cultural heritage are, with very few exceptions, clearly unjustifiable and condemnable.[6] That said, it is not clear what kind of military responses are morally required or permitted in order to protect cultural heritage against such attacks.

Defensive military action, which aims at protecting cultural heritage, can threaten harm to three different groups of people. First, it is likely to inflict

---

[6] The destruction of the Nazi icon could be an example of one such exception.

harm on those who are targeting the cultural heritage in question, that is, culpable aggressors. Members of this group will be the natural targets of defensive action aiming at the protection of threatened cultural heritage. The second group of people is the civilians who happen to live within dangerous proximity to the area of defensive military operations. It is often very difficult, if not impossible, for defensive force to avoid collaterally harming members of this group. The third group consists of members of the military defensive force themselves. As combatants in action, members of the latter group are very likely to be exposed to the risk of serious harm. In what follows, I will consider each of the three groups in turn and ask whether it is morally permissible to subject the members of each group to the risk of serious harm in order to protect cultural heritage.

3. Culpable Aggressors

Culpable aggressors present the weakest moral challenge to the permissibility of defensive harm in protection of cultural heritage. Most people, I suppose, grant that it is morally permissible to inflict some harm on those who aim at destroying cultural heritage, when doing so is necessary for its protection. For example, I presume that it would be morally permissible, in the eyes of most people, for the armed guards at the Louvre to open fire at anyone trying to destroy sections of the museum, if that is the only way to prevent destruction or serious damage to the museum.[7] Similarly, most people would say that it is morally permissible for the guards at the Notre-Dame Cathedral to target anyone trying to set the cathedral on fire, if that is the only way to prevent the burning down of the cathedral.

Although it is morally permissible to harm culpable aggressors in order to protect cultural heritage, this does not suffice to establish that cultural heritage or property has any special moral status that distinguishes it from other types of property. The French police are also morally permitted, for example, to use lethal means against anyone trying to set fire to a newly built car factory, even though the latter would not be classified as cultural heritage. As Frowe and Matravers write:

---

[7] It is likely that some might not accept this claim or share the intuition behind it. Nonetheless, it should remain of interest, even to the skeptic, to explore the underlying grounds, as well as the implications, of such intuitions.

56 HERITAGE AND WAR

> One must also be sure not to conflate what we can call law and order justifications for harming with harming for the sake of heritage. For example, we might agree that if someone were going around a museum or gallery methodically destroying every piece of art, it could be permissible to kill her if this were the only way to stop her....But this permissibility could be explained by our interest in maintaining law and order rather than the value of cultural artifacts. After all, it seems similarly permissible to prevent the destruction of other types of property. (Frowe and Matravers 2019: 23)

Thus, in order to show that cultural heritage has special status beyond that attaching to ordinary property or other types of financial assets, one needs to show either that (1) one may inflict more harm on culpable aggressors, or other categories of people, for the sake of protecting cultural heritage compared to protecting ordinary assets (when they have equal financial value), or (2) defensive harm can be permissible even against non-aggressors for the sake of protecting cultural heritage, whereas defensive harm against non-aggressors for the sake of protecting ordinary assets is not morally permissible.

The second claim concerning the permissibility of harming non-aggressors for the sake of protecting cultural heritage is addressed below. Let us consider the first claim, namely that it is permissible to inflict significantly more harm on aggressors for the sake of protecting cultural heritage than for the sake of protecting regular assets.

Consider a group of people who are trying to destroy an item with significant cultural value, say a collection of paintings by Vermeer. Let us contrast this with the case of another group of aggressors who are trying to destroy items with no cultural significance, say a collection of expensive cars whose overall financial value is equivalent to that of the Vermeer paintings. Would it be permissible to inflict more harm in order to protect the paintings than for the sake of protecting the cars? Most people would likely agree that, other things being equal, protecting the paintings should take priority over protecting the cars, in case a choice between them has to be made. Such ascription of priority could be based on the irreplaceability of the paintings in question, as compared to that of the cars. The priority we give to protecting the paintings over the cars does not strictly entail that it is permissible to inflict more defensive harm, especially lethal harm, against culpable aggressors in the former case than in the latter one. But it can still provide plausible grounds for claiming that the proportionate harm one is permitted to inflict in order to prevent the destruction of the Vermeers is higher than that which one is permitted to inflict for the sake of preventing the destruction of the cars.

4. Non-Culpable Civilians

Let us consider now the second category of people who might be harmed by military action aimed at protecting cultural heritage, namely non-culpable civilians.

It's permissible to impose significant collateral harms on some people in order to avert substantially worse harms to others. If imposing collateral harm on innocent civilians were impermissible, it would be difficult to justify almost all modern warfare. By contrast, it does not seem morally permissible to inflict serious collateral harm on non-culpable civilians in order to protect regular property or financial assets. It would not be morally permissible, for example, to collaterally kill or seriously harm a number of innocent bystanders in order to prevent a bank robbery.

What is true about ordinary assets in this regard, it might be argued, applies equally to cultural heritage. Consider again the situation where the only way to protect Notre-Dame Cathedral from the approaching fire would involve inflicting serious harm on a group of children near the site. Or suppose, for example, that a rocket has been launched at the cathedral which, unobstructed, will cause serious damage to the cathedral. Suppose also that the only way to protect the cathedral is to shoot down the rocket, where pieces of the obstructed rocket would fall to the ground, killing and injuring a number of civilians. It would be impermissible to save the cathedral under the conditions present in the two latter cases, if we think it is morally impermissible to save the cathedral instead of saving a group of innocent children (see Section 2 above). If it is wrong not to prevent some harm under a given circumstance, then, other things being equal, it must be at least as wrong to inflict that same harm under these same circumstances. Thus, if it is morally wrong to save the cathedral instead of saving a number of innocent children, then it must be equally bad, or worse, to inflict harm on an equal number of non-culpable civilians in order to protect the cathedral.[8]

---

[8] This does not rule out the claim that, under certain circumstances, it might be morally permissible to inflict serious harm on non-culpable civilians in order to protect cultural heritage. This might be the case when the number of non-culpable civilians in question is very small and/or the cultural heritage at stake is of sufficiently great significance.

58 HERITAGE AND WAR

4.1 Cultural Self-Determination

Nonetheless, the permissibility of inflicting collateral harm on non-culpable civilians in order to protect cultural heritage can be justified on the basis of protecting the right of cultural self-determination against cultural cleansing. So far, we have appealed to isolated cases of threats to cultural heritage. Such threats are not, however, always isolated events. They can be part of a pattern that has different meaning and implications. The destruction of cultural heritage, as pointed out earlier, can be part of an attempt to change the cultural landscape of a certain territory and, hence, deprive the local population of their material cultural heritage. Such cultural cleansing is sometimes pursued through military aggression. But it could also be pursued via 'lawful' and 'peaceful' means by authoritarian regimes[9] or by an elected parliament dominated by extreme nationalist parties, who have no regard for the interests and rights of the minority whose cultural heritage they aim to cleanse.

When some groups or communities are faced with the threat of cultural cleansing, it would seem morally permissible for them to resist and defend themselves against such a threat. It would be morally permissible for them to do so against military and violent aggression. It would also seem permissible to do so against a 'peaceful' policy of cultural cleansing. Moreover, it is not clearly impermissible for the targeted group to resort to armed resistance in order to defend themselves against cultural cleansing, when other more peaceful options are exhausted.

More importantly, such armed resistance or defensive effort against cultural cleansing may be seen as permissible, even if it involves causing serious collateral harm to non-culpable civilians. If the right to cultural self-determination is treated as part of the right of political self-determination in general, and if defending the latter right justifies resorting to military action even when doing so involves inflicting serious collateral harm on non-culpable civilians, then resorting to military action in order to prevent cultural cleansing may also justify inflicting harm on non-culpable civilians. This view also entails that the right of the local population to use force, in order to resist cultural cleansing, is not dependent on maintaining law and order. The targeted community may be morally permitted to resort to armed resistance even against their own government. This might be more applicable to the

---

[9] An example of such cultural cleansing is the destruction of religious buildings and monuments in Albania under the communist regime of Enver Hoxha. In 1967 alone, more than 2,000 Ottoman heritage sites were destroyed, including 750 mosques (Ermal 2012).

protection of intangible heritage such as language, as it usually requires interfering with people. But it is also applicable to tangible heritage such as monuments and landscapes. From this perspective, cultural cleansing is seen in a similar light as ethnic cleansing.

While the latter aims at forcing a group out of their own territory, the former aims at changing the cultural nature of the territory itself, perhaps as a way of changing the cultural identity of its residents. Thus it can be said that, while ethnic cleansing takes, or pushes, the local residents away from their territory, cultural cleansing takes the territory (in terms of its cultural features) away from its residents.[10]

However, it might be argued that even if we accept the above view concerning the permissibility of, or resorting to, armed resistance against cultural cleansing, this does not show that there is something special about cultural heritage that distinguishes it from regular assets. The right of the local population to resort to armed resistance is not dependent on the fact that the aggression in question aims at cultural cleansing. Armed resistance would be justified even if the aggression aims only at the destruction of infrastructure.

If the above alleged symmetry between cultural heritage and ordinary assets holds, then it would undermine or weaken the claim that cultural heritage has special value that distinguishes what is morally permitted in its defense from what is morally permitted in defense of other assets. Such symmetry does not, however, undermine the claim that it is permissible to resort to military action in defense of cultural heritage, even when doing so would involve imposing collateral harm on innocent civilians. The symmetry only extends this permissibility to ordinary assets.

Despite the above symmetry claim, however, there remains an important difference between what it is permissible to do to prevent cultural cleansing and what is permissible to do to prevent harm to infrastructure and other such assets. There is an element of urgency in defending cultural heritage that does not exist in the case of defending ordinary assets. This can be illustrated as follows. Suppose that threats, either to cultural heritage or to ordinary assets, are not of a military or violent nature, but are pursued through peaceful but oppressive policy. Compare the two following possible situations. In the first case, the authorities pursue a discriminatory and oppressive policy against an ethnic minority by ordering the destruction or dismantling of most of the cultural heritage sites that are of significance to the minority in

---

[10] Clearly, the success of this view depends on the aptness of the analogy between ethnic cleansing and cultural cleansing.

60   HERITAGE AND WAR

question. In the second, the authorities pursue a discriminatory and oppressive policy against an ethic minority by ordering the destruction or dismantling of a sizable portion of the infrastructure in the territory of the targeted minority. Let us assume that defending the targeted assets in both situations, be it cultural heritage or ordinary infrastructure, can be accomplished only through resorting to armed resistance. Under such circumstances, there are stronger grounds for resorting to armed resistance in the case of defending the threatened cultural heritage than in defending the threatened infrastructure. First, normally most cultural heritage has intrinsic value that makes it less replaceable than purely instrumental infrastructure or any other such ordinary assets. Hence, there is more urgency in protecting cultural heritage. Second, cultural cleansing, but not the destruction of infrastructure, affects the sense of identity and self-expression of the targeted group.[11] Hence, it strikes closer to the heart of self-determination of the targeted group. Therefore, if one thinks it is sometimes morally permissible for a community to resort to war or armed resistance in order to defend their right to self-determination, then there are more grounds to do so in defending cultural heritage than in defending infrastructure or any other ordinary assets of the sort.[12]

5. Cultural Interveners

So far, we have looked at the permissibility of inflicting harm on culpable aggressors as well as innocent civilians in order to protect cultural heritage. This leaves a third category of people who might be harmed in the effort to protect cultural heritage, namely those engaged in the military effort to protect cultural heritage. Members of the latter group might be exposed to risks of harm in trying to accomplish their task. Hence, a question arises as to whether it is permissible to expose potential military defenders of cultural heritage to such risk.

---

[11] It should be noted that distinguishing heritage from infrastructure is not always a straightforward matter. The marketplace might seem more like infrastructure, but destroying local markets can have a massive effect on identity and cohesion. In this regard, defending the market would be included among the things that would contribute to the permissibility of inflicting lethal harm.

[12] The presence of the above additional grounds for resorting to armed resistance in defending cultural heritage does not establish that these grounds do indeed succeed in justifying such resistance. It only shows that, in general, there are stronger reasons for armed resistance in the case of cultural heritage than in the case of ordinary infrastructure.

A positive answer to the above question may be grounded on the role-based duties that combatants take upon themselves. By becoming a member of the armed forces or police, one accepts taking on certain duties and tasks, along with the risks associated with them. An important part of these duties is to maintain peace and order, as well as to protect public and private property from all forms of unlawful aggression.

Members of security forces are expected to take risks, not only to protect cultural heritage and human lives, but also to protect ordinary assets. Thus, for example, police and firefighters are expected to take some risk in order to prevent a group of aggressors from burning down a car factory, even assuming that the fire will not claim human casualties. Similarly, the French police are expected to take some risk in order prevent the destruction of the Notre-Dame Cathedral.

Given that members of the army and other security forces are required to take risks in order to protect ordinary assets, nothing special is established about cultural heritage by simply showing that security forces are required to take risks in order to protect it. It does not seem unreasonable, however, to claim that greater risk is expected in protecting cultural heritage than regular assets. The irreplaceability of cultural heritage could provide grounds for taking more risks in protecting it.[13] A difference in degree, however, does not necessarily amount to a difference in kind. In order to establish a difference in kind, we need to show that protecting cultural heritage can justify exposing security forces to harm under circumstances or situations that are not also applicable in the case of protecting regular assets. Thus, it would be useful in this regard to consider the situation where the cultural heritage in need of protection is located in other countries and outside the jurisdiction of the potential protectors. Absent any mutual defense agreement, it is doubtful that it would be morally permissible to expose one's own soldiers to serious risk simply in order to defend regular assets in another country. Thus, it would be relevant to our inquiry to see whether it is permissible for a government to expose members of its own armed forces to harm in order to protect cultural heritage that is located outside its jurisdiction; that is, whether it is permissible to engage in 'humanitarian cultural intervention' with the risk of exposing one's own combatants to serious harm.[14]

---

[13] The irreplaceability of cultural heritage might be due to the value people attach to its historical origin. In this sense, cultural heritage is treated similarly to the way original art is treated, where a mere copy is considered significantly less valuable.

[14] This would amount to asking whether the defense of cultural heritage can be a just cause for war.

62   HERITAGE AND WAR

The claim that the protection of cultural heritage may warrant military intervention in other countries is at the core of the recent interest in expanding the scope of humanitarian interventions to include the protection of cultural heritage. This interest is triggered by attacks orchestrated by various radical Islamist groups against significant cultural heritage sites in Afghanistan, Mali, Iraq, and Syria. These attacks led some to press for the need for the international community to intervene, even militarily, in order to protect cultural heritage.

Thomas G. Weiss and Nina Connelly (2017) argue in favor of expanding the justification for humanitarian military intervention to include the protection of cultural heritage. However, as Frowe and Matravers argue, Weiss and Connelly conflate an instrumental justification for the protection of cultural heritage as a way of protecting human lives, with an intrinsic justification for forcefully protecting heritage, and ultimately "offer no account of the permissibility of harming people for the sake of heritage" (Frowe and Matravers 2019: 35).

Focusing on the permissibility of humanitarian cultural interventions without conflating it with the protection of human lives, the question should be framed as follows: Is it permissible to expose combatants to the risk of serious harm merely for the sake of protecting cultural heritage outside their own country? In addressing this question, I will assume that ordinary humanitarian interventions, that is, interventions that aim at protecting human lives, are morally permissible (under certain circumstances and conditions), even when such interventions would expose the intervening combatants to serious harm. With these assumptions in mind, I will examine the extent to which such permissibility extends to humanitarian cultural interventions. In order to answer the above question, it is helpful to distinguish between at least three types of cultural interventions.

In the first type of intervention, the cultural heritage under threat has value mainly for the local population, but not for the intervening side or for the wider international community. In the second type, the threatened cultural heritage has value mainly for the intervening side, but not for the local population or for the international community at large. Finally, in the third type of cultural intervention, the cultural heritage under threat has value for the international community but is of no special value to the local population (apart from economic value, perhaps) or to the intervening side.[15] We need to

---

[15] It should be pointed out that these are not the only possible types of humanitarian cultural interventions. There are other possible combinations, as well as various different degrees in which the

KILLING FOR CULTURE   63

examine each of these types of humanitarian cultural interventions in order to assess the moral permissibility of exposing the intervening forces, as well as others, to the risk of harm.

5.1 Locals-Centered Cultural Intervention

Let us start with the first type of humanitarian cultural intervention, where the cultural heritage under threat matters mainly for the local population. In this type of cultural intervention (call it Locals-Centered Cultural Intervention), the intervening force would be acting on behalf, or for the benefit, of the local population. Hence, such interventions are similar in this respect to ordinary humanitarian interventions where the intervention takes place in order to protect the lives and safety of the local population. Under locals-centered cultural interventions, the local population is the main beneficiary of the intervention. Thus, it could be argued that the risks such interventions impose on the local population are justified on the grounds that the latter group would prefer to be subjected to the risks of intervention rather than suffer the risks of non-intervention. Moreover, as has been argued, given that the local population is the main beneficiary of the intervention, it is required to shoulder more of the risk of the intervention. Thus, the intervening force would be permitted, in comparison with wars of self-defense, for example, to shift more of the risk away from their members and towards the local population.[16]

Locals-centered cultural interventions share the above features of ordinary humanitarian interventions. Nonetheless, there is an important difference between the two. It is less controversial to assume that the threatened local population is more likely to accept the risk of ordinary humanitarian intervention than a cultural one. If, for example, a given humanitarian intervention would reduce the deaths among the threatened population from 1,000 to 20, then members of the threatened population might well prefer the intervention to take place, even when the intervention itself will cause 10 of these 20 deaths. It is safe, after all, to assume that people would prefer less risk to their lives and limbs. The same is not necessarily true, however, with respect to cultural humanitarian interventions. Unlike ordinary humanitarian interventions, in cultural interventions members of the local population are not

---

cultural heritage in question matters to the local population, the international community, or the intervening force.

[16] For a defense of this view, see McMahan (2010). For an opposing view, see Christie (2018).

64 HERITAGE AND WAR

making an *ex-ante* comparison of risks to their lives or limbs between intervention and non-intervention. Instead, they are making an *ex-ante* comparison between risks to their cultural heritage in the case of no intervention, and risks to their lives and limbs in the case of an intervention. While it is unreasonable for people to choose more, rather than less risk of harm to their lives and limbs, it is not obviously unreasonable for one to choose more risk to cultural heritage rather than more risk to one's life and limbs. Thus, it cannot be taken for granted that the local population are *ex-ante* beneficiaries of, or would consent to, humanitarian cultural intervention on the grounds that it would protect cultural heritage, when such intervention would increase the risk of harm to their lives and limbs.

Notwithstanding the above important difference between ordinary humanitarian interventions and locals-centered cultural interventions, the latter may still be morally permissible. If we accept the view, discussed above, that the local population is permitted to resort to military means in order to defend their cultural heritage against cultural cleansing, even when doing so would impose a risk of serious harm on non-culpable civilians, then it should also be permissible for outside interveners to provide military assistance to the local population under the same conditions. It may be permissible for the intervening force to inflict harm on non-culpable civilians for the sake of protecting cultural heritage when the threat to heritage rises to the level of cultural cleansing.

The argument would only show that the interveners in locals-centered cultural interventions are morally permitted to impose risks of harm on the local civilian population. It would not show that it is morally permissible to expose members of the intervening force themselves to the risk of significant harm. Hence, a question remains as to whether it is permissible to expose members of the intervening force to significant risk, when the cultural heritage under threat has little direct value to them. This is a challenge that needs to be met by advocates of cultural intervention.

A positive answer to the above question might be defended on the following grounds. If, in resisting cultural cleansing, it is permissible to inflict collateral harm on non-culpable civilians, then it should be also permissible to expose members of the intervening force to a similar degree of harm in order to prevent cultural cleansing.[17]

---

[17] It is more accurate to say the intervening combatants in such a case are ordered to incur risk to themselves, rather than being exposed to risk.

In response, it might be objected that there is a morally relevant difference between collateral defensive harm against non-culpable civilians, on the one hand, and exposing members of the intervening force to harm on the other. The civilians whose collateral harm is unavoidable in a just war (be it humanitarian or defensive), present an obstacle to the achievement of the just ends of the war. In this respect, these civilians resemble the person on the sidetrack in the standard 'trolley problem' and whose presence makes it impossible to save the five people on the main track without inflicting harm on her. Similarly, the presence of civilians often makes it impossible to achieve the ends of a just war without harming them. The same is not true of the humanitarian interveners, regardless of whether the intervention aims at protecting lives or cultural heritage. The interveners provide an opportunity for, rather than an obstacle to, protecting the threatened lives or objects. In this respect, the position of the intervening force resembles more the person standing on the footbridge in the standard trolley case, who can save the five trapped on the railway track by being pushed in front of the approaching trolley. Most people would think that it is morally impermissible to push the person on the footbridge, even when this is the only way to save the five others.[18] The same can be said to be true of humanitarian interveners.[19] They are usefully exposed to risks of harm (even if harms to them are not themselves useful). Thus, exposing them to harm by sending them into military action for the sake of defending the lives and rights of the threatened population requires weightier justification than that required for exposing civilians to collateral harm for the same purpose.

Moreover, it might be argued, there is a further morally relevant difference between humanitarian interventions and cultural ones, which makes it harder to justify exposing members of the intervening force to harm in the latter case. The value of human lives and other related basic rights is something that members of the intervening force should directly recognize. On the other hand, the value of cultural heritage that matters only to the local population can be appreciated only indirectly by combatants of the intervening force. It is conditioned on attitudes that the local population has towards the threatened cultural heritage. The moral reason for intervening in order to protect such cultural heritage is thus one step removed in contrast with the reason to intervene for the sake of protecting human lives. This leaves the potential

---

[18] For this view, see Øverland (2014).
[19] Again, it would be more accurate to say that the interveners are ordered to jump in this case, rather than being pushed.

66 HERITAGE AND WAR

interveners with a significantly weaker moral demand to risk their lives in the case of protecting cultural heritage.

In response, it can be argued that the first alleged moral asymmetry between exposing non-culpable civilians to harm and exposing humanitarian interveners to harm, applies to ordinary interventions as well as to cultural ones. Thus, it might be argued that rejecting the permissibility of exposing one's own combatants to harm in order to prevent cultural cleansing would also imply the impermissibility of exposing these combatants for the sake of preventing widespread violations of basic human rights. Hence, there is nothing different in this regard between ordinary humanitarian interventions and cultural ones.

As to the second alleged asymmetry, it can be argued that cultural interveners are not simply asked to take risks for the sake of protecting cultural heritage that matter to the local population, but are asked to take such risks in order for the local population to enjoy the right of shaping and determining their lives and the cultural environment in which they live. In other words, the interveners are not asked to make sacrifices for the sake of fulfilling the mere desires of the local population, but rather to ensure that the latter are able to enjoy an important right.

The success of the latter argument, in justifying exposing the cultural interveners to significant risk, depends on assuming that the right of self-determination, in the sense relevant for the protection of cultural heritage, is significant enough to generate a requirement on others to take on significant cost to ensure its fulfillment. The truth of this assumption is far from obvious, however. While preventing mass atrocities and widespread violations of basic human rights would generate a requirement that involves taking significant risks, it is not at all clear that the prevention of cultural cleansing, and the self-determination associated with it, would generate such a requirement.

5.2 Interveners-Centered Cultural Intervention

The second type of cultural intervention is where the threatened cultural heritage matters mainly to the intervening side, but not for the local population. Such interventions (call them 'interveners-centered cultural interventions') would be more akin to wars of self-defense than humanitarian interventions, since the aim of the military action is to defend the interests of the intervening side rather than to defend the interests of the local population. An example of this type of cultural intervention is the Turkish military operation in Syria in early 2015, which, according to the Turkish government, aimed at protecting the tomb of Sulayman Shah. The latter monument is considered of significance to Turkish people, but not so much to the Syrians. Given that the local population stands to gain little from the intervention, the intervening Turkish force would be less justified in inflicting harm on non-culpable local civilians for the sake of protecting the tomb.

An appeal to Turkish interests in protecting the tomb can hardly provide justification for inflicting collateral defensive harm on innocent local Syrian civilians. Moreover, the possible destruction of the tomb is not part of a campaign of cultural cleansing against Turkish cultural heritage, and its destruction would not affect, in any significant way, the ability of the Turkish people to preserve their cultural landscape and maintain their cultural practices and identity. One can safely assume that the right of the Turkish people to cultural heritage is fully secure within the territories of the Turkish borders. Not only here, but elsewhere as well, it is rarely the case that the right to cultural heritage (even the purely material one) depends on what happens within the borders of other countries.

While it is difficult to justify inflicting harm on the local population in order to protect the cultural heritage that matters mainly to the intervening side, it is easier to justify exposing the intervening force to such harm. Members of the military forces have a role-based duty to protect the legitimate interests of their country and, hence, accept the risks associated with doing so. A question, of course, remains as to whether the protection of the cultural item or site in question (the tomb of Sulayman Shah, in our example) is of sufficient significance to the concerned group (the Turkish people) to justify exposing members of its armed forces to serious harm.[20]

5.3 Non-Centered Cultural Intervention

Finally, we come to the third type of cultural intervention. In this case, the threatened heritage has value to people in general, including the local population and the intervening side, but is of no *special* value to any of the latter two groups (call it Non-Centered Cultural Intervention). The calls for the international community to intervene militarily in Syria, in order to protect

---

[20] According to reports, the Turkish operation to protect the tomb of Sulayman Shah did not cause any casualties among civilians. However, one Turkish soldier was killed during the operation (Kilford 2015).

68 HERITAGE AND WAR

Palmyra from damage and destruction by the advancing ISIS fighters, falls to some extent within this category of cultural interventions.

There is no doubt that Palmyra is a very significant cultural site. Its significance is not premised, however, on the special role it plays in the lives of the population living around it, or on the role it plays in the lives of the Syrian people in general. Similarly, Palmyra is also not of special significance to any given group outside of Syria (other than a small group of archeologists and historians). Thus, while Palmyra has undeniable value, it does not have additional special value, either to the local population or to the potential intervening side.[21]

As with the case in the locals-centered and interveners-centered cultural interventions, we have two issues to address in relation to the third type. The first is whether it is permissible for the outside interveners to put non-culpable local Syrian civilians at risk of serious harm in order to protect Palmyra from ISIS fighters. The second is whether it is permissible to expose combatants of the intervening force to the risk of serious harm in order to protect Palmyra.

With respect to the first question, it seems plausible to maintain that it is less justifiable to collaterally harm members of the local population in the third type of cultural intervention, than to justify doing so in locals-centered cultural interventions where the threatened cultural heritage has special value to the local population. Given that the third type of intervention does not aim at defending the rights and interests of the local population in particular, it is less justifiable to make them carry a significant share of the burden of the intervention.[22]

As for the second question concerning the cost that it is permissible to expose the intervening side to, it is also less justifiable to expose members of the latter group to harm in the third type of cultural intervention, than to do so in interveners-centered cultural interventions where the threatened cultural heritage has significant value to the intervening side. Given that there is nothing especially at stake for the intervening combatants in the third type of

---

[21] It might be argued that, although Palmyra plays no significant role in the cultural practices of the Syrian local population, it might still be of special value to them as a source of local and national pride. To the extent that this may be true, my claim that Palmyra has no special significance for the local population would no longer hold.

[22] It might be argued that the local population would still have a special responsibility to protect the cultural heritage in question on the grounds that it is located within their territory. In other words, it might be argued that the Syrian people have a natural custodianship towards the cultural heritage located in their territory, even if the cultural heritage in question is not one that has special value to them.

cultural intervention, it would not seem justifiable to ask them to carry any serious burdens or risks associated with such intervention.

6. Conclusion

Protecting cultural heritage from damage and destruction may sometimes require military action. Such action is often morally problematic as it is likely to expose human lives to the risk of serious harm. In examining the permissibility of resorting to military action that aims at protecting cultural heritage, I distinguished three groups of people that might be harmed by such military endeavor: culpable aggressors, non-culpable civilians, and cultural interveners, that is, combatants who are engaged in the military effort of protecting cultural heritage.

I argued that it is morally permissible to impose harm on culpable aggressors who aim at damaging or destroying cultural heritage. However, this does not provide a clear way of distinguishing the treatment of cultural heritage from that of ordinary assets, given that culpable aggressors against the latter may be also liable to defensive harm. As for non-culpable civilians, I argued that exposing them to harm may be grounded in the prevention of cultural cleansing, which is in turn grounded in the right of self-determination. This is especially the case when these non-culpable civilians are part of the group that is being defended against cultural cleansing.

As for cultural interveners, I argued that exposing them to harm may be justified by (1) the role-based duty these interveners have to protect the cultural heritage that matters to the rights and legitimate interests of the citizens in the countries on whose behalf they act, and, to a weaker extent, by (2) the protection of other citizens or groups against cultural cleansing. However, I have pointed out that while the role-based duty presents plausible grounds for exposing combatants to harm, it is less likely to provide such grounds for defending cultural heritage outside the jurisdiction of the military force in question. It is unlikely, or exceptional, that cultural heritage that exists outside the territory of a given state is of such importance for the fulfillment of the rights and significant interests of the population of the state in question.[23]

---

[23] The protection of highly significant religious sites, such as Mecca and the Vatican, might provide such exceptional cases.

References

Chakrabortty, Aditya. (2019), 'The Lesson from the Ruins of Notre Dame: Don't Rely on Billionaires', in *The Guardian*, July 18, accessed June 30, 2020, https://www.theguardian.com/commentisfree/2019/jul/18/ruins-notre-dame-billionaires-french-philanthropy.

Christie, Lars. (2018), 'Distributing Harm in Humanitarian Interventions', in R. Jenkins, M. Robillard, and B.J. Strawser (eds.), *Who Should Die?* (Oxford: Oxford University Press), 186–201.

Committee on Culture and Education. (1995), 'War Damage to the Cultural Heritage in Croatia and Bosnia-Herzegovina', Doc. 7431, accessed February 19, 2022, https://assembly.coe.int/nw/xml/XRef/X2H-Xref-ViewHTML.asp?FileID=6989.

Crossette, Barbara. (2001), 'Taliban Explains Buddha Demolition', in *The New York Times*, March 19, accessed June 30, 2020, https://www.nytimes.com/2001/03/19/world/taliban-explains-buddha-demolition.html.

Ermal, Nurja. (2012), 'The Rise and Destruction of Ottoman Architecture in Albania: A Brief History Focused on the Mosques', in A.Z. Furat, and H. Er (eds.), *Balkans and Islam Encounter, Transformation, Discontinuity, Continuity* (Electronic resource, Cambridge Scholars Publishing), 204–205.

Frowe, Helen, and Matravers, Derek. (2019), 'Conflict and Cultural Heritage: A Moral Analysis of the Challenge of Heritage Protection', in J. Paul Getty Trust Occasional Papers in Cultural Heritage Policy, 3 (Los Angeles, CA: J. Paul Getty Trust).

Gore-Langton, Robert. (2012), 'Wipe Out Britain's Historic Cities!', in *Express*, April 21, accessed June 30, 2020, https://www.express.co.uk/expressyourself/315749/Wipe-out-Britain-s-historic-cities.

Kilford, Chris. (2015), 'Operation Shah Euphrates—A Short Military Analysis', in *Today Zarman*, March 2.

McMahan, Jeff. (2010), 'The Just Distribution of Harm between Combatants and Noncombatants', in *Philosophy and Public Affairs* 38/4: 342–379.

McNicoll, Tracy. (2019), 'Notre-Dame Fire Donations Pour In, Spark Controversy', in *France 24*, April 18, accessed June 30, 2020, https://www.france24.com/en/20190418-france-paris-notre-dame-cathedral-fire-donations-controversy.

Øverland, Gerhard. (2014), 'Moral Obstacles: An Alternative to the Doctrine of Double Effect', in *Ethics* 124/3: 481–506.

Singer, Peter. (1972), 'Famine, Affluence, and Morality', in *Philosophy and Public Affairs* 1/1: 229–243.

Singer, Peter. (2009), *The Life You Can Save: Acing Now to End World Poverty* (New York: Random House).

Stoilas, Helen. (2019), 'Nearly €1bn Raised for Notre-Dame over Two Days', in *The Art Newspaper*, April 18, accessed June 30, 2020, https://www.theartnewspaper.com/2019/04/18/nearly-euro1bn-raised-for-notre-dame-over-two-days.

UNESCO. (1954), *Convention for the Protection of Cultural Property in the Event of Armed Conflict*, 2 249 UNTS 240 (Paris: UNESCO).

UNESCO. (1970), *Convention on the Means of Prohibiting and Preserving the Illicit Import, Export and Transfer of Ownership of Cultural Property* (Paris: UNESCO).

Unger, Peter. (1996), *Living High and Letting Die: Our Illusion of Innocence* (New York: Oxford University Press).

Weiss, Thomas G., and Connelly, N. (2017), 'Cultural Cleansing and Mass Atrocities: Protecting Cultural Heritage in Armed Conflict Zones', in J. Paul Getty Trust Occasional Papers in Cultural Heritage Policy, 1 (Los Angeles, CA: J. Paul Getty Trust).

5

Cultural Icons and Reasons of Culture

Dale Dorsey

1. Introduction

Imagine this:

> In the great Anglo-French War of 2163, the British soldiers charged with capturing Paris faced a stark choice. The French insurgents had hidden a large cache of laser blasters, computer malware, and mind control devices in the lowest levels of *Le Théâtre du Grand Guignol*. Ultimately, these soldiers decided that they would preserve the theater, rather than destroying it, prolonging the war by weeks. They chose to do so, given the cultural significance of the theater itself and its importance for French and Parisian history.

Most would argue that the British behavior in this sci-fi scenario was not unreasonable or irrational. Or, at the very least, not the sort of thing for which the British lacked reason, even if (depending, one supposes, on the other sacrifices made to protect the theater) it is not ultimately supported by sufficient reason. We seem to face reasons to protect cultural values such as those represented by the Grand Guignol. Not only do we face such reasons, these reasons seem to be weighty. Imagine, for instance, that it was clear that a blockade of the theater, rather than the destruction of the theater, would cost additional noncombatant casualties. Surely the British would, at the very least, be *justified* in adopting the blockade if the sacrifice of lives were limited enough. And, indeed, I am tempted to say something much stronger: not only is the blockade justified, it is required.

But this seems puzzling. Why should the protection of cultural landmarks, objects of cultural significance, and so forth, be worth the cost of human life, even a single human life? What, to put the point somewhat differently, are the reasons that would justify, even require, the British to accept additional casualties for the sake of the protection of this old theater?

Dale Dorsey, *Cultural Icons and Reasons of Culture* In: *Heritage and War: Ethical Issues*. Edited by: William Bülow, Helen Frowe, Derek Matravers, and Joshua Lewis Thomas, Oxford University Press. © Dale Dorsey 2023.
DOI: 10.1093/oso/9780192862648.003.0005

CULTURAL ICONS AND REASONS OF CULTURE   73

In this chapter, I will critique several answers to this question and offer a possible (though sketchy and tentative) solution. I hold that we should reject the suggestion that reasons to preserve cultural icons can be reduced to welfarist, aesthetic, or historical considerations. Furthermore, I argue that we should reject the claim that such reasons are simply given by the *sui generis* fact that a given icon is of cultural significance. Rather, or so I argue, we respect and preserve items of cultural significance out of a genuine *moral* concern for participants in the culture in question. Properly taking individuals into moral account, or so I argue here, will entail taking seriously the valuing attitudes they have *given* the cultural roles they occupy.

So that's the plan. The roadmap runs as follows. First, I disambiguate a number of questions we might ask about the normative significant culture for the purposes of clarifying the particular question I seek to answer here. In Section 3, I discuss three forms of reductivism about the significance of cultural icons: welfarist, aesthetic, and historical reductivism. In Section 4, I discuss two versions of a *sui generis* approach to cultural icons. And in Section 5, I introduce a final possibility, viz., that the normative significance of cultural icons is a result of a form of *moral* reductivism. I refine and defend this proposal in what remains.

2. Some Questions We Might Ask about Culture, Disambiguated

The question of why culture and cultural institutions should be preserved is, to my ears, hopelessly ambiguous. It can be broken down into many questions, not all of which are guaranteed to have the same or even similar answers. For instance, it may be pertinent to consider:

1. *The Culture Itself*: we may face reasons to preserve the practice of a given culture. Why? And what reasons?
2. *The Cultural Icons*: we may face reasons to preserve objects, landmarks, etc., with significance for a given culture. Why? And what reasons?
3. *The Cultural Practice*: we may face reasons to conform to cultural expectations, or engage in culturally sanctioned behavior. Why? And what reasons?

These are clearly different questions and, I think, could, in principle, permit of very different answers. The first asks why we ought to preserve the existence of a culture *as practiced by individuals*. The second asks why we

74   HERITAGE AND WAR

should preserve objects, artifacts (broadly, "icons"), given their cultural significance, or their significance for the practice of a given culture. The third asks why we should conform to certain internal norms of cultures *assuming* that said culture exists and is practiced. Indeed, notice that the "we" in such questions may very well refer to different people. The first question seems to apply not just to participants in culture *x*—that is, "we" may face reasons to preserve our culture and its transmission—but also to outsiders. For instance, if we find that a particular culture is endangered, we may face reasons to take steps to make sure that it is or can be preserved. We may rationally regret, for instance, that a particular culture or set of cultural practices goes out of existence, even if it is not our own. The second question seems to apply not just to cultural participants, but also to outsiders. Indeed, this seems to apply to the British soldiers in the case under discussion, as well as participants in the culture for which the Grand Guignol is an important aspect or symbol. The third, however, seems to apply specifically to cultural *insiders*—those who participate in a given culture or cultural practice (I will call these people "denizens" of a particular culture).

In this chapter, I'm interested mainly in the second question. And this is significant, in part because this question is in some ways more difficult to answer than the other two. For instance, consider the first question. Famously, some (including, e.g., political communitarians) have argued that individuals have a kind of "right" to the culture of which they are a participant (see, e.g., Taylor 1994). Others have denied this, arguing instead that individuals have (at most) a right to some culture or other or to an "equal capacity," but not equal achievement, of some culture or other (see, e.g., Barry 2002; Sen 1999: ch.10). But even if we accept the stronger claim that individuals maintain rights to a particular culture as it is, it's hard to see how this would provide, for example, the British reason against destroying the Grand Guignol. Cultures—even very specific cultures—survive the destruction of particular cultural icons. But if this is correct, then even a broad commitment to individuals' ability to conform to the cultures in which they participate does not yet answer the question concerning the preservation of particular icons.

In addition, it should be clear from the above remarks that even if, say, Parisians face particular reasons to conform to Parisian culture (and perhaps to form relevant pro-attitudes and so forth that reflect Parisian culture), this does not provide the *British*, non-Parisian as they are, reason to conform to the demands of Parisian culture. But, if in fact we (either as denizens or outsiders) do, why should we face reasons to preserve or protect cultural icons such as the Grand Guignol?

3. Reductivism

The first family of answers I consider here falls under the general heading of "reductivism." By this is meant the proposal that the reasons we face to preserve or protect cultural icons has to do with the value they possess when considered from other, more familiar, standards or standpoints. For instance, if the Grand Guignol were destroyed, we might imagine that there would be a tremendous loss of well-being value. People's lives, especially those who care a lot about the theater would be made worse. Surely we have reason to make people's lives better rather than worse, to not harm others, and so on. Given this straightforward fact, we may be tempted to accept:

Welfarist Reductivism: the reasons to preserve, protect, and so forth, particular cultural icons are derived from the reasons we have to protect and advance the welfare of people.

Second, one might imagine that cultural elements such as this might be assimilated into the domain of aesthetic value. We have reason to preserve, for example, the works of Shakespeare, Big Ben, the music of James Brown and the Famous Flames because they are sublime, they have tremendous value *qua* aesthetic object. Call this view:

Aesthetic Reductivism: the reasons to preserve, protect, and so forth, particular cultural icons are derived from the reasons we have to protect and advance objects of aesthetic value.

Third, we may consider the possibility of:

Historic Reductivism: the reasons to preserve, protect, and so forth, particular cultural icons are derived from the reasons we have to protect objects of historical significance.

For instance, it may be that cultural icons such as the Pyramids of Giza or the village of Machu Picchu are worth preserving, given their historical significance.

A few notes regarding the forms of reductivism I've just proposed. First, I don't mean them to be an exhaustive list of potential forms of reductivism (indeed, I will propose a fourth later on). These, however, seem to me initially plausible for explaining our reasons to protect and preserve cultural icons.

76 HERITAGE AND WAR

Second, while it is likely to be uncontroversial—or near enough—that we have reasons to protect and advance the welfare of people, it may nevertheless be controversial whether we face genuine *aesthetic* reasons,[1] or historical reasons. Nevertheless, I propose to set aside these concerns, insofar as I hold that *even if* such domains generate genuine reasons (even in conjunction), they do not do so in a way that would justify protecting or preserving cultural icons.

3.1 Welfarist Reductivism

To begin, for any reductivist proposal, we can and should ask whether it supports the variety of reasons we seem to have in the face of such questions of preservation. Now, it's unquestionably true that many objects of cultural significance are important for the well-being of people. Cultural practices are important for the quality of many people's lives, and to the extent that the loss of certain cultural icons blights their ability to fully engage in such practices, this will diminish their overall well-being.

However, reductivism of this kind cannot seem to deliver the results that seem plausible in a range of cases. For instance, it would seem implausible to hold that one should simply be indifferent when comparing the destruction of the Grand Guignol, together with modest but equivalent welfare compensation, and the maintenance of the Grand Guignol. Of course, the way we conceive of this case will differ markedly between different theories of welfare. But imagine that for each person who is affected by the destruction of the Grand Guignol, they take a welfare burden of degree d. And also imagine that one could benefit each of these persons by degree d by some other means. It would seem odd to say that there's no reason whatsoever to choose to preserve the cultural landmark rather than destroy it and compensate those who are burdened by its destruction. There's normative, shall we say, *leftover* between the significance of the Grand Guignol and its specific welfarist significance.

Now this argument might be challenged. One might respond by saying that the welfare benefits that individuals maintain, *given* the existence of cultural institutions such as the Grand Guignol, has a kind of lexical or incomparable welfare value.[2] That is, no amount of *other* welfare benefits could make up for the welfare-based loss of the Grand Guignol. But this proposal faces a number

---

[1] Though, of course, there are very strong reasons for thinking that genuine aesthetic reasons exist. See, for instance, King (2018).
[2] For further discussion of lexical dominance relations, see Arrhenius (2005), Dorsey (2009), and Griffin, (1986).

of challenges. First, it would have to be vindicated by specifying exactly *what* welfare benefits individuals maintain, given the existence of the Grand Guignol. Notably, however, these benefits cannot be construed to be *participation in the relevant culture itself*, especially given that—as we have already noted—culture survives the loss of individual cultural icons, at least in typical cases. Of course, one might imagine that there are hedonic, or other mental-state related benefits maintained. But this proposal is problematic insofar as hedonic benefits seem to be eminently fungible. (For instance, one could provide the same degree of welfare benefits—if the loss is to be construed as strictly hedonic—to individuals by, for example, buying them a vacation, or repairing their cobblestone streets, and so forth.) Alternatively, one might hold that the welfare benefits derive from the desires or other pro-attitudes that cultural denizens maintain toward, for example, the Grand Guignol. But what specific desires are we talking about here? Surely I, as a Parisian, will desire to preserve the Grand Guignol, to have it survive, not to have it destroyed, and so on. And, indeed, I may be prepared to sacrifice in blood and toil for its survival. But notice here that we must make a distinction in such pro-attitudes. Not all such attitudes are plausibly welfare-relevant. I may, for instance, as a distant observer, desire that the Notre Dame cathedral be rebuilt to its former splendor. But this desire is not plausibly relevant to the quality of *my* life. And this seems to me what is *typically* (though, perhaps, not always) going on in the case of pro-attitudes toward cultural icons. Generally, if and when I desire to preserve the Grand Guignol, I do it out of a concern for the culture, the city I love, or perhaps the theater itself. It is generally not an attitude I maintain *for my own sake*. But we should not hold that desires I maintain simply for the sake of others, or cultures, or, as it were, buildings, are welfare-relevant pro-attitudes (cf. Dorsey 2012a; Parfit 1984, app.1; Sobel 1998).

On balance, welfarist reductivism is implausible as a theory of reasons to preserve cultural icons. Now, I must be careful here. I am not arguing that there are no welfare-based reasons to preserve cultural icons. However, it seems right to say that welfarist reductivism does not capture the whole story: it does not provide a complete catalog of the reasons we have to preserve cultural icons.

3.2 Aesthetic Reductivism

In light of the failure of welfarist reductivism, we may wish to offer an aesthetic reduction. After all, many cultural icons have tremendous aesthetic value. But, of course, the problems with this proposal should be immediately

78   HERITAGE AND WAR

manifest. While many cultural icons surely have substantial aesthetic value, not all do. One might imagine, for instance, that in the year 2163, the Grand Guignol is a dilapidated, ugly shell of its former self. But this doesn't seem to eliminate the reasons the British soldiers may have had to protect it, even at the cost of death and disability for the military and civilian population. Of course, it may reduce the facts that count in favor of their so doing—the beauty of the building is no longer such a reason. But this does not entail that there is no reason, *given* its status as a cultural icon.

Here's another example. Just south of Lawrence, Kansas there is a large swath of largely unremarkable swampland, the sort that seems ripe for economic development. However, for more of the history of this land, consider the following passage:

> The United States Indian Industrial Training School, [later referred to as the Haskell Indian Nations University], was one of the first boarding schools and opened in 1884 with the goal of giving American Indian students the vocational skills necessary to assimilate in order to "kill the Indian and save the man." Haskell began its boarding school with twenty-two Indian students from various tribes across the U.S., first focusing on agricultural trades. Student life was rigid and inflexible: if a child was caught speaking their tribal language, practicing traditional customs, or not adhering to the militaristic standards of school behavior, cruel and unusual punishments were utilized to deter their "deviant" behavior—which sometimes resulted in the death of the child.
>
> The school was located on wetlands to use land that white settlers did not want, yet the wetlands became a place of comfort and ceremony for many of the students forced into this harsh new way of life. The wetlands served as a place of farewells, where elders left children with words of advice and prayer, and a meeting place for students to reunite with their families and friends when they were homesick. Students often went to the wetlands to perform ceremonies, pray, commune with nature and the environment, and even to bury their dead. The children's deaths were caused by disease, suicide, sometimes the environment itself, as runaway students died of exposure in the wetlands. Students were secretly buried in the wetlands by their fellow students, who performed spirit release ceremonies using a lock of hair. Thus the area has always been a site of resistance, a fact recognized by school officials, who tried to "kill" the wetlands—cutting down vegetation and draining the water—in order to prevent the cultural activities which took place there.   (Seyler and Corbin 2004)

It is clear, then, that the relevant wetlands has tremendous cultural significance for the Native American population in and around Lawrence. And, indeed, this cultural significance came to be a major flashpoint when a bypass road, intended to connect Topeka, Lawrence, and Kansas City, was to be constructed on the land, destroying the graves located there. Whether or not it is ultimately acceptable to build such a road (it was eventually constructed), it seems right to say that the cultural significance of the land is at least *a* reason to preserve it. But notice that this has nothing to do with the aesthetic significance of the wetlands, which is, as noted, unremarkable.

3.3 Historical Reductivism

In this subsection, I consider the possibility that we may have *historical* reasons to preserve cultural icons, and that the reasons to do so may be reduced to such reasons. Now, the very nature of historical reasons is not altogether clear, at least to me. However, it seems plausible to hold that *the fact that x is historically significant* is in fact a reason to, for example, preserve or protect it, and I will treat "historical reasons," in essence, as being facts of this kind: facts of historical significance.

With this out of the way, it seems to me at least plausible to hold that the fact that some thing, that is, a building, artwork, and so forth, has historical significance is a reason to preserve or protect it. For instance, we may think there is good reason to preserve the engrossed copy of the United States' Declaration of Independence. And surely the reason to do so is that this document has such profound historical significance. If this is correct, which I will allow for the purposes of argument here, then it seems quite right to believe that we have reason to preserve many cultural icons, given their historical significance. This may plausibly apply to, for example, the Grand Guignol, as well as, for example, Stonehenge, or the Bamiyan Buddha statues, destroyed by the Taliban in 2001. Furthermore, it may be that some cultural icons that lack specific aesthetic value could, in principle, be protected, given reasons of historical significance, such as the aforementioned wetlands.

However, it's hard for me to see how or why reasons to protect cultural icons can or should be limited to their historical significance. First, clearly not all cultural icons will maintain historical significance. For instance, we might think that the Washington Monument is worthy of protection. But it is not because the monument *itself* has historical significance. Indeed, this fact seems to me commonplace of cultural icons, including cultural icons that are

80 HERITAGE AND WAR

relatively new—such as, for example, the London Eye—and cultural icons that, while old in age are nevertheless not significant as a matter of history.

Of course, one could simply respond that even if such icons lack historical significance, they may nonetheless maintain, for example, aesthetic or welfarist significance. Fair enough. Indeed, reductivists may sensibly claim that while neither historical, aesthetic, nor welfarist reductivism can capture all of our reasons to preserve cultural icons, these sets of reasons are nonetheless jointly sufficient to do so.[3] But, or so it seems to me, we should reject this claim, as well. Take again the Wetlands. Plausibly, it lacks aesthetic or welfarist significance. And while it may very well maintain historical significance, even this fact is not sufficient to fully capture the normative significance of its preservation. While we may seek to preserve the Wetlands as a historical matter, were the Wetlands to be lost, this loss would be felt not simply as a loss "of history." It would be felt as a loss *to a culture*—the loss of a particular cultural icon that, given this fact, matters. To put this another way, we don't preserve the Haskell-Baker Wetlands out of (or at least *entirely* out of) a concern for its *historical* significance. We preserve the Haskell-Baker Wetlands *at least in part* because of the *special* significance this land has for the Native American culture whose icon it is.

4. Sui Generism

I think the aforementioned forms of reductivism cannot fully account for the normative significance of cultural icons and their preservation. This may cause us to supplement reductivism and suggest that we also face certain *sui generis* reasons with respect to the preservation or protection of culturally significant icons.

There are a few ways one might be a sui generist about cultural icons; one could be an axiological sui generist or a normative sui generist. The first form of sui generism of this kind holds that cultural items, landmarks, etc., have specifically *intrinsic value*: they are valuable, period, and generate reasons for being valuable in this way. Of course, G.E. Moore thought that all intrinsic value supervened on the intrinsic properties of valuable states (Moore 1993). But that can't be right in the case of cultural artifacts, states, etc. After all, one might imagine a universe containing only the Grand Guignol. Would that be better or worse than a state containing nothing? If we abstract from any, say,

---

[3] Thanks to Joshua Thomas and Derek Matravers for helpful comments here.

aesthetic value the theater maintains, then the answer is obviously 'no'. And, indeed, there's good reason for this. Cultural artifacts of this kind have their *sui generis* cultural value, if value there is to be had, through their *relational* properties, as a result of contextual factors, including interaction with cultural denizens in various ways, that render it an object of cultural significance. It cannot be valuable all by itself.

But maybe that's not a big deal for axiological sui generism. Recall that whether or not all intrinsic value supervenes on intrinsic properties is a controversial hypothesis, one that many (including Hurka 1998, Korsgaard 1997, Kagan 1998, and myself 2012b) have argued against. In light of this, one possibility might be that, say, the Grand Guignol has intrinsic value—but its intrinsic value is explained at least in part by its status as a cultural institution, by the fact that, for example, it has significance in Parisian culture. Call this an *axiological* sui generism.

Note, however, that this is simply one form of sui generism. This form might be compared with a view that takes no general stand on the axiological value of cultural icons, but holds instead that there is a *reason* to preserve them and that—and hence the sui generism—this reason just *is* the fact that the particular object in question is a cultural icon. Call this a *normative* sui generism.

But both forms of sui generism seem unsatisfactory. Consider a dead culture for whom a particular rock formation had cultural significance. There are no adherents to the culture, no one whose welfare will be diminished by removing or rearranging the rock formation, it has no aesthetic or historical significance, and so on. Do we have any reason to preserve this rock formation? I'm struggling to see that we do. Of course, we do sometimes preserve cultural landmarks of dead cultures: ancient cave paintings, for instance. But in those cases we don't seem to preserve, or think we have reason to preserve, the landmarks because of their cultural significance *per se*, but rather, say, their historical significance or the insight they provide for us of long-dead civilizations. Or, perhaps, their *current* cultural significance (i.e., the cultural significance Stonehenge may have for current Europeans).

Of course, one might seek to revise both forms of sui generism to focus specifically on live cultures, cultures who actually have adherents. After all, one might say, the intrinsic value of certain cultural icons needn't be eternal. Sometimes cultural icons, objects, and states (and so forth) can lose intrinsic value (or cease to be reason-generators) insofar as they are no longer objects of cultural significance. But on reflection this doesn't seem right, or at least doesn't seem the way we'd describe the particular objects involved.

82   HERITAGE AND WAR

In describing the rock formation, it seems sensible to say that it never lost the status of being culturally significant. It just so happens that it is culturally significant only in the context of an unpracticed culture, a culture for whom there are no denizens.

What I think is going on here is better described as focusing not on the fact that the object in question is a cultural icon—this fact seems to me eternal—but rather the fact that certain people—extant people—*in fact* seem to care about it. To put this another way, the difference between the Grand Guignol and the rock formation is not that one of them is not a cultural icon. Rather, the difference is that there are *people for whom* the Grand Guignol is a cultural icon, there are no such people in the case of the rock formation. We care less about the object itself, given its status as a cultural icon—instead, we care about the *people for whom* that object is significant. Consider, again, the Haskell-Baker Wetlands. As noted above, we care to preserve the Wetlands not out of a concern for, say, its historical significance. Its historical significance is not of special interest for any *particular* individual or group of individuals. But we preserve the Wetlands (at least in part) out of a concern for the Native Americans whose cultural icon it is, out of a concern for those people who care about it.

But if this is correct, then we appear to have a substantial shift in the way we understand the reasons stemming from the intrinsic value *of the object* to a general concern for the people for whom the cultural icon is, in fact, an icon. And, on reflection, this seems right. In protecting the Grand Guignol, it's hard to see how we care, unless we are Parisians, about the Grand Guignol *per se*. Rather, we seem to care about the Grand Guignol only derivatively—given its significance for real, live, Parisians.

5. A Modified Derivative View

By way of a proposal, I'd like to first consider *how*, for example, the Grand Guignol has significance for real, live, Parisians. Surely this must, in some sense, be mediated by the Parisians' valuing attitudes. If, for instance, most Parisians simply didn't care at all about the Grand Guignol, its artistic history, and so on, it seems right to say that any further reason the British may have to preserve it *qua* cultural institution ceases. (Though they may have other reasons to preserve it, i.e., aesthetic or historical reasons.) Or, at the very least, the reasons are significantly diminished in significance. This doesn't mean that the Grand Guignol ceases to be a cultural institution.

Rather, it ceases to be *valued as such*, it ceases to be a cultural institution *for the people of Paris*.

To put the point somewhat bluntly, but perhaps accurately, for the Grand Guignol to be a cultural icon, it must be the object of the valuing attitudes of the people of Paris *insofar as* those people are denizens of that culture. But if this is right, it seems possible to offer a modified derivative account of the reasons we face to preserve cultural icons. Call this:

The Value-Based View: the reasons to preserve, protect, and so forth, particular cultural institutions, objects, landmarks, etc., are derived from the reasons we have to respect the valuing attitudes of those for whom those landmarks are valued *qua* cultural institutions.

Note that we should distinguish the *Value-Based View* from *Welfarist Reductivism*. Even if we accept a preferentist or value-based view of welfare, as I do myself, recall that not all preferences, were they to be satisfied, have an influence on the quality of a person's life. Some preferences have welfarist content, others do not. Here, or so it would seem, while some may value the Grand Guignol for the sake of their own welfare, it seems right that many who care about the Grand Guignol will not care about it for their own sake, but rather for the sake of the culture itself. And hence the form of reductivism involved here is not a welfarist reductivism *per se*, but rather a form of reductivism that grants normative status to cultural icons, given the valuing attitudes of cultural denizens.

One might wonder, after all, why *mere* valuing attitudes, if these valuing attitudes are not welfare-relevant, should be significant in determining the normative status of cultural icons. The answer runs as follows. Plausibly, there are reasons—perhaps even straightforward moral reasons—to take seriously the valuing attitudes of agents, even if the satisfaction of those valuing attitudes does not help to determine the welfare of the person whose attitudes they are. Take a simple example. It may matter to me a great deal that my favorite easy chair is handed down to my eldest daughter upon my death. Now, that it is so handed down isn't going to make a difference to my welfare. After all, I am—or will be at the relevant time—dead as a doornail. But it seems right to say that there are good reasons to take my preference seriously and act in accordance with it out of a moral concern for me.

Indeed, this proposal is reflected in a number of important views of moral consideration. For these views, we properly take people into moral consideration if we seek to advance their ends, preferences, or goals. Views like this

84   HERITAGE AND WAR

are suggested by Kant and Kantians[4] (consider, for instance, the injunction to take the ends of others as one's own), as well as some consequentialists, such as David Sobel (1998). Thus it does not seem implausible to hold that the *Value-Based View* is a kind of *moral* reductivism: reducing reasons to preserve and protect cultural icons to the method by which we properly take individuals into moral account. In addition, if we accept the *Value-Based View*, we can plausibly distinguish the Grand Guignol—which we appear to have reasons to preserve, from this rock formation—which we don't.[5] In the latter case, there are no people who maintain preferences or valuing attitudes regarding the rock formation as a cultural landmark. In the former case, there are (or so we presume for the sake of argument).

However, there is a problem with the *Value-Based View* as stated. Consider the following supposition. Imagine that no Parisians care about the Grand Guignol *qua* cultural institution. But there is, nonetheless, a group of dedicated North Dakotans who are steadfastly committed to the preservation of the Grand Guignol *insofar as it is an aspect of Parisian culture*. They are committed, in other words, to a certain vision of Parisian culture, of which the Grand Guignol is a part, and care deeply about its preservation on those grounds. It would seem, given the *Value-Based View*, that the British have reason to preserve the Grand Guignol, given the commitments of these decidedly non-Parisians. After all, their preferences are to preserve this theater insofar as it is an aspect of Parisian culture, and the *Value-Based View* indicates that we have reason to respect such preferences. This seems too strong.

Now, of course, the problem here is clear. North Dakotans are not denizens of Parisian culture, or, at least, none of the North Dakotans I know. Only the preferences of the *member* of the culture do we have reason to respect as they concern the aspects of that culture. But while this is a plausible view, in saying this we lose the *Value-Based View*'s plausible link to a general theory of moral consideration. After all, if the North Dakotans really take as their end the preservation of the Grand Guignol, isn't this something we have special reason to accept?

---

[4] Cf. Immanuel Kant, *The Groundwork of the Metaphysics of Morals* 4:430: "but there is still only a negative and not a positive agreement with *humanity as an end in itself* unless everyone also tries, as far as he can, to further the ends of others. For, the ends of a subject who is an end in itself must as far as possible be also *my* ends, if that representation is to have its *full* effect in me."

[5] Perhaps that's too strong. We may have reasons to preserve it, but these reasons plausibly stem only from the historical or aesthetic significance of the formation, not its cultural significance. Thanks to Joshua Lewis Thomas.

6. The Role Principle

The problem here is to be found in the *Value-Based View as a theory of proper moral consideration*. I have critiqued this view elsewhere in some detail (Dorsey 2018), so I won't really go into it here much, but there is an alternative account that seems more promising, contained in a principle I call:

The Role Principle: in addition to the welfare of individuals, moral consideration requires a moral agent x to take into consideration a person y's valuing attitudes *insofar as* these valuing attitudes are reflected in the normatively significant roles that y occupies.

Here's an easy case that illustrates the way the *Role Principle* works:

Fire Rescue: Matt and his daughter Alice are trapped on a high floor of a burning building. Eventually, a firefighter, Dawn, appears who (for all anyone knows) could only save one of them. Matt insists that Dawn save Alice, leaving himself behind.

Here Dawn saves Alice, surely in part out of consideration for Alice, but also out of consideration *for Matt*, in particular, out of consideration for Matt's status *as a father to Alice* which is itself a normatively significant role, given that Matt faces practical reasons to behave toward Alice in certain specific ways, given that he is Alice's father. The *Role Principle* reflects this: for Dawn, in this case, proper moral consideration of Matt is derived from the preferences he has given his role as a father to Alice.

There are (at least) two ways one might doubt the *Role Principle*.[6] To begin, one might doubt that a person has the power, given their preferences (whether or not role-related), to change the moral landscape in the way I describe. To see this, consider two examples. First,[7] one might imagine that the choice is not between Matt and Alice, but between Alice and an unrelated person, Reggie. But one might imagine that Matt (out of harm's way) is calling audibly for Dawn to save Alice. Plausibly (though contentiously), Dawn should ignore Matt's shouts, and hence his role as Alice's father. And while I'll grant this for the sake of argument, this doesn't tell against the *Role Principle*, but is rather

---

[6] For a much more thorough defense of my position against some of these objections, see Dorsey (2018).

[7] Thanks to Helen Frowe.

86 HERITAGE AND WAR

an illustration of the claim that, in this case, Matt is not to be taken into deliberative consideration. It doesn't tell us *how* Matt is to be taken into deliberative consideration—which is what the *Role Principle* dictates—insofar as he *is*. Second,[8] one might imagine that Matt, Reggie, and Alice are all in the burning building together. Reggie insists on being saved, but Matt directs Dawn to save Alice. One might think it implausible to hold that Dawn now has greater reason to save Alice than Reggie, just because Matt "threw his weight" (cf. Sobel 1998) behind Alice's well-being. Of course, it would still plausibly represent a moral failure if Dawn failed to take Matt's preferences into account, but only because Matt has, at best, a power to take himself *out* of moral consideration, not to add to the reasons to save Alice.[9]

Note that my intuitions differ on this case, but I'll offer a more general suggestion in response. To hold that Matt simply has the power to take himself out of moral consideration would seem to entail that once he expresses his preferences, his preferences no longer have any effect on what Dawn ought to do (beyond, obviously, not saving himself). But this can't be correct. To see this, imagine that a former Mayor of New Orleans is dying of cancer. A friend offers to pay a considerable amount of money to keep the Mayor comfortable and in the best possible care up until the end. The Mayor refuses, and insists that the friend instead donate that money to assist in the rebuilding of a failing New Orleans primary school. This would seem to provide reason for the friend to donate *specifically* to the primary school, *given* the preferences of the Mayor (and given the fact that the Mayor has a special role in relation to the school). The Mayor may also have instructed the friend to donate specifically to, say, cancer research (which obviously the Mayor has a special role in relation to), with the effect on the reasons being similarly transferred. The idea here is that when the Mayor refuses assistance, at least in this case, she doesn't take herself out of consideration; her preferences help to determine what proper moral consideration of her amounts to. The same, or so I claim, is happening in the case of Matt and Alice and, indeed, in the case of Matt, Reggie, and Alice.

Further, one might hold that while preferences are relevant in determining proper moral consideration, they need not be specifically linked to a person's normatively significant roles. Couldn't Reggie insist that Alice be saved, and shouldn't Dawn take Reggie's preference seriously? If this is correct, why believe that Matt's role *as a father* is relevant? In response to this, it is clearly

---

[8] Thanks to Joshua Lewis Thomas.
[9] For illuminating discussion of this point, see Parry (2017).

true that the preferences that can help to form proper moral consideration of a person are not unrestricted in content. An abused woman may, even quite autonomously, prefer the welfare of her abuser to her own (Cf. Dorsey 2018: 39–47). But even if she does, this would not entail that proper moral consideration *of her* would be to advance the welfare of her abuser. I might, even quite autonomously, prefer the welfare of Brad Pitt to my own, just because I'm such a huge fan. But this does not mean that a would-be benefactor of me has reason to privilege the welfare of Brad Pitt. Now, this just entails that some preferences are or should be ruled out as helping to determine proper moral consideration. Why think it is the role-based preferences, specifically, that are doing the work here? I think the answer runs as follows. In suggesting that it is role-based preferences specifically doing the work, rather than, for example, preferences that reflect, say, agent-neutral reasons, we capture the sense in which proper consideration of a person is proper consideration *of them*. It is *their specific normative circumstances*, that is, the normatively significant roles *they occupy*, that are reflected in proper moral consideration (cf. Dorsey 2018: 49). Now, this does not entail that Reggie's preferences are irrelevant to Dawn's deliberation. But the best explanation for this is that Reggie's preferences do something different: they activate a power to take oneself out of moral consideration—they do not help to determine what proper moral consideration *of Reggie* happens to be, insofar as he is to be considered morally.

A number of questions, at this point, arise. First: what is a normatively significant role? I interpret this notion somewhat broadly, but in essence the suggestion is this. A person p occupies a normatively significant role r to the extent that p faces practical reasons or *stronger* practical reasons, *given p's* occupancy of r—reasons that other, non-r-occupiers do not face. Thus *being Alice's father* is a normatively significant role of Matt's.[10] After all, he faces reasons, given his maintenance of this role (i.e., reasons derived from Alice's welfare, her development, and so on), reasons that other people lack or that are comparatively weakened. Sometimes such reasons are simply the fact of the role itself. For instance, one such reason faced by Matt, given that he is Alice's father, *is the fact that Matt is Alice's father*.

Normatively significant roles are numerous and have different constitutive norms, reasons, and so on, that help to determine their normative significance. Being a judge, for instance, is a normatively significant role (one that, arguably,

---

[10] Indeed, though I'd be tempted to resist, one could permissibly interpret the nature of a role to include Reggie's relationship to Alice, that is, as a fellow participant in a life-or-death situation. This may help to assuage some concern about the *Role Principle* while nevertheless ruling out the possibility that just any old preference counts.

88   HERITAGE AND WAR

provides reasons for the judge to treat the law with greater normative significance than non-judges [*pace* Brink 1985]). Being a professor is a normatively
significant role (one that, arguably, provides reasons for the professor to treat
academic considerations with greater regard than non-professors), and so on.
Furthermore, different normatively significant roles will provide reasons of
greater strength. It may be plausible to say that Matt, as a father, is *required*
to ask Dawn to save Alice.[11] But a professor, arguably, is not always *required* to
take academic considerations as decisive.[12]

But what about the case of the Grand Guignol? Here I suggest that *being a
cultural denizen* is a normatively significant role. This is, in part, given point
(3) discussed in Section 1: we seem to face reasons to conform to the practices
of the culture we are engaged in, just as Matt faces special reasons to look after
his daughter that others do not. As cultural denizens, we seem to face reasons
(though mostly non-decisive) to behave in certain ways, to preserve and protect the practice of the culture we are engaged in. And if this is correct, then
the preferences of cultural denizens *insofar as they are cultural denizens* will
have significance in our moral consideration.

7. The Role Principle and the Grand Guignol

How, then, does the *Role Principle* vindicate the decision of the British to preserve the Grand Guignol at the cost of life and limb? In basic terms, the story
runs something like this. Because Parisians, as denizens of Parisian culture,
value the Grand Guignol, and insofar as the British have moral reasons to
take Parisian citizens seriously and to accord them moral consideration, the
British soldiers have reasons to respect and fulfill the valuing attitudes of
Parisians, *given* the roles Parisians occupy. Put bluntly, the British soldiers
take the Parisians seriously not just in terms of their interests or well-being
but also under the auspices of the particular roles they occupy, viz., denizens
of the Parisian civic culture. And insofar as the denizens of the Parisian civic
culture prefer that the Grand Guignol survive rather than be destroyed (or so
we shall stipulate here), the British have moral reason to preserve it, weighed,
of course, against the other reasons they may face.[13]

---

[11] Thanks to Helen Frowe.

[12] For evidence: consider the widespread, and normatively justified, relaxing of academic standards
during the COVID-19 pandemic.

[13] Of course, this does not entail that the British *must* lay down their lives in this way. There are
many reasons that must be weighed here. But it does entail, plausibly, that the British have *reason* to
do so, given the preferences of the Parisians in this case. Thanks to Joshua Lewis Thomas, whom I
suspect will not agree with my intuitions here.

Now, this establishes a reason to preserve the Grand Guignol. But it does not yet say anything about the weight of such a reason. Why think that the reason to preserve this cultural icon can tell against the (surely significant) reasons to preserve life and limb? Here the answer is likely to be found, at least as a rough guide, in the valuing attitudes of the Parisians themselves. Here is one plausible scenario:

Scenario One: The cultural denizens of Paris would prefer that the Grand Guignol be saved, even at some cost to Parisian life and limb.

Here it seems quite right that proper moral consideration of the cultural denizens would entail preserving the Grand Guignol even at some reasonable cost to life and limb. Of course, it would be difficult to spell out the precise cost, but this makes little difference here. And, indeed, it's clear that the reasons involved can be as weighty as this. After all, one need only consult *Fire Rescue*.

However, one might also consider:

Scenario Two: The cultural denizens of Paris would prefer that Parisian life and limb be spared to the preservation of the Grand Guignol.

In this case, it would seem that the reasons involved clearly tell in favor of *not* risking additional deaths for the sake of the preservation of the Grand Guignol. After all, the cultural denizens of Paris do not value the Grand Guignol highly enough to spill blood to preserve it.

Of course, these are ideal cases, where all individuals agree, or maintain the same preferences. In real life cases there will be disagreements among cultural denizens concerning the weight of particular reasons, their individual preferences, and so on. But this is no problem. This simply entails that moral consideration requires a careful weighting of individual preferences in determining the proper way to treat a large number of individuals. And this just is a commonplace problem of making aggregative moral judgments, a problem I will (mercifully) not broach here.[14]

Furthermore, the *Role Principle* clearly assuages worries about the preferences of non-cultural denizens. While North Dakotans are surely denizens of some culture or other, and should have their preferences respected in that

---

[14] I don't mean to suggest here that there are not very serious issues that arise when aggregating individual preferences. See, for instance, Parry (2017). I just mean to say that this particular issue is an instance of a more general problem, and doesn't present any *particular* problem when it comes to the *Role Principle*.

90   HERITAGE AND WAR

way, they are not—or so the stipulation goes—denizens of particularly *Parisian* culture. They do not maintain *that role*. And so any preferences they have *qua* Parisian culture do not command the same respect as the preferences denizens of Parisian culture actually command. Furthermore, the *Role Principle* accommodates the intuition that we preserve, for example, the Haskell-Baker Wetlands, not out of a concern for its aesthetic or historical value, but rather for the sake of those members of the culture who care about it. We have reason to preserve these Wetlands *because we are concerned about the Native Americans for whom they are culturally significant*. Because they are cultural denizens, because being a cultural denizen is a normatively significant role, we have reason to preserve these Wetlands out of a moral concern *for them*.

8. Conclusion

In summary, I have here investigated the reasons we have to preserve, protect, and so on, cultural institutions, landmarks, objects. I argued that these reasons are not derivative of, for example, welfarist or aesthetic considerations. They also cannot plausibly be explained by the intrinsic value of the cultural institutions, etc., themselves. Rather, or so I claim, respect for cultural institutions turns out to be derivative of the normative consideration we owe *people*, insofar as they embody the role of cultural denizens.

If this is correct, then answers to the other two questions that arise when it comes to cultural preservation and practice may suggest themselves. First, we have reasons to engage in cultural practices because to be a cultural denizen is a normatively significant role. Second, we may face reasons to preserve the practice of a given culture, given the preferences of cultural denizens that it be so preserved. Of course, this doesn't entail that we ought to preserve certain cultural practices at the cost of well-being for, for example, future generations and so on; obviously welfarist considerations and other morally relevant considerations must trade off against the reasons generated by the preferences of cultural denizens.

References

Arrhenius, Gustaf. (2005), "Superiority in Value," in *Philosophical Studies* 123/1–2: 97–114.

Barry, Brian. (2002), *Culture and Equality* (Cambridge, MA: Harvard University Press).

Brink, David O. (1985), "Legal Positivism and Natural Law Reconsidered," in *The Monist* 68/3: 364–387.

Dorsey, Dale. (2009), "Headaches, Lives, and Value," in *Utilitas* 21/1: 36–58.

Dorsey, Dale. (2012a), "Subjectivism without Desire," in *Philosophical Review* 121/3: 407–442.

Dorsey, Dale. (2012b), "Intrinsic Value and the Supervenience Principle," in *Philosophical Studies* 157/2: 267–285.

Dorsey, Dale. (2018), "The Focus of Interpersonal Morality," in M. Timmons (ed.), *Oxford Studies in Normative Ethics, v.8* (Oxford: Oxford University Press).

Griffin, James. (1986), *Well-Being: Its Meaning, Measurement, and Moral Importance* (Oxford: Oxford University Press).

Hurka, Tom. (1998), "Two Kinds of Organic Unity," in *Journal of Ethics* 2/4: 299–320.

Kagan, Shelly. (1998), "Rethinking Intrinsic Value," in *Journal of Ethics* 2/4: 277–297.

Kant, Immanuel. (1785), *Groundwork of the Metaphysics of Morals.*

King, Alexandra. (2018), "The Amoralist and the Anaesthetic," in *Pacific Philosophical Quarterly* 99/4: 632–663.

Korsgaard, Christine. (1997), "Two Distinctions in Goodness," in C. Korsgaard, *Creating the Kingdom of Ends* (Cambridge: Cambridge University Press).

Moore, G. E. (1993), "The Conception of Intrinsic Value," in T. Baldwin (ed.), *Principia Ethica* (Cambridge: Cambridge University Press).

Parfit, Derek. (1984), *Reasons and Persons* (Oxford: Oxford University Press).

Parry, Jonathan. (2017), "Defensive Harm, Consent, and Intervention," in *Philosophy and Public Affairs* 45/4: 363–366.

Sen, Amartya. (1999), *Development as Freedom* (New York: Anchor Books).

Seyler, Alicia, and Corbin, Amy. (2004), "Haskell-Baker Wetlands," *Sacred Land Film Project*, accessed February 19, 2022, https://sacredland.org/haskell-baker-wetlands-united-states/.

Sobel, David. (1998), "Well-Being as the Object of Moral Consideration," in *Economics and Philosophy* 14/2: 249–281.

Taylor, Charles. (1994), *Multiculturalism* (Princeton, NJ: Princeton University Press).

6

Cultural Heritage Protection and the Reconciliation Thesis

William Bülow and Joshua Lewis Thomas

1. Introduction

Cultural heritage is frequently damaged or destroyed during armed conflict, often constituting a considerable loss for both the local population and a wide variety of stakeholders further afield, including religious, scientific, and artistic communities, amongst others.[1] Preventing these harms provides strong reasons to protect cultural heritage during war. However, for those who oppose the destruction of heritage, a further argument is also commonly made: that cultural heritage ought to be protected, in part because doing so can help to secure lasting peace and reconciliation post-conflict. For example, Irina Bokova, former Director-General of UNESCO, holds that the protection of cultural heritage is a security imperative because, amongst other things, "[w]e need culture and heritage for reconciliation and resilience, to build confidence—to achieve peace and understanding" (Bokova 2016: 9). Similarly, Thomas Weiss and Nina Connelly argue that heritage should be defended in war, in part because damage to heritage "impedes or destroys the basis for post-conflict peacebuilding and eventual economic development" (2017: 11). Two core claims underlie statements of this sort: (1) that warring states should aim to establish a lasting peace post-conflict; and (2) that this provides a strong reason for them to protect cultural heritage from harm throughout the conflict. In the absence of a better name, we call this the *Reconciliation Thesis*.

Our aim in this chapter is to take a closer look at the Reconciliation Thesis in order to examine its plausibility and its implications for cultural heritage protection in war. We begin by discussing the extent to which belligerents

---

[1] We are thankful to Helen Frowe, Derek Matravers, and Emma Cunliffe for constructive and helpful comments on earlier drafts of this chapter, which was written during our time as postdoctoral research fellows in the Heritage in War project, funded by the Arts and Humanities Research Council (grant number AH/P015077/1). We have each contributed equally to the chapter.

William Bülow and Joshua Lewis Thomas, *Cultural Heritage Protection and the Reconciliation Thesis* In: *Heritage and War: Ethical Issues*. Edited by: William Bülow, Helen Frowe, Derek Matravers, and Joshua Lewis Thomas, Oxford University Press. © William Bülow and Joshua Lewis Thomas 2023. DOI: 10.1093/oso/9780192862648.003.0006

have reason to aim at a lasting peace and what this amounts to in the context of armed conflict. We argue that combatants have a strong reason not to jeopardise the prospects of such a peace and post-war reconciliation (Section 2). We then turn to the proposal that the protection of cultural heritage is important for reconciliation. We identify three ways in which heritage might be instrumental to this end: (i) Economic Rehabilitation; (ii) Educational Uses; and (iii) Return of Displaced Populations (Section 3). Putting these things together, it appears as though combatants may well have an instrumental reason to protect cultural heritage during armed conflict in order to promote post-war reconciliation. However, as we argue, it is not clear how strong this reason is, especially when weighed against competing values and interests (Section 4). In particular, it remains unclear whether, in virtue of the Reconciliation Thesis, combatants should be prepared to put innocent lives or other vital parts of civilian infrastructure at risk for the sake of protecting cultural heritage. To explore this issue, we argue that the Reconciliation Thesis can explain another claim frequently made in the literature on cultural heritage and war, which we refer to as the *Inseparability Thesis*.[2] This thesis, which is often evoked in order to justify the protection of heritage during armed conflict, states that there is no need to choose between saving lives and preserving cultural heritage since they are inseparable projects.[3] While it is possible to interpret this claim in a number of different ways, one interpretation, we argue, is in terms of the Reconciliation Thesis; essentially, to the extent that defending heritage can help to safeguard human lives and interests in the future via the promotion of reconciliation, it can be seen as serving the same end as the direct defence of human life. Nevertheless, even if there is a sense in which protecting heritage can amount to protecting lives, it is not obvious that combatants should always be prepared to directly risk lives (or other things of moral significance) for the sake of heritage. Rather, as we argue, this claim too faces some important challenges.

2. The Importance of Aiming at a Lasting Peace

Some philosophers argue that states must aim to bring about peace and that a war cannot be just if its occurrence, or the way it is fought, undermines or

---

[2] Here we take a cue from Matthes (2018), who refers to this claim as the 'Principle of Inseparability'.
[3] For critical discussion of the Inseparability Thesis, see Matthes (2018) and Frowe and Matravers (2019).

94   HERITAGE AND WAR

threatens the prospects of peace (see e.g., Rawls 1999). While we are sceptical of whether the prospect of securing a lasting peace provides an absolute moral constraint on waging war, we find it intuitively plausible that warring states have reason to aim at a lasting peace, or at the very least not to jeopardise it when such peace is possible. One reason for this is that obtaining peace arguably serves the good of the community; and, as Suzanne Uniacke points out, the legitimacy of political leaders, as well as their authority to declare war, depends on their acting for the good of the community. By declaring war, political leaders act on behalf of others for whom they are responsible and thus, given their responsibility, a legitimate authority has the right to wage a war only if this will also serve the good of the community (Uniacke 2014). Admittedly, it is open for discussion what exactly constitutes the good of the community in various scenarios. However, it is at least reasonable to think that it will sometimes require more than merely fending off an attack, and that warring states have further important responsibilities, including, when feasible, securing a lasting peace (2014).[4]

Besides this, political leaders also have more general moral reasons to attempt to preserve the prospect of post-conflict peace, independently of their role-specific responsibilities. In brief, if a war ends but a stable peace cannot be built, this increases the chances of a future war that will inflict, as war invariably does, a variety of serious harms on innocent people. Granting that such harms are of moral significance, the leaders of warring states have weighty reasons to support the possibility of establishing a lasting peace whenever possible.

Insofar as political leaders have the reasons outlined above to aim at a lasting peace, it follows that their preferred aim should be to create what peace scholars refer to as 'positive peace', as long as doing so is feasible. Positive peace involves more than the mere absence of fighting. Rather, it is characterized by active cooperation and coexistence between former belligerents (Fabre 2016). Thus, assuming that this type of relationship would provide better conditions for the citizens of each nation than a relationship of mere ceasefire, the same reasons which support the pursuit of peace support the pursuit of positive peace to an even greater extent. Securing positive peace is

---

[4] To be sure, securing a lasting peace might not always be possible. For example, a state that is facing a genocidal attack might have no prospects of securing a lasting peace with its attacker. This does not mean that waging a defensive war is thereby impermissible. To the contrary, waging a defensive war might still be required for the sake of the good of the community even if securing a lasting peace is unlikely.

likely to be a more demanding task, however. For instance, it presupposes some form of reconciliation between the fighting parties, where reconciliation is understood both as a process and an outcome. As a process, reconciliation amounts to the formal or informal procedure in which bad feelings, suspicions, or harms that have been created by the conflicts and injustices of the past are properly addressed (Radzik and Murphy 2020). As an outcome, reconciliation amounts to an improvement in the relations amongst parties who were formerly at odds with one another. Understood this way, reconciliation encompasses the process of building more just relationships as well as the improved relations that result from this.

Granting the above argument, that warring states have reasons to aim at positive peace, it seems reasonable to hold that combatants also have strong reasons not to jeopardise the prospects of such a peace and post-war reconciliation. Even if there are good grounds for believing at the start of a war that a lasting peace is achievable, these prospects can be undermined by the way combatants carry out the war—for instance, if their actions stoke anger or resentment in the enemy population. Similarly, a war might render future reconciliation unlikely if it is fought in a manner by which important opportunities and resources for achieving post-reconciliation are lost. Consequently, our above discussion is relevant not just to military or political decision makers; combatants also have reasons to conduct the war in ways that preserve the chances of future reconciliation.

This claim might sound strange. After all, combat seems directly opposed to peace. Nevertheless, this does not mean that just combatants should refuse to fight or lay down their arms. Indeed, while all combatants have strong reasons to preserve the prospect of peace, just combatants also have reasons which favour continuing to fight. For instance, they may be fighting to defend their territory from invasion, or to defeat a dangerous and unjust aggressor. Moreover, since they are *just* combatants, we are assuming that their cause is sufficiently weighty to justify their going to war in the first place. Thus, their reasons to pursue peace, while substantial, will not be sufficient to prohibit their fighting, at least for the time being. Their reasons to pursue peace will, however, generate some constraints on the *way* they fight. Specifically, these reasons indicate that just combatants should fight with a particular kind of restraint that limits the effect of the war on the prospect of future peace and reconciliation. To be clear, we are not claiming that combatants have reasons to *personally* reconcile with, say, the enemy soldiers they were fighting. Rather, the kind of peace and reconciliation which combatants have reason to preserve is that which is necessary to prevent conflict re-emerging in the future, that is, reconciliation between their nations as wholes.

While our focus up to now has been on wars of national defence, we should note that the reasons that favour the pursuit of peace and reconciliation are also relevant to other types of conflict. For example, if a state is involved in a war of humanitarian intervention in a distant territory, its leaders and combatants have reason to preserve the prospect of post-conflict peace between themselves and the other nations involved—if not for the good of their own community, then certainly because doing so would minimise the possible harm posed to innocent people in the future. Moreover, this latter factor would also give the intervening state reason to promote and preserve the prospect of peace *between* the other warring nations. Indeed, in any conflict where there is a likelihood that violence and war will re-erupt, military leaders and combatants all have reason to support peacebuilding, and to defend the things which are necessary for it, no matter which nation they belong to or what part their nation plays in the conflict.

In summary, it appears reasonable to hold that both combatants and other military decision makers have strong reasons to avoid causing harm of the sort that is likely to provoke anger and resentment or to deprive people of the sorts of things that help to promote peace in the long run. Importantly, this might lend support to the Reconciliation Thesis, insofar as heritage is instrumental to post-war reconciliation. In order to assess this claim, however, we need to say something about how heritage could be instrumental to this end.

3. Heritage and Peacebuilding

Those who champion the importance of preserving heritage during war often motivate this position by arguing that the loss of heritage can undermine the long-term prospects of peace and reconciliation. This argument should be distinguished from appeals to the *short-term* negative consequences of heritage destruction, such as the immediate unrest and retaliation which deliberate attacks on heritage can sometimes cause. One example here is the bombing of the Al-Askari Mosque in Iraq in 2006, which exacerbated tensions between groups already under the stress of a foreign invasion and led to a "significant rise in violence, deaths, and reprisal attacks" (Cunliffe, Fox, and Stone 2018: 6). This factor may offer some support to those who wish to defend the prioritisation of heritage protection during armed conflict. However, our focus in this chapter is squarely on the Reconciliation Thesis, so we will not discuss the prospects of this alternative strategy any further.[5]

Having granted that combatants have a reason to preserve the prospects of future reconciliation, the relationship between heritage preservation and reconciliation now needs to be established. Here we will concentrate on three ways in which heritage has been said to be important—economic rehabilitation, educational use, and encouraging the return of displaced populations—before examining what each means for the Reconciliation Thesis.

3.1 Economic Rehabilitation

It is widely claimed that the destruction of heritage can harm an area's post-conflict economic development (Weiss and Connelly 2017; Cunliffe, Fox, and Stone 2018). Heritage can support economies through the creation of jobs and the attraction of income in the form of tourism. Weiss and Connelly see this as one of the losses that is often overlooked in debates surrounding the protection of heritage in war. With the loss of tourist attractions, they argue, "comes the concomitant loss of investment opportunities as well as the loss of jobs related to care and upkeep, and revenue derived from a healthy tourism industry" (Weiss and Connelly 2017: 13). To take one example, a 2014 Historic England report claims that heritage tourism provided the United Kingdom with 134,000 direct jobs and £5.1 billion in economic output in 2011 (Historic England 2014: 3). Although all countries are different, this gives a sense of the potential impact that heritage can have on an economy. Some heritage sites, such as historic marketplaces, also play an important role in local economies by facilitating trade. For instance, it has been argued that the destruction of the Al-Madina Souq was harmful to Aleppo's economy and that rebuilding the marketplace "will be essential if Aleppo is to recover its previous vitality" (Montoya-Guevara 2017: 3).

The economic harm caused by heritage destruction is serious in its own right and has implications for reconciliation. Empirical studies suggest a strong correlation between poor economic development and the resurgence of war (Oetzel et al. 2010: 362). Eight of the ten poorest countries in the world have recently experienced, or are currently experiencing, violent conflict

---

[5] In brief, we believe that this short-term focused argument might be somewhat successful, but that it also suffers from many of the weaknesses of the reconciliation-based argument (to be discussed in Section 4).

98 HERITAGE AND WAR

(Stewart 2002: 242). Of course, as Oetzel et al. point out, the relationship between poverty and war is likely multidirectional, with war clearly leading to widespread economic insecurity; however, it is also widely accepted that poverty increases the chances of further war as well (Oetzel et al. 2010: 362, 361–364). Indeed, recent World Bank research found that some countries can be caught in a 'fragility trap'—a vicious cycle where conflict begets weak economic growth which in turn begets more conflict (Andrimihaja et al. 2011).

A survey of case studies and statistical analyses found several routes through which economic insecurity can motivate conflict (Stewart 2002: 343). First, there is the *group motivation hypothesis*. This thesis holds that one reason groups go to war is because there is serious economic inequality between them: "In this situation relatively deprived groups are likely to seek (or be persuaded by their leaders to seek) redress [...] Where political redress is not possible they may resort to war" (2002: 343). The corresponding *private motivation hypothesis* suggests that individuals who are personally suffering from low income and employment opportunities may be drawn to war to gain employment as soldiers, or for the other economic opportunities which war provides, such as looting, arms-trading, profiteering, and so on (2002: 343). Finally, very poor economies can generate a sense of the *failure of the social contract*. Specifically, it is thought that government authority is weakened when it is seen as failing to provide an acceptable level of services and economic conditions such as employment opportunities. If things get too bad in this regard, "the social contract breaks down, and violence results" (2002: 343).

The importance of economic stability for peacebuilding is why, as Cunliffe, Fox, and Stone point out, "armed forces now frequently find themselves tasked to help deliver an economically viable and stable post-conflict country before they can withdraw" (Cunliffe, Fox, and Stone 2018: 9). A stable economy lays the foundation for a strong and lasting peace and the opportunity for past enemies to cooperate rather than return to violence. Thus, to the extent that heritage can help support a country's economy through employment, tourism, or other means, armed forces may find themselves with a strong reason to take care of it and defend it from harm.

3.2 Educational Uses

Besides its economic value, it is frequently argued that cultural heritage that survives a conflict might be put to use as an educational tool to promote cooperation between communities. Indeed, several organisations have made use of cultural heritage across the Balkan region to teach previously antagonistic groups about each other's cultures in an attempt to promote understanding and reconciliation. The general idea is that by exposing people to heritage belonging to another group, they can learn more about that group—their beliefs, history, and values—and this enriched understanding will contribute to better relations between the groups overall. This seems to be the rationale behind the work of Cultural Heritage without Borders (CHwB) throughout the Balkans. In the words of Eaton and Hadžić,

> CHwB believes that cultural heritage has an important role to play in [post-conflict recovery], providing a safe place for people to encounter, discover, learn about and, in some cases, confront and overcome their heritage, both good and bad. For this reason, CHwB wants to restore, conserve and interpret cultural heritage, building networks and dialogues amongst professionals and trust and collaboration within communities. (2013: 6–7)

In Kosovo, a similar project was carried out by Intersos, an Italian NGO (Wolferstan 2007: 285). In 2004, they began offering tours around local heritage sites belonging to both Serbians and Albanians. At first these events kept the different ethnic groups separate, but eventually they began offering mixed tours. The groups would visit heritage sites and then take part in "dialogue sessions that used cultural heritage as a starting point to discuss the importance of identity" (2007: 285). According to Wolferstan, these sessions led to a variety of collaborative initiatives and projects between the groups (2007: 286). She continues: "Visiting such sites allowed the dialogue tourists to remember how their respective communities interacted with the site in the past, helping them to transform their role from the aggressor/victim binary to seekers of peace" (2007: 287).

There is also a way in which exposure to certain types of heritage might help to reconcile warring groups even if the heritage does not exclusively belong to any of their cultures. Here we are specifically thinking of heritage which reminds them of (or teaches them about) an identity that they *share* or, at least, certain elements of history or culture which the groups have in common. In such a case, their cultural identity would be something which brings them together and connects them, rather than something which separates them. For example, Amr Al Azm (2018) argues that peace and reconciliation in Syria will only be achieved by identifying "common ground amongst the opposing sides". Fortunately, he continues,

100 HERITAGE AND WAR

> Syria has a resilient identity based on shared citizenship around a common history, supported by a long and rich cultural heritage...Syrians' shared cultural heritage transcends ethnic, sectarian or tribal differences and therefore presents an attractive and effective method for unifying the Syrian people and ensuring the future stability of their state...Museums, ancient sites and monuments effectively become the vehicle for identity creation, community outreach and cohesion.   (2018)

Granting the above, one path to peace in Syria could be to promote engagement with the ancient sites and artefacts which predate the modern sects of Syrian society. By doing so, a sense of belonging and affinity might be generated between antagonistic groups as they begin to appreciate their shared history and origins. Of course, any projects which inspire groups to reflect on the things they have in common might be beneficial here but, given the relationship between heritage and identity formation, it stands out as a particularly useful tool.

3.3 Return of Displaced Populations

Another way in which heritage protection could enhance reconciliation is by encouraging the return of populations displaced by the war. This is particularly relevant for conflicts involving groups which cohabited peacefully prior to the conflict but were forced to flee as a result of the violence. For instance, before the Yugoslav wars, Muslims lived alongside Serbians and other groups in mixed towns in Bosnia Herzegovina. Nevertheless, when conflict broke out, many civilians were killed and a great deal of Muslim architecture was deliberately targeted and destroyed. Perhaps the most famous instance of heritage destruction was the shelling of Mostar's famous Old Bridge, but many less-famous sites, such as small local mosques, were demolished as well.[6] Because of this conflict, large numbers of Muslims ended up leaving their homes to find safety elsewhere.

These attacks were likely intended as a method of cultural cleansing—that is, as an attempt to create a new version of Bosnia without Muslims (Bevan 2016: 12). Indeed, during testimony at a Hague tribunal, wartime president of the Sokolac Municipal council Milan Tupajić reported that, "There is a belief

---

[6] Reportedly, many other religious buildings, such as Catholic and Orthodox churches, were also damaged or destroyed during the war, though to a lesser extent (Cano 2008).

among the Serbs that…by destroying the mosques, the Muslims will lose a motive to return to the villages" (Šušnica 2019). This policy was, sadly, effective in many instances: a large proportion of the Muslim population have not yet returned to their hometowns, and those who have, typically did so only after their most significant heritage sites were rebuilt, many years later (Lostal and Cunliffe 2016: 250). As Ascherson writes, "the presence of certain monuments can seem to affirm the right to space through their presence across time. When they are knocked down—as a mosque is blown up—the resulting fear and insecurity can be intense" (2005: 22). Moreover, in the absence of these physical anchors or "pegs of safety", any survivors of the conflict may feel they face only two options: "either integrate with us, or get out" (2005: 22).

The general point is this: a part of what makes our homes familiar, comforting, and inviting are the physical sites and monuments we are used to, particularly those with which we share some personal or cultural connection. Without those sites or monuments, home might no longer feel like home. More significantly, under the awareness that they were deliberately attacked by other groups, the disappearance of these sites will feel especially unwelcoming and even threatening. If such heritage were protected, however, things might be different. The presence of, say, their local mosque, might silently convey to residents that they still have a place in the village they were forced to flee from, at least in some respects. It might also encourage any individuals who remained throughout the conflict to stay rather than move elsewhere (Loosley 2005: 593–595).

The implications for reconciliation should be fairly clear. While there is a kind of peace in a post-conflict situation wherein one belligerent group has entirely expelled another from the territory, this is not what we would call a 'just peace' nor a true reconciliation. Although the fighting has ended, one group has been wrongly forced from their homes by the other, and this wrong still stands, likely fuelling further resentment. A just peace would require, amongst other things, those who were expelled being allowed and assisted to return as (partial) compensation for the harm they have suffered. Similarly, the ideal outcome with regard to reconciliation—making a return to violence less likely—would presumably involve the two groups reintegrating and moving forwards as friends (or at the very least, not as enemies). Reaching this kind of complete reconciliation would be impossible while one group remains in exile, however. As such, granting the above, we find another possible benefit of heritage protection if, without their valued heritage, members of an exiled or persecuted group will be less willing to return or remain.

102   HERITAGE AND WAR

Naturally, this consideration will not move the fighting parties who aim to carry out cultural cleansing. Indeed, it is precisely one of their motivations for attacking heritage in the first place. Nevertheless, when conflict drives people from their homes, any military force with eventual reconciliation between belligerent groups as one of its goals would have some additional reason to defend and protect heritage from damage, regardless of how the damage might be caused. If they fail to do so, displaced populations would be more likely to stay displaced, and full reconciliation would become that much more distant.

4. The Reconciliation Thesis and Its Implication for Cultural Heritage Protection in War

In Section 2 we argued that combatants have a strong reason to aim at post-war reconciliation and in Section 3 we identified three ways in which heritage might contribute to post-war peacebuilding and reconciliation. Put together, this suggests that the Reconciliation Thesis is at least initially plausible, and that combatants have reason to protect cultural heritage during armed conflict for the sake of its instrumental value for post-war reconciliation. Certainly, it seems that combatants ought to avoid causing deliberate or malicious damage to heritage. Military forces should also take measures to ensure that heritage is not damaged accidentally, such as drawing up no-strike lists and giving their combatants heritage awareness training (Rush n.d.). Combatants should also prevent others from looting or inflicting damage on heritage where possible.

Nevertheless, the strength of this reason for protecting cultural heritage is not clear, especially when weighed against other valuable priorities and interests. Are combatants expected to put their own lives at risk or sacrifice significant military objectives in order to protect cultural heritage? And how do their reasons for protecting heritage compare to their reasons for protecting other things, such as vital parts of the civilian infrastructure? Even if one accepts the rather general moral claim about the reconciliation-based reasons for protecting heritage, articulated above, it is not clear that these reasons provide combatants with much moral guidance. To give another important example, these reasons do not determine how to proceed when one is confronted with the choice between avoiding harm to a cultural heritage site and directly saving, or avoiding harm to, the lives of civilians or one's fellow combatants.

Those who defend the importance of cultural heritage protection in war often seem to overlook these types of issues. Sometimes they even dismiss them.[7] For example, Weiss and Connelly (2017) argue that the protection of people and the protection of culture are inseparable. Culture, they argue, is just as essential to life as water and air. Hence, "there is no need for a hierarchy of protection" between cultural heritage and human lives, since the choice between the two is false (2017: 5). Similarly, Bokova argues that "there is no need to choose between saving lives and preserving cultural heritage: the two are inseparable" (2015: 294). This type of claim, which we referred to above as the Inseparability Thesis, is ambiguous and it is rather unfortunate that its proponents rarely explain precisely what they mean by it (to say the least). One way of understanding the thesis is as a claim that culture is a constitutive part of human life and that therefore protecting cultural heritage and protecting human lives are inextricably linked (Matthes 2018; Frowe and Matravers 2019). This claim can easily be dismissed if taken literally. Alternatively, if the claim is merely that cultural heritage is amongst the sorts of things that make people's lives go well, it is questionable whether it is sufficiently important to justify risking lives (Frowe and Matravers 2019; Bülow 2020; Haydar, Chapter 4 in this volume).

However, one possible interpretation of the Inseparability Thesis which is of particular interest here involves understanding it along the lines of the Reconciliation Thesis. This also seems to be what some proponents of the Inseparability Thesis have in mind. For example, one of the reasons that Weiss and Connelly provide in favour of the Inseparability Thesis is that cultural heritage "plays an important role in the restoration of civil society and the revitalization of local economies postconflict" (2017: 6). Even though they do not say so explicitly, someone who shares Weiss and Connelly's view could perhaps argue that protecting heritage is, in itself, an instrumental way of discharging the duty to protect innocent civilian lives. That is, one could argue that we should balance the immediate harms to human beings during conflict against the benefits of safeguarding heritage and thereby protecting people in the future by preserving a lasting positive peace. This means that, at least when calculations suggest it would save more lives overall, we should give priority to saving cultural heritage over saving individual lives because of heritage's long-term peace-promoting consequences. Doing so is not merely a matter of protecting cultural objects, but a matter of safeguarding human lives.[8]

---

[7] For a discussion of this issue, see Frowe and Matravers (Chapter 3 in this volume).

[8] The Inseparability Thesis is sometimes understood more strictly as claiming that there can be absolutely no conflict between heritage and human lives, even when the conflict boils down to, essentially, whether to save lives directly or save lives *via* saving heritage. Those who interpret the

104   HERITAGE AND WAR

This claim has important practical consequences. If saving heritage amounts to protecting the lives of innocent people in the future, then this might justify risking the lives of innocent human beings, or other things of moral value or significance, in order to avoid causing harm to heritage. Moreover, if it is true that heritage is indeed vital for the restoration of civil society and peacebuilding, and thus for protecting people, then this might even provide a reason for deploying military force in order to prevent the deliberate destruction of cultural heritage. That said, we believe that this type of argument for the protection of heritage, even at the cost of human lives, is unconvincing. In what follows, we point to some problems with this argument before evaluating the overall strength of the Reconciliation Thesis.

4.1 Opportunity Costs

Even if belligerents have a strong reason to aim at reconciliation, this does not entail that they must, by any means, attempt to save everything that could possibly be useful for promoting reconciliation and peacebuilding in the future. What matters, or so it seems, is that combatants fight, to the extent to which they are able, in a way that preserves the best prospects of long-term peace. But this may be compatible with causing or allowing *some* harm to the built environment, given that the loss of a single building or two (unless they are particularly important) is unlikely to have a significant effect on future peace. In such cases, the reconciliation-related reasons combatants have in favour of protecting heritage can be satisfied by merely protecting *enough* heritage; they do not have to save all the heritage they can. In other words, while the destruction of heritage might generally render future reconciliation less likely, combatants can tolerate some harm befalling heritage so long as these harms will not tangibly diminish the chances of future peace.

Furthermore, allowing or causing such loss of heritage will sometimes be justified, because there are circumstances in which militaries lack the resources or opportunities to achieve their critical goals while also safeguarding heritage. That is, protecting heritage might come with serious opportunity

---

Inseparability Thesis in this way will object to our discussion above, since our observations about reconciliation do not rule out the possibility of those sorts of conflicts. Nevertheless, here we interpret the Inseparability Thesis as a much more moderate claim, which would be vindicated to some extent by the truth of the Reconciliation Thesis. In brief, this claim holds that saving heritage is not in a deep or profound conflict with saving lives, since saving heritage amounts to saving lives in one sense. We are thankful to Helen Frowe for raising this point.

costs. Most relevantly, a force that focuses too much on defending heritage might be unable to pursue other effective means for promoting or preserving peace, since heritage protection is not the only factor that influences this outcome. As Stewart (2002) suggests, there are several factors that can be seen as root causes of conflict. We have already discussed some in Section 3, such as economic stagnation or poverty on an individual level. However, Stewart also highlights, for instance, the *green war hypothesis*, which holds that environmental degradation, particularly when it affects the productivity of agriculture, can lead to disputes about land or water rights (2002: 343). Additionally, as mentioned in relation to economic conditions, the perceived failure of governments to provide adequate services, and the subsequent weakening of the social contract, can also contribute to increasing tensions and violence (2002: 343). Consequently, if combatants aim to preserve the prospects of post-conflict reconciliation, they may find themselves torn between mutually exclusive courses of action—for example, attempts to prevent the environmental damage which war can inflict, attempts to support governments struggling to maintain authority and stability, and attempts to prevent harm to heritage.

Determining which option would be most beneficial with regard to long-term peace is a very difficult challenge. And yet those who defend the Reconciliation Thesis as a moral justification for prioritising heritage need to show the maximal effectiveness of heritage preservation in order to support the claim that combatants have compelling reason to protect heritage over other means for promoting reconciliation (and, indeed, over the direct protection of lives). This is, of course, very hard to prove to a satisfactory degree of certainty, not least since there are further reasons to doubt the Reconciliation Thesis, to which we now turn.

4.2 Does Heritage Protection Always Promote Post-war Reconciliation?

Consequentialist calculations, in general, encounter difficulties when dealing with situations of great uncertainty.[9] Alongside this broad worry, the Reconciliation Thesis faces a number of further epistemic problems. To start with, there are reasons to be sceptical about the strength and reliability of the

---

[9] Consequentialist calculations are also subject to a range of traditional challenges regarding, for instance, how different values are weighed and whether value in the distant future is discounted at all. However, we will put these other concerns to one side here.

relationships between heritage preservation and the three mediating factors established in Section 3.

First, while heritage can be valuable for the sake of economic recovery, as Weiss and Connelly suggest, this does not show that protecting heritage should be a military's priority for securing that end. Heritage protection is neither the only, nor necessarily the most important, factor for maintaining a stable economy. For instance, if economic recovery is what matters, it might be much more effective to protect those parts of the infrastructure that facilitate production or trade, such as factories, roads, and ports. It is also debatable to what extent protecting heritage *does* secure economic recovery in various cases. For example, it has been reported that while Aleppo's centuries-old bazaar is slowly being rebuilt, the two souks that were first to reopen were struggling to attract customers a year after reopening. For the most part they were largely empty, and tourists were non-existent (Mroue 2019). It is, of course, difficult to know whether things would have been better had they survived the conflict intact. However, we cannot merely assume that they would have, nor that saving heritage will always help tourism.

As for the displacement of populations, we should note that merely saving their cultural heritage might not be enough to motivate them to come back. That is, while saving or rebuilding heritage is a significant factor in promoting this end, it is unlikely to be sufficient. The same seems true for the educational aspect of heritage, which is often conditional and depends on a number of other background factors. For instance, it arguably depends on whether there are opportunities to educate people, which in turn requires that their basic needs are satisfied. The mere existence of heritage is evidently not enough by itself to educate and reconcile communities at odds with one another. If it were enough, then presumably there would have been no conflict in the first place. Thus, the fact that important cultural heritage monuments or sites are still standing does not guarantee that they will facilitate post-war reconciliation. More specifically, the educational potential of heritage can be called on as a justification for protecting heritage at the cost of human lives only if there is some credible chance that successful insight and dialogue-generating projects will actually be undertaken once the fighting has subsided.

A final complication is the possibility that a military's attempts at heritage preservation will backfire. Some heritage is problematic and divisive, such as monuments commemorating injustice or controversial figures or events. Preserving this kind of heritage might have either no effect or a negative effect on future peace in the region. Similarly, while some attempts to preserve heritage might be beneficial for a military's reputation and relationships with civilians, others might be damaging. For example, a military moving heritage elsewhere for safety might be perceived as stealing it. Likewise, a military could be criticised for apparently having misplaced priorities if they chose to defend heritage sites instead of important infrastructure or human lives, potentially undermining any authority or goodwill they had mustered. All in all, the details of any attempt at heritage preservation must be scrutinised before any broad claims can be made about its benefits for post-conflict peace and reconciliation.

4.3 The Possibility of Reconstructing Heritage

When weighing human lives versus heritage, we should also note that human lives cannot be replaced while heritage can, at least sometimes, be rebuilt. Of course, many would argue that there are important elements of value that are lost when original heritage buildings are destroyed, and that cannot be recovered through the creation of replicas (Sagoff 1978; Janowski 2011; Korsmeyer 2019). Nevertheless, what matters with regard to the Reconciliation Thesis is whether reconstructing damaged heritage would have the same or a comparable impact on reconciliation and peacebuilding as would preventing that damage in the first place.

This is again a difficult empirical question to answer, and the answer will likely differ depending on the specifics of the heritage being considered. However, there is some reason to think that reconstructing heritage would do at least some good in many cases. A rebuilt museum or heritage site is likely to attract tourists and could be used for inter-group educational projects. Similarly, a rebuilt place of worship could encourage displaced people to return home. The value of reconstructed heritage might be somewhat weaker than preserved original heritage in these cases—tourists may prefer to visit originals, and displaced groups may be less moved by replicas of their cherished sites—but we could expect it to have at least some instrumental value for peacebuilding. This is important; to the extent that rebuilding is a practical option and to the extent it would be instrumentally valuable in this way, the reconciliation-based justification for sacrificing things of moral significance in order to defend heritage will be correspondingly weaker.

108 HERITAGE AND WAR

4.4 The Implications for the Reconciliation Thesis

To be sure, our overall point in this section is not that the empirical premise in the Reconciliation Thesis—that heritage can facilitate reconciliation—is false. In fact, we do think that cultural heritage is relevant for peacebuilding and post-war reconciliation, and that there are strong reasons to address the destruction and damage of cultural heritage amongst the conditions of transitional justice.[10] However, from what we have argued here, we believe that we should be cautious about the anticipated benefits of saving heritage and the extent to which its protection is necessary in order to secure a lasting peace. If the relationship between the defence of heritage and the prevention of future conflict is as weak as it appears to be then it is doubtful that heritage protection is sufficiently important to outweigh, for instance, preventing the deaths of innocent individuals; there will be a reconciliation-related reason to protect heritage but, unless we have some clear reason to believe otherwise, it will typically be overridden by the duty to directly protect people's lives.

The point here is simple: it is not enough that the protection of heritage *can* be useful for post-conflict peacebuilding. Rather, in order to morally justify causing innocent people's deaths or sacrificing other significant military goals, we should have compelling reasons to think that safeguarding heritage will *in fact* protect a sufficient number of human lives in the future, and more so than any other alternative plan of action. Yet, as we have just discussed, there are various philosophical and epistemic grounds for doubting this in any particular case. First, the reconciliation-related reason we have discussed requires only that the prospect of positive peace be maintained, and this goal might be adequately secured by protecting some, but not all, heritage in an area, or even by ignoring heritage in order to focus on other more effective peace-promoting factors. Second, there is always a possibility that saving some heritage might fail to secure any substantial peace-related benefits and could even contribute to an increase in unrest. Third, it is plausible that at least some of the peace-related benefits of heritage could be obtained through rebuilding post-conflict, thus freeing militaries from the riskier task of protecting it during conflict.

Before concluding, we should stress that the difficulties we have identified here are not conclusive. However, as it stands, we have reason to be sceptical

---

[10] For discussion of this issue, see Lostal and Cunliffe (2016).

of the Reconciliation Thesis, especially if it is evoked as a justification for imposing serious risks on civilians or one's fellow combatants. Thus, our conclusion here is that even though proponents of the Reconciliation Thesis do point to an important aspect of cultural heritage that ought to be taken into consideration during armed conflict, this alone provides us with little guidance for resolving the difficult moral dilemmas that are unfortunately evident in war. Nor does it show that one might be morally justified in intervening militarily for the sake of protecting heritage, as some of its proponents imply (e.g., Weiss and Connelly 2017). This does not mean that it is never morally justified to give priority to cultural heritage over human lives, but rather that those who believe that such priority is sometimes justified need to either strengthen the reconciliation-based argument or find support for their view elsewhere.

5. Conclusion

Our aim in this chapter has been to examine the Reconciliation Thesis—that is, the claim that combatants have reason to protect cultural heritage in war, grounded in the importance of heritage for post-war reconciliation. In order to examine this thesis, we first discussed whether belligerents have a reason to aim at reconciliation. We argued that they do indeed have such a reason, grounded in the general moral obligation not to cause harm to innocent individuals and, for military leaders, in their responsibility to act for the good of their community. We then identified three reasons why protecting heritage can be important for post-war reconciliation—Economic Rehabilitation, Educational Uses, and Return of Displaced Populations. While we grant that each of these shows that heritage might be important for a future reconciliation process, it is debatable whether any of these reasons shows that it is morally permissible to protect cultural heritage at the expense of human lives, or that protecting cultural heritage ought to be given priority over protecting other parts of a state's infrastructure or pursuing victory. In response, proponents of the Reconciliation Thesis might argue that protecting heritage is simply another way of protecting innocent civilian lives. However, this claim faces a number of important challenges. Hence, we have reason to be sceptical of the Reconciliation Thesis, especially when it is evoked as a justification for imposing serious risks or costs on persons, or sacrificing other significant military objectives.

References

Al Azm, Amr. (2018), 'The Importance of Cultural Heritage for Post Conflict Stabilization and Reconciliation', *Antiquities Coalition*, 15 February, accessed 5 May 2020, https://theantiquitiescoalition.org/post-conflict-stabilization-reconciliation/.

Andrimihaja, Noro Aina, Cinyabuguma, Matthias, and Devarajan, Shantayanan. (2011), 'Avoiding the Fragility Trap in Africa', World Bank Africa Region Policy Research Working Paper 5884, accessed 18 February 2021, https://papers.ssrn.com/sol3/papers.cfm?abstract_id=1961471.

Ascherson, Neal. (2005), 'Cultural Destruction by War and Its Impact on Group Identities', in Nicholas Stanley-Price (ed.), *Cultural Heritage in Postwar Recovery*. Papers from the ICCROM Forum held 4–6 October 2005: 17–25.

Bevan, Robert. (2016), *The Destruction of Memory: Architecture at War* (2nd ed.) (London: Reaktion Books).

Bokova, Irina. (2015), 'Culture on the Front Line of New Wars', in *Brown Journal of World Affairs* 22/1: 289–296.

Bokova, Irina. (2016), 'Uniting Humanity around Heritage: The Role of Museums', in Kurt Almqvist and Louise Belfrage (eds.), *Cultural Heritage at Risk: The Role of Museums in War and Conflict* (Axel and Margaret Ax:son Johnson Foundation: Stockholm), 9–11.

Bülow, William. (2020), 'Risking Civilian Lives to Avoid Harm to Cultural Heritage?', *Journal of Ethics and Social Philosophy* 18/3: 266–288.

Cano, Nadzida. (2008), 'Bosnian Muslims Sue Serbs over Destroyed Heritage', in *Balkan Insight*, 10 April, accessed 5 May 2020, https://balkaninsight.com/2008/04/10/bosnian-muslims-sue-serbs-over-destroyed-heritage/.

Cunliffe, Emma, Fox, Paul, and Stone, Peter. (2018), 'The Protection of Cultural Property in the Event of Armed Conflict: Unnecessary Distraction or Mission-Relevant Priority?', *NATO OPEN Publications*, 2/4.

Eaton, Jonathan, and Hadžić, Lejla. (2013), 'Restoration, Reconciliation, Hopes for the Future: Cultural Heritage Without Borders—17 years in the Western Balkans', Cultural Heritage without Borders—Albania, presented at the Conference "The Politics of Heritage and Memory" in Zadar, Croatia, 9–10 October.

Fabre, Cecile. (2016), *Cosmopolitan Peace* (Oxford: Oxford University Press).

Frowe, Helen, and Derek Matravers. (2019), 'Conflict and Cultural Heritage: A Moral Analysis of the Challenges of Heritage Protection', in J. Paul Getty Trust Occasional Papers in Cultural Heritage Policy, 3 (Los Angeles, CA: J. Paul Getty Trust).

Historic England. (2014), 'Heritage Counts 2014: The Value and Impact of Heritage', *Historic England*, accessed 4 May 2020, https://historicengland.org.uk/content/heritage-counts/pub/2014/value-impact-chapter-pdf/.

Janowski, James. (2011), 'Bringing Back Bamiyan's Buddhas', in *Journal of Applied Philosophy* 28: 44–64.

Korsmeyer, Carolyn. (2019), *Things: In Touch with the Past* (Oxford: Oxford University Press).

Loosley, Emma. (2005), 'Archaeology and Cultural Belonging in Contemporary Syria: The Value of Archaeology to Religious Minorities', *World Archaeology* 37/4: 589–596.

Lostal, Marina, and Cunliffe, Emma. (2016), 'Cultural Heritage that Heals: Factoring in Cultural Heritage Discourses in the Syrian Peacebuilding Process', in *The Historic Environment: Policy & Practice* 7/2–3: 248–259.

Matthes, Erich Hatala. (2018), 'Saving Lives or Saving Stones: The Ethics of Cultural Heritage Protection in War', in *Public Affairs Quarterly* 32/1: 67–84.

Montoya-Guevara, Camilo. (2017), 'Aleppo's Al-Madina Souq: Post-Conflict Reconstruction of Its Social Functions', *The Aleppo Project*, 15 February, accessed 5 May 2020, https://www.thealeppoproject.com/papers/aleppos-al-madina-souq-post-conflict-reconstruction-social-functions/.

Mroue, Bassem. (2019), 'Centuries-old bazaar in Syria's Aleppo making slow recovery', *AP News*, August 5, 2019, accessed 2 November 2022, https://apnews.com/article/71578382fb274bc88a7e78f9d1f2f7c0.

Oetzel, Jennifer, Westermann-Behaylo, Michelle, Koerber, Charles, Fort, Timothy L., and Rivera, Jorge Rivera. (2010), 'Business and Peace: Sketching the Terrain', in *Journal of Business Ethics* 89: 51–37.

Radzik, Linda and Murphy, Colleen. 'Reconciliation', *The Stanford Encyclopedia of Philosophy* (Fall 2021 Edition), Edward N. Zalta (ed.), https://plato.stanford.edu/archives/fall2021/entries/reconciliation/.

Rawls, John. (1999), *The Law of Peoples* (Cambridge, MA: Harvard University Press).

Rush, Laurie. (n.d.), 'Cultural Property Protection as a Force Multiplier: Implementation for All Phases of a Military Operation', *The Blue Shield*, accessed 1 May 2020, https://theblueshield.org/download/military-cpp-reports-and-documents/.

Sagoff, Mark. (1978), 'On Restoring and Reproducing Art', in *Journal of Philosophy* 75: 453–470.

Stewart, Frances. (2002), 'Root Causes of Violent Conflict in Developing Countries', in *British Medical Journal* 324: 342–345.

Šušnica, Srđan. (2019), 'Narrative: "Targeting History and Memory" Presented in Banja Luka', *Sense*, accessed 29 July 2019, https://www.sensecentar.org/activities/narrative-targeting-history-and-memory-presented-bana-luka.

Uniacke, Suzanne. (2014), 'Self-Defence, Just War, and a Reasonable Chance of Success', in Helen Frowe and Gerald Lang (eds.), *How We Fight: Ethics of War* (Oxford: Oxford University Press), 62–75.

Weiss, Thomas G., and Connelly, Nina. (2017), 'Cultural Cleansing and Mass Atrocities Protecting Cultural Heritage in Armed Conflict Zones', in J. Paul Getty Trust Occasional Papers in Cultural Heritage Policy, 1 (Los Angeles, CA: J. Paul Getty Trust).

Wolferstan, Sarah. (2007). 'Community Participation in Heritage in Post-conflict Kosovo. Promoting Democracy, Dialogue and Reconciliation through Cultural Heritage', in Interpreting the Past. The Future of Heritage. Changing Visions, Attitudes and Contexts in the 21st Century. Selected Papers from the Third Annual Ename Colloquium, Belgium, March 2007. Accessed October 29, 2022 from http://ucl.academia.edu/sarahwolferstan/Papers.

7

Responding to Cultural Wrongs in Palestine and Israel

Victor Tadros

1. Introduction

Lydda was a historic town in Palestine that played a significant role in recent historical, political and literary discourse in the context of the conflict in Israel/Palestine. After the creation of the state of Israel, Lydda was renamed Lod. Whether Lydda and Lod are different names of the same town or different towns is difficult to resolve, but we can leave the metaphysics of towns aside. Lod is 15km to the southeast of Tel Aviv.

Lydda was one of the most significant commercial towns in Palestine. It had a long history dating back to at least 600 BC, but it developed significantly during the British mandate, partly due to its position on the route from Jerusalem to the main port of Jaffa. The main commercial activities were olive oil and soap production, but there were also significant citrus groves that had been developed for generations by the Palestinian inhabitants of Lydda. The population was almost solely Arab Muslims and Christians—of the 20,000 inhabitants of Lydda in the years prior to 1948, around 18,500 were Muslims, and almost all the remainder were Christians. Fewer than 100 Jews lived in Lydda. In the partition plan, Lydda was intended to be incorporated into the Arab-controlled part of Israel/Palestine.

During the war of 1948 between the new state of Israel and surrounding Arab states, the vast majority of the Arab population of Lydda was 'removed'. The poorly defended town was quickly overrun by Israeli forces, who then rounded up the local population. Some were cabined in the Great Mosque where at least 100 innocent civilians were murdered, including women and children who clearly formed no part of the fighting force. Most of the remaining population was marched from the town. Removing the Arab population was in accordance with the policy of the Israeli political authorities, under the

Victor Tadros, *Responding to Cultural Wrongs in Palestine and Israel* In: *Heritage and War: Ethical Issues.*
Edited by: William Bülow, Helen Frowe, Derek Matravers, and Joshua Lewis Thomas, Oxford University Press.
© Victor Tadros 2023. DOI: 10.1093/oso/9780192862648.003.0007

114   HERITAGE AND WAR

direction of David Ben Gurion, which indicated that if Jewish fighters met with resistance in Arab settlements, the local population would be expelled.[1] Only around 1,000 Arabs remained, and they were initially imprisoned behind guarded wire fences, without adequate supplies of water. They were allowed to stay, though, due to the need for labour (see Jacobi 2004).

In negotiations, Jordan demanded that Lydda be placed under its control, and that Palestinian refugees be permitted to return, but the negotiations failed, and Israel retained control of Lydda. Jewish immigrants were settled there, mostly at first from Tunisia and Morocco, as well as some from Europe, and later, mainly in the 1990s, from the Soviet Union. By 1950, around 8400 Jewish people were settled in Lod (see Morris 2004: 390). Many of the Jewish immigrants who settled there left their home countries, partly because of the wave of antisemitism that was rife in the Arab and North African world in the immediate aftermath of the creation of the state of Israel, and which persists today, and partly because they were encouraged to come by the new Israeli government. Israeli political leaders were particularly keen to encourage Jews from the region to come to Israel, as they were concerned that underpopulation of the new state, and especially the lack of manual labour, would hamper the state-building project.

This resulted in a very significant decline in the number of Jews in the Middle East and North Africa outside Israel. For example, around 265,000 Jews lived in Morocco in 1948, whereas only around 2,000 Jewish people live there now. Jews and Muslims largely lived peacefully together in Morocco for centuries, though Jews (as well as Christians and others) were sometimes discriminated against, including some attacks on Jews in Morocco in the early twentieth century. Complex social and legal arrangements facilitated a partly integrated community of Muslims and Jews. There were some separate legal rules governing their arrangements, but also a complex set of practices to foster commercial and social engagement (see Boum 2014; Marglin 2016). After the creation of Israel, riots broke out against Jews, resulting in the murder of over 40 people. Around 18,000 Jews left Morocco in 1948/9. Tunisian Jews have a similar story—with long periods of peaceful coexistence, with some tensions, followed by mass exodus from 1948, and especially in the 1960s. Whilst some North African Jews went elsewhere, most notably to France, the majority moved to Israel. A large proportion of Jewish immigrants in the immediate post-1948 years were settled in houses previously owned and

---

[1] See Golan (2003: 125) and, for the more general attempt to remove Arabs from towns and settlements to be replaced with Jews, see Morris (2004).

occupied by Palestinians to solve a housing crisis in the new state (see Morris 2004). And the desire to house Jewish immigrants was the central reason why the Israeli Defence Force tempered the destruction of Palestinian villages towards the end of 1948 (see Morris 2004: chapter 6).

Lod was considered a major site for settlement of Jewish immigrants to Israel, especially as housing in the new state was short, and there was insufficient labour to build more. The perceived need to use Arab houses to house immigrants was considered a sufficient reason, explicitly given by the Israeli government, not to respect the right of Palestinians to return. As Israeli Foreign Ministry Director General Eytan put it: 'Generally, it can be said that any Arab house that survived the impact of the war...now shelters a Jewish family. There can be no return to the status quo ante' (see Morris 2004: 550).

Over time, buildings in Lydda/Lod were demolished and new ones created. The small remaining Arab population was compelled to live in segregation in some parts of the town, and this *de facto* segregation still exists—the Arab population is now largely separated from the Jewish part of the town by a 3-metre wall. The Israeli authorities have heavily controlled the daily lives of Arabs, and the latter have had little say in the planning and development of their town.

Whilst there was a plan to develop Lod into a modern industrial town, this was unrealistic in the early days of Israel, and agriculture and olive oil production were reactivated as sources of employment for Jewish immigrants as well as for the remaining Arab population. Whilst some of the farms and orchards were destroyed, others were occupied and developed. And the state funded the development of new farms and orchards, primarily to employ immigrants who were without work. Infrastructure and employment, however, could not keep up with the rapid immigration of Jews in the 1950s, and many were left in transit camps without employment. During the 1950s, Lod did not develop economically as had been hoped. Significant numbers of its more educated and ambitious inhabitants found employment in nearby Tel Aviv, and as a result left, but this occurred along racial lines; as well as the few remaining Arabs, those remaining in Lod were mainly non-European Jews from North Africa and the Middle East, who typically had lower levels of education than European Jews. And the exodus of wealthy families was accompanied by a lack of funding to develop the town. As some other towns in Israel became more like modern industrial European towns, Lod was left behind.

Lod was also fundamentally transformed in a physical way in the 1950s, and not to good effect. The historic centre, which had been developed over several thousands of years, was flattened to create the space for a more modern

116   HERITAGE AND WAR

European-style city. Whilst some historic buildings still exist there, the integrity of the old city was significantly eroded at that point. But the vision of a well-functioning modern city has never been realised.

A new Arab population began to migrate to Lod in the 1950s, searching for work. Lod is now sometimes described as a 'mixed' city, in that it is one of relatively few cities in Israel that has substantial populations of both Arabs and Jews—around 30 per cent of the population is Arab, compared with 20 per cent of the overall population of Israel. Lod has a notoriously high crime rate, as well as high levels of poverty and drug use. There are significant inequalities between the Arab and Jewish populations, with little being done to ensure adequate security, education and basic housing facilities for Arabs. For example, policing is very limited in Arab areas, and very few housing permits have been granted, so Arabs who build houses to improve their living conditions are at risk of having them destroyed, which occurs regularly. Many have the impression that the Israeli government has little interest in reducing the crime rate, or improving the social and living conditions of the Arab community, because Arabs have been largely separated from Jews.

But some also see Lod as having the potential for the growth of stronger relationships between Arabs and Jews in Israel—to overcome, at least in part, the fissures and conflicts that arose from the 1948 war and that have plagued the region ever since. There is some weak indication that the Israeli authorities finally recognise the need to invest in both Arab and Jewish communities, though optimism remains limited.

2. Embedded Living Culture

What can we learn about the significance of heritage in war from Lydda and Lod? Obviously, heritage is not the only important concern when we focus on Lydda and Lod; and it is not the most important concern. But, as we will see, that concern is intertwined with the concerns that arise from the violations of more basic and important rights that occurred in 1948. Let us focus first on the value of the heritage of Lydda and Lod, and then on the rights and duties that different people have to respond to that heritage in the aftermath of the 1948 war.

When we think about the value of heritage, and our moral response to it, we tend to focus on famous monuments—those iconic buildings, statues and artefacts that can be seen as representing a country or community—think of Italy, think of the Colosseum; think of France, think of the Eiffel Tower; think of Egypt, think of the Pyramids; think of India, think of the Taj Mahal; and so on. Destruction of these things can seem to have great significance because of what they represent nationally and internationally. The national, but also international, outpouring of sorrow and grief as Notre-Dame Cathedral burned captures the significance that people give to iconic buildings of this kind.

These icons are amongst the heritage sites that are recognised internationally—those that are protected by the Blue Shield that designates property as worthy of protection in the theatre of war. The Hague Convention for the Protection of Cultural Property in the Event of Armed Conflict (UNESCO 1954), which has effectively been incorporated into UK law, defines cultural property as:

> movable or immovable property of great importance to the cultural heritage of every people, such as monuments of architecture, art or history, whether religious or secular; archaeological sites; groups of buildings which, as a whole, are of historical artistic interest; works of art; manuscripts, books and other objects of artistic, historical or archaeological interest; as well as scientific collections and important collections of books or archives or of reproductions of the property defined above; and so on.

What is interesting for my purposes is not whether Lydda fell within this definition, and so would have been protected by the convention. Perhaps it might have, given the historical importance of the town, and the historically and religiously significant buildings that were there, and, to some extent, still are. Rather, my interest is in the way in which something counts as significant cultural property.

The Convention states the ambition to protect those things 'of great importance to the cultural heritage of every people'. And there is a sense in which this is right—a derivative sense. The primary significance of the culture of Lydda, though, was not due to its importance for 'every people', but rather for the people who lived in the town or were directly connected with it. The architecture of the town structures the life of the people who live there. The historic significance of the buildings for humanity captures only a small part of their role in the lives of the people who live there.

Furthermore, in debates about cultural property in war, we have often been concerned with the question of whether we should sacrifice lives for cultural property. If the only way to protect cultural property is to kill either innocent people, or those who attack it, is it ever permissible to kill for the sake of cultural property? Is it even permissible not to save a life in order to protect

118 HERITAGE AND WAR

it? Many people doubt that. Suppose that I was able either to save Notre-Dame from destruction or save the life of a child. I'd choose the child every time.

Because of this reaction to the comparative importance of lives and cultural property, those who are concerned to protect cultural property in war often emphasise the idea that there is no conflict—protecting cultural property and protecting people typically go together. But this is often not true with respect to the iconic monuments that those interested in cultural heritage have primarily been concerned with. Iconic monuments may not be especially important to the lives of people who are affected in war. They may care little for the destruction of the monuments that have great historical significance for people outside their communities.

For example, many members of my Egyptian family couldn't care less about the historical monuments of Ancient Egypt and can't understand why anyone wants to go to see them. They may value them as a source of income for the country, and perhaps, to some extent, they help to represent Egypt and Egyptians on the international stage, but their historical importance leaves many Egyptians unmoved—the society which gave them meaning is now dead. Their main importance is to preserve our understanding of an ancient society: both its amazing achievements and its bizarre attitudes, practices and beliefs. The people of modern Egypt have a rich cultural heritage, but one that is largely disconnected from Ancient Egypt. Religion, and therefore religious buildings, for example, are important to their everyday lives. And religion helps structure communities in Egypt. And Egyptians value central aspects of the towns they live in—they build their lives around the shops, markets, cafes, beachfronts, businesses, and so on, in their towns.

Several contrasts between different kinds of culture help us to understand it, and I cannot provide a general account of the significance of culture here. But here are two crude contrasts that help us to understand different ways in which culture can be significant. First, we might distinguish iconic from embedded culture. The importance of iconic culture is in its symbolic representation on the national and international stage. It typically has symbolic significance for people in a political community, but it is also important in helping to represent and distinguish people in the international community. Our main ambition is to preserve it in its iconic form, which is often as it was created. Cultural artefacts of this kind are often no longer evolving, or they are doing so only very slowly. A building might become iconic whilst it is still in the process of being built or added to, for example—but that is not the normal case.

Embedded culture, in contrast, primarily has significance for a people by being embedded in their everyday lives. Embedded culture is not primarily valued by people for what it represents, but for how it structures their lives. For that reason, its primary value is for the people whose lives it structures. Everyone has reason to care about and value embedded culture though. For everyone has reason to care about and value everyone else. We all have reason to value the value that embedded culture gives to the people whose lives it structures. Of course, the same cultural object can have both iconic and embedded cultural value.

Second, we might contrast living and dead culture. Dead culture is culture that is no longer evolving or developing. Ancient Egypt, for example, had both iconic and embedded culture. The embedded culture is now dead. With respect to the icons of Ancient Egypt, though, things are more complex. They will have seen some of their monuments as iconic, and those monuments still have some iconic significance in Egypt today, though their meaning for Ancient and modern Egypt is quite different—their meaning for modern Egypt is in the fact that an ancient culture is historically and geographically connected to modern Egypt. Although there is a great deal of Ancient Egyptian culture that is now dead, we can respond to the cultural value of both the iconic and embedded culture of Ancient Egypt. We might value the latter, for example, by understanding its value for the people of Ancient Egypt—the different kinds of iconic and embedded cultural value it had for them.

Living culture, in contrast, continues to evolve through people's activity. A market, for example, might have central importance for the culture of a town. It continues to evolve as people find new goods to buy and sell, and new ways of buying and selling. There is less ambition to preserve embedded living culture as it was initially created.

The value of embedded culture is often most deeply appreciated by people whose culture it is, and who participate in its evolution. For many people, their living embedded culture is much more important than the icons of their state. Threatening these icons is significant because it symbolises other threats they face—not only to their living culture, but also to their political and human rights.

From the little that I know of the law in this area, there seems to be a tension between the initial ambitions of the Hague Convention, which were primarily concerned with iconic culture, much of which was dead, and more recent ambitions to protect cultural heritage, which are more concerned with

120   HERITAGE AND WAR

the relationship between iconic culture and living embedded culture. In other words, there is an emphasis on the relationship between heritage, cultural property and cultural rights, which is increasingly focused on the lives of people whose culture it is.

Consider, for example, the recent Joint Statement on Cultural Rights and the Protection of Cultural Heritage, agreed on by a very wide range of countries. The UN Special Rapporteur for Cultural Rights, in her first report on the impact of cultural property on human rights, suggested that destruction of cultural property in armed conflict:

> [c]an constitute an aggravating factor in armed conflict and may also represent major obstacles to dialogue, peace and reconciliation, for instance when they interfere with the right to manifest one's religion by limiting access to places of worship.   (2016: para. 3)

The idea here is less about ensuring that iconic cultural objects and artefacts, which have significance for the whole world, are protected, and more about ensuring that a people who live in a place, and who are affected by war, do not have their culture eroded in such a way as to hamper the culturally significant features of their way of life. There is no reason why the kind of iconic culture that the Hague Convention is primarily concerned with, either necessarily or uniquely, has the impact on a people in the way that this account suggests.

Now, let us focus on the cultural impact of driving most of the Arab population from Lydda, and fundamentally altering the architecture of the town, in the light of the distinctions I have drawn. The cultural lives of the people who lived there were profoundly changed as a result. The cultural history of the town continued to have significance for the people who lived there prior to being driven out, and who developed that culture in their everyday activities. As can be seen from the early twentieth-century history of Lydda, this did not mean that the inhabitants merely replicated the way of life of their ancestors; the town expanded and developed in that period. Their culture was embedded and living. But at the same time, developments in the town grew from the history of the town, and modern development was integrated into the cultural life of the town. Thus, Lydda had a narrative cultural history, where new developments in its culture are best understood as evolving from previous cultural developments and achievements. The events in Lydda in 1948 effectively put an end to that cultural narrative and began a new one.

It is hard to discover exactly what happened to the particular people who were driven from Lydda. But we do know that those in Palestinian refugee camps in, for example, Gaza and Lebanon, organised themselves according to the towns from which they came. They held on tightly to the particular communities they lived in, and aimed, insofar as they could, to sustain some of the culture of those towns, with the longer-term ambition of retaining and developing their living culture as far as they could. They also aimed to pass on their cultural ambitions to their children. That intergenerational feature of Palestinian refugee communities still exists, and I have argued elsewhere that it has political significance—it helps to ground the right of return.[2] But their developing cultural life in Lydda was ruptured, and even if they clung on to their culture as refugees, they could no longer develop it in the flourishing and integrated way that they did prior to 1948.

3. Contribution to Culture through the Generations

In this way, Lydda also helps us to understand the intergenerational significance of living culture. Our response to Lydda is not restricted to those of the particular generation who were driven out. Both their ancestors and their descendants occupy our minds when we respond to the cultural destruction that occurred there. Previous generations created the conditions which the current generation responds to in fostering and evolving an embedded living culture. Future generations have reasons to respond to that culture by responding to the cultural achievements of the current generation and previous generations. A generation develops a living culture that was created and sustained by previous generations; it does it not only for the sake of the people in that generation, but also for the sake of future generations, with the ambition that future generations will develop that culture in their own way.

Both iconic and living culture have intergenerational significance, but typically in different ways. The cultural status, identity and value of iconic objects is generated and sustained over generations. When Notre-Dame Cathedral was burning, I saw an interview with an elderly Parisienne, who suggested that the tragedy was in part that this generation had failed those who had contributed to the development of the Cathedral, and preserved it, over the generations. The idea that I intend to capture, then, is that a current culture or

---

[2] I briefly sketch out those arguments below. For the fuller arguments, see 'The Persistence of the Right of Return' (Tadros 2017) and 'Inheriting the Right of Return' (Tadros 2020).

122   HERITAGE AND WAR

aspect of culture has its value in part because of its having been developed over generations, and that the people whose significance we fail to respect when we destroy a culture include those who were involved in developing it.

But I also intend to emphasise a feature of culture that is not best understood by reflecting on great historical monuments, such as Notre-Dame. I suggested that the main way in which we respond to iconic culture is through preservation. The aim is to make accessible to people a past cultural achievement—in this case, involving the preservation of a building in its current form. That achievement might be the achievement of generations of people, some of whom generated the iconic culture, and some of whom preserved it and fostered our understanding of it.

The ambition to preserve Notre-Dame itself developed over generations, and it was to preserve it for future generations. The fire thus undermined this ambition, and it now requires the current generation of French citizens imaginatively to respond. In that case, there is a dilemma between the extent to which people ought to attempt to recreate the Cathedral as it was, or to reinvent it with their own imaginations. And there may also be an ambition to retain signs of the tragic burning of the Cathedral, to historically recognise this event. But the role of the cultural value of the Cathedral itself, as it was, is primarily conservative. Our imaginations are engaged because these conservative ambitions will inevitably be thwarted, at least to some degree, by the fire.

The main ambition that we typically have when living culture is our own, in contrast, is to constantly imaginatively reinvent that culture by reflecting on the past and creating for the future. People contribute to culture in a range of ways—by developing things of cultural value, by participating in practices that involve engaging with and valuing things of cultural value, by promoting and protecting it, and so on. The evolution of cities, towns, communities and countries occurs over generations, primarily through the cultural and political engagement of inhabitants as well as political leaders over time. And the lives of new generations, as they unfold in cities, towns, communities and countries, are shaped by the development, sustenance, promotion and protection of their cultures over generations. Each generation contributes to the lives of the next, not only by preserving what was of value in the past but also by imaginatively responding to the past to improve, develop and evolve the culture. Older generations pass on aspects of their culture, but also learn new ways of reinventing them from younger generations.

Different living cultures have different rates of change. Some are more conservative, where participants in those cultures primarily aim to preserve traditions more or less unchanged. Others are less conservative—participants are encouraged to radically reimagine the culture. Even with the most conservative cultures, though, there is almost always some ambition for each generation to reinvigorate the culture in a new way.

The culture of towns is an instance of this general idea that living cultures are changing cultures. There is no reasonable expectation that central features of the cultural identity of a town remain static, and are protected, in the way that we protect historical artefacts. But nevertheless, new generations can respect the culture of their town, even whilst reimagining life in that town. Respecting the culture of a town can be an imaginative activity, where the town is developed in the light of its historic cultural features. For it is part of the culture of a town that it develops over time through the imaginative activities of its inhabitants.

Indeed, this dynamic and evolving feature of the culture of communities and towns is necessary for life in a town to be just. Previous generations have a duty to ensure that each future generation can creatively participate in the development of their culture. Those who attempt to ossify their cultural achievements in a way that is too restrictive of the autonomous cultural activities of future generations violate that duty. Intergenerational respect, then, requires future generations to respond appropriately to achievements of the past, but this does not normally require simple preservation and repetition of the culture.

There is thus an important contrast between imaginatively developing a culture and destroying that culture in order to create a new one. That distinction is partly a matter of the intentions of participants, who reflect on the value of a culture in order to discover what in it to preserve, what to leave behind and what to alter and develop. But it is also a matter of integrating the activity of developing the culture across generations who engage with previous and future generations in a cooperative way.

In the light of this observation, why should we care that Lydda was around 4,000 years old? I doubt that it is primarily because the long duration of the town matters much in itself, or even that there were buildings of historic significance that needed preservation. Rather, the evolution of the town across the generations involves the complex development of a way of life between people, who both respond to their ancestors, and shape their futures in the light of what their ancestors have achieved. When we respect the life of a historic town, we respect this complex intergenerational development of a cultural practice that involves the communicative activity of people across time.

This also provides an extra dimension to the wrongness of removing a people from the location where they live. In her important contribution to

124 HERITAGE AND WAR

territorial rights, Annie Stilz has emphasised the importance of located life plans in grounding the right of people to remain in a territory, and not to be forcibly removed from it.[3] I doubt location has universal significance, and I think that plans are not always located. So, although I agree with Stilz that such plans are central to territorial rights, I may not give them the prominence that she does in the overall picture. But even in acknowledging that located life plans are not universally important, it is worth noting that, even with record high levels of migration, only around 3.5 per cent of the world's population live outside the country where they were born (UNDESA 2019).

Of course, migration is expensive, and difficult, and many people who would like to migrate don't have the opportunity to do so. But many who do have the opportunity choose not to, because their life plans are so firmly connected to the particular community in which they live, and it is normally impossible to move a whole community and recreate it elsewhere without great damage to the lives, and loss of the way of life, of the people whose community it is.

And we can now see a further reason why migration proves difficult for people. A person's attachment to a location is often intergenerational. People foster and develop the culture of their ancestors through engagement with the present population, in order to create the platform for future generations to continue that culture. And they often do this in a way that is importantly attached to particular locations that preserve practices, memories and narratives for future generations to reflect on and respond to. The wrong of displacing people, as happened in Lydda, is partly the wrong of disrupting or destroying this intergenerational project.

4. How Should Settlers Respond to the Cultural Value of Lydda?

Let us now reflect on the obligations of those who were involved in the displacement of the Palestinians—both those who were directly or indirectly involved in displacing them, and those who occupied their land, homes and businesses after they were displaced. Different Jewish people living in Israel had different obligations post-1948, partly due to their different roles (if any) in the violation of Palestinian rights, and partly because they were not all equally placed to respond to those violations once they had occurred. Perhaps

---

[3] For her most recent and complete development of this view, see Stilz (2019).

the most interesting group to focus on are the Moroccan and Tunisian Jews who occupied Lydda post-1948, and who lived in the houses of Palestinians who had been driven out.

4.1 Value and Response

Start with the standard view that those who act wrongly owe a response to the wrongdoing. A response to wrongdoing is made appropriate, in part at least, because the response is appropriately guided by the values that were set back by the wrongdoing. For example, suppose that I wrong you, and my conduct was made wrong by the fact that I set back your welfare. I respond appropriately to the wrong when your welfare guides my response in the appropriate way. This helps to explain two central ways in which we ought to respond to wrongdoing, which are usefully distinguished by Adam Slavny (2014): by either negating or counterbalancing its wrong-making features.

A person who acts wrongly might have an opportunity to negate at least some of the negative effects of her wrong, and of that which made the conduct wrong. And, if taking that opportunity is not too onerous, she has a duty to do that. For example, suppose that I wrongly poison your drink in an attempt to kill you. The appropriate response is to pour the drink away, or if I cannot do that, to give you the antidote. In that way, I negate the potential negative effects of my conduct that made it wrong. I then also ensure that I have not committed some kind of wrong: I am an attempted murderer rather than a murderer.

Often, though, negation is not possible. Where that is so, I have a duty to counterbalance the effects of my conduct. For example, if I break your arm, I cannot negate the harm that I have caused. But I can counterbalance it, perhaps by running errands for you, or providing you with financial compensation. Even in this case, counterbalancing involves improving the welfare of the same person that I have harmed. That is so because people are distinctively valuable, and it follows that we cannot simply substitute welfare for one person with welfare for another. There is thus at least some reason to focus on the victim of our own wrongdoing, rather than providing equivalent welfare to others.

As Slavny (2014) suggests, the duty to negate normally has priority over the duty to counterbalance, other things equal. This is especially true in the case of aesthetic or cultural value. For example, suppose that I wrongly damage a painting. My primary obligation is to rectify the damage to that painting,

126   HERITAGE AND WAR

rather than counterbalance the loss by restoring another. Of course, if I cannot rectify the damage I have caused, perhaps I should restore another, or do something else in response. But my primary obligation concerns the distinctive value of the painting that I damaged; the distinctive value that underpinned my wrong.

This priority of negation over counterbalancing is related to a more basic distinction: that between respecting and promoting value. One way of understanding the deontic significance of value is that we have reason to advance value as much as possible. But this does not seem the only way to respond to value; perhaps not even the most important way. Value must be respected as well as promoted. That is why I am required to restore a painting that I have damaged, rather than restoring a different damaged painting of equal value, other things being equal. To do the latter would ensure that I have not set back the value quantitatively, but it would involve a lack of respect for the distinctive value of the painting I have damaged.

4.2 Involving the Wronged

The most obvious way to respond to the displacement of Palestinians from Lydda was to permit them to return. They had the right of return for a range of reasons, but one of them was their interest in the living embedded culture that had been developed across generations in their town, and that they were involved in sustaining and developing. With most people, I believe they had the right of return after the conflict ceased, and the Israeli authorities violated this right following the 1948 war.

A more difficult question, and one which I have addressed elsewhere, is whether that right passes between generations. I have offered two different arguments in support of the intergenerational right of Palestinians to return. First, the legitimate political struggle to return can be sustained across generations, as descendants legitimately intend to assist their ancestors in their struggle to return with their children (Tadros 2017). Second, the original Palestinians who were removed in 1948 had an interest in sustaining their way of life by passing their culture on to their children in the region where they lived, and the appropriate way to respond to the wrongful setback to that interest is to recognise their ability to pass their occupancy rights on to their children (Tadros 2020).

Those who continue to exclude Palestinians from return, or who participate in and sustain political, social and legal practices that have this effect, infringe the rights of Palestinians. Whether they violate those rights is a difficult matter, to do with the consequences of permitting return, and how return could be managed in a way that would reduce conflict. There are strong reasons to believe that the right of return should have been honoured post-1948, and that it should be honoured today, so that those who participate in excluding the Palestinians from Israel violate the right of return.

However, in contrast with the Israeli authorities, and the military who were directly involved in excluding the Palestinians from their town, it is less clear that the Jews who occupied the homes of Palestinians in Lydda post-1948 either infringed or violated the right of return of Palestinians. Even if they did not, they still had positive obligations to respond to the violation of Palestinian rights by others.

But there is also a basis of their having powerful reparative obligations. First, let us consider a clearer case where Jewish immigrants violated the rights of Palestinians: the rights of those Palestinians who remained in Lydda. Presumably, they could have done a great deal to ensure that Palestinians were not the victims of wrongful segregation. They could at least have attempted to ensure that they were allowed to live in their homes. And Palestinians were made to work in the businesses that they had owned. Moroccan Jews who lived in Lydda from 1948 could have done much more than they did to ameliorate or eliminate these injustices. By living in the homes of Palestinians, they incurred obligations to ameliorate the violations of the rights of Palestinians that led to these homes being available. This is especially so as they were the intended beneficiaries of the wrongdoing perpetrated against these Palestinians.

Did they violate any other rights of Palestinian refugees—those who lived in refugee camps? Perhaps it might be argued that they ought not to have occupied the homes of Palestinians. The moral considerations are tricky though. One argument for the view that Moroccans ought not to have lived in these houses is that Palestinians who owned them were owed consent-sensitive duties that others not reside in them. In general, it is wrong to live in my house, whilst I am away, without my consent. The Palestinians obviously did not consent, and presumably would not have done so had they been asked.

But there are considerations against the view that consent was required. First, it was unrealistic for Moroccan Jews who arrived post-1948 to attempt to seek the consent of the Palestinians. They had no way of contacting them. It might be thought, because of this, that they were required not to live in these houses—where a person is owed a consent-sensitive duty, and consent cannot be secured, the person must comply with the duty. But second, had

128   HERITAGE AND WAR

they sought their consent, the Palestinians may have been required to consent; or at least they may have been required to consent in return for rent.

Here is why the Palestinians may have been under such a duty. These Jewish immigrants would be left with insufficient accommodation without occupying their homes, and the Palestinians could not benefit from these homes by living in them, at least not immediately. Where one person has significant need for accommodation, and another cannot use that accommodation, the first ought to consent to the second using it. This seems true even if the reason why the first cannot use her accommodation is that she has been unjustly excluded from it.

Perhaps it might be argued that Moroccan Jews causally contributed to the exclusion of Palestinians by occupying their land, homes and businesses. Jewish immigrants to Israel ensured that the Israeli authorities were able to develop their state whilst excluding the Palestinians.[4] This does, I think, affect the rights of these immigrants—they had a special obligation to ensure that their conduct did not reinforce disadvantages that Palestinians suffered at the hands of the Israeli authorities. But even so, there is a question of whether this was sufficient to make it wrong for them to occupy empty Palestinian houses.

Perhaps it might be argued that these Moroccan Jews would bear responsibility for their own plight if they were left without housing, as they decided to emigrate to Israel. But this view is hard to believe—even if voluntary choice is a reason not to alleviate a person's burden, they had inadequate information about the circumstances in Israel that they were moving to, and the antisemitism in their own country gave them powerful reasons to leave.

However, even if Moroccan Jews had a right temporarily to live in the houses of Palestinians, they were wrong to claim ownership over these houses, even where ownership was granted by the Israeli authorities—something that happened quite systematically in the early years of the state of Israel. Palestinians owned these homes, and there are strict limits to the possibility of co-owning property. By claiming ownership over this property, Moroccan Jews implied that Palestinians lacked ownership rights—rights that they had, and that were being violated by the Israeli authorities.

Some might object that only legal authority determines a person's ownership over property, and that as soon as they were denied legal ownership, the Palestinians were no longer moral owners of the property. This view, though, is completely implausible. A state can wrongly deprive its citizens of their

---

[4] I am grateful, here, to Helen Frowe for discussion.

RESPONDING TO CULTURAL WRONGS IN PALESTINE AND ISRAEL   129

legal ownership rights. It is hard to believe that when it does so, it successfully deprives them of their moral ownership rights. Legal ownership should normally be restored, and that should guide decisions by political actors who take the reins in states that have behaved unjustly.

Furthermore, Moroccan Jews may have been permitted to live in these houses only on condition that they fight for the Palestinian right of return, at least insofar as doing this was consistent with the security of Moroccan Jews. They were permitted to benefit from the houses of Palestinians, but only to the extent to which this is consistent with the prior, and more stringent, rights of the Palestinians, and only on condition that they do what they can, within reason, to respect those rights, and to ensure that others respect them. It may seem hard to imagine Moroccan Jews fighting for the Palestinian right of return in 1948. I don't find this so far-fetched, though.

At any rate, my main interest is not in whether Moroccan Jews wronged Palestinians by living in their houses. It is, rather, in the cultural obligations they had, and whether these obligations were owed to the Palestinians. Those who arrived in Lydda must have been aware that they were entering a town where a large Arab population had, until recently, lived. And they also must have been aware that this population was driven away, either intentionally, or by the conflict. Furthermore, they must have been aware that the Palestinian population wanted to return and that the property and occupancy rights of Palestinians were either being violated, or at least infringed, by the Israeli government, army and officials. Finally, they must have been aware that the long-standing culture of the Palestinians was tied to the town and was being eroded or destroyed by their having been driven out.

Given that the Palestinians had the right of return, one obligation that Jewish settlers had, at least initially, was to preserve the town, including the homes they lived in, ready for return. Although it was perhaps unlikely that the Palestinian right of return would be fully respected in the near future, given the animosity that had been generated in the previous decades and by the 1948 war itself, there was certainly a chance that Lydda would be placed under the control of the Jordanians, and the Palestinians would then have been granted the right to return there.

As time passed, though, the chance of return diminished, and with that the possibility of adequately responding to the legitimate cultural ambitions of Palestinians also diminished. This is because of the kind of culture that they enjoyed in Lydda—a living embedded culture of the kind described earlier. Lydda had already substantially developed dynamically under the mandate from the late nineteenth century, as it increasingly became an important hub

130   HERITAGE AND WAR

of economic activity, given its fortuitous location between Jerusalem and Jaffa. It had a rich and historic culture, but it was far from frozen in aspic.

The ambitions of at least some of the population of Lydda, then, were presumably to develop the town further, and this will have included the transformation of traditional modes of employment. This would probably have been accompanied by a transformation in the modes of living of ordinary Palestinians, which was already underway in the mid-twentieth century. As we find everywhere, there would no doubt have been disagreement between Palestinians about how to transform the town, including the extent to which traditional ways of life must be respected and preserved against the opportunities that would have presented themselves in the second half of the twentieth century. It is very hard to know what opportunities would have presented themselves, and how the Palestinians would have responded, under just political conditions, not least because it is a very contentious matter what just political conditions would have involved.

Furthermore, it is an odd way to respond to a person's interest in living embedded culture to do what they would have done had they been permitted to develop their culture. The value of a living embedded culture is in its actual development by people who are appropriately connected to it. Nothing resembling that value is realised by others aping the conduct that Palestinians would have engaged in had they not been driven out.

And yet, it also cannot be appropriate to respond to Lydda as one might respond to iconic culture. The idea that the new Jewish population of Lod would have been required to freeze Lydda in a pre-1950s state, ready for the Palestinians to return, is absurd, not least because the lives of Palestinians have substantially evolved in that time—those who now argue for the right of return are strongly culturally connected to their ancestors, of course, but their lives are also significantly different from their parents and grandparents, who were driven from towns like Lydda in 1948.

Furthermore, we must recognise the cultural rights of Moroccan Jews themselves. They had their own cultural challenges, as the state of Israel was being developed with the ambition to be a kind of European state in the Middle East. The culture of Moroccan Jews was in some ways much closer to Palestinians than Jews who came from Europe, so in some ways it would have been easier to respond to their cultural ambitions without further eroding the cultural ambitions of Arabs beyond what had already been done to them by the authorities. But they were also involved in a struggle to develop their own cultural practices and ambitions in the face of wealthier and more powerful Jewish people from Europe who discriminated against them.

Still, Moroccan and Tunisian Jews were surely not permitted to ignore the living embedded culture of Palestinians that had been eroded or destroyed by their mistreatment in 1948. Perhaps the most appropriate way to respond to the culture of Lydda was to place Palestinians at the heart of the development of Lydda, to the extent that this was possible, and to engage with them as Moroccan and Tunisian Jews had engaged with Muslims and Christians for generations. Respecting their right to be involved in the development of the cultural life of Lydda need not have come at the exclusion of the rights of Jewish Moroccans and Tunisians to develop their own culture, as it was part of their historic culture to engage with people of different religions, and to find ways of accommodating their different faiths within complex commercial, legal and cultural structures.

There were at least some Palestinians, still living in Lydda, who were deprived of their basic rights of property and employment—their houses were occupied, and their businesses were taken over by the new Jewish inhabitants who employed them as labourers. And further Arabs arrived, looking for work. It is still not too late, I think, for some kind of respect for Palestinian culture in what has become Lod. The sad fragmentation of the city, and the divisions within it, might still be overcome in a way that might show respect, not only for the Palestinians who were driven away, and their descendants, but also for the Jews who moved there from North Africa, who had a tradition of compromise and accommodation with others.

5. Conclusion

The domination of political groups who are deeply disrespectful of the rights and culture of Palestinians in Israel continue to aim at the expansion of Israel's territory, with the ambition of ensuring that the Palestinians remain largely invisible to Israelis. Rather than reflecting on the appropriate way to respond to the remaining threads of Arab culture, the aim is the further destruction and replacement of Palestinian culture. This project is deeply disrespectful of the cultural life of Palestinians. But it is also deeply disrespectful of the cultural life of Jews. Respect for the different cultural traditions in the region requires imagining a future life together, where hostility, racism and exclusion are challenged through integrated political structures. This requires imagination, but that is just what history demands.[5]

---

[5] I am grateful to participants in the conference on Heritage in War at Cambridge in 2019 and the Heritage in War Core Research Group at Kings College London. I am also grateful to Cécile Fabre, Helen Frowe and Adam Slavny for helpful conversations and written comments.

References

Boum, A. (2014), *Memories of Absence: How Muslims Remember Jews in Morocco* (Stanford, CA: Stanford University Press).

Golan, A. (2003), 'Lydda and Ramle: From Palestinian Arab to Israeli Towns, 1948–1967', in *Middle Eastern Studies* 39: 121–139.

Jacobi, H. (2004), 'In Between Surveillance and Spatial Protest: The Production of Space in the "Mixed City" of Lod', in *Surveillance and Society* 2: 55–77.

Marglin, J. M. (2016), *Across Legal Lines: Jews and Muslims in Modern Morocco* (New Haven, CT: Yale University Press).

Morris, B. (2004), *The Birth of the Palestinian Refugee Problem Revisited* (Cambridge: Cambridge University Press).

Slavny, A. (2014), 'Negating and Counterbalancing: A Fundamental Distinction in the Concept of a Corrective Duty', in *Law and Philosophy* 33: 143–173.

Stilz, A. (2019), *Territorial Sovereignty: A Philosophical Exploration* (Oxford: Oxford University Press).

Tadros, V. (2017), 'The Persistence of the Right of Return', in *Philosophy, Politics, and Economics* 16/4: 375–399.

Tadros, V. (2020), 'Inheriting the Right of Return', *Theoretical Inquiries in Law* 21/2: 343–367.

UNDESA (Department of Economic and Social Affairs). (2019), 'The number of international migrants reaches 272 million, continuing an upward trend in all world regions, says UN', 17 September, accessed 8 June 2020, https://www.un.org/development/desa/en/news/population/international-migrant-stock-2019.html.

UNESCO. (1954), Hague Convention for the Protection of Cultural Property in the Event of Armed Conflict of May 14, 1954, 2 249 UNTS 240.

UN Special Rapporteur for Cultural Rights. (2016), *Joint Statement On Cultural Rights and the Protection of Cultural Heritage*, accessed 8 June 2020, https://www.ohchr.org/Documents/Issues/CulturalRights/JointStatementCyprus 21Mar2016.pdf.

8

When Damage Becomes Memorial

Carolyn Korsmeyer

1. Introduction

So identified are societies with their artistic and technological accomplishments that, from antiquity to the present, warring parties have deliberately destroyed material artifacts almost as much as they have targeted peoples (Gamboni 1997). In addition to whatever military objectives might be achieved, motives for such actions include iconoclasm, revenge, and psychological warfare, on the assumption that by demolishing treasured objects, the sentiments that sustain cultural continuity, community, and resistance may be undermined. Material heritage is also collateral damage when wholesale assault is wreaked upon entire cities, leaving behind relics that become emblems of both loss and survival. While war's destruction often targets monuments long venerated for their artistry and history, even an undistinguished building can become valued if it is the only thing left standing.

Any society must rebuild after the devastation of war to meet the needs of the living, thereby erasing signs of conflict as new buildings rise from the ashes. Reconstruction often strives to return a place to what it was before, replicating familiar appearances and preserving artifacts too valuable to lose—or what is left of them. In certain cases, preservation is also an effort to halt degradation that has accrued for centuries, for when an artifact is ancient, the question of what stage of its 'life' should be represented in repair is salient. This decision pertains both to individual artifacts and whole regions. For example, after agents of ISIS destroyed Roman sites in Palmyra, Syria, the Institute for Digital Archaeology recreated the triumphal arch of Septimus Severus to look the way it had appeared, not when first erected, but just before it was destroyed. When much of the city of Warsaw was mined at the end of World War II, the famous Old Town was reconstructed largely in the style that had developed by the eighteenth century, although the city is much older than that (Matravers 2020).

Carolyn Korsmeyer, *When Damage Becomes Memorial* In: *Heritage and War: Ethical Issues*. Edited by: William Bülow, Helen Frowe, Derek Matravers, and Joshua Lewis Thomas, Oxford University Press.
© Carolyn Korsmeyer 2023. DOI: 10.1093/oso/9780192862648.003.0008

134   HERITAGE AND WAR

In recognition of the inevitable destruction wrought by time, some argue that many old artifacts damaged in war simply ought to be left to decay (Scarbrough 2020). If their latest injuries are sufficiently grave, reparative efforts are likely to be fruitless. Furthermore, the marks of time, natural disaster, and armed conflict can be important to retain because they are a part of the history of an object that future generations ought to remember. Against the latter recommendation is the fact that technological achievements and valuable works of architecture also need to be remembered, and if their repair or reconstruction enhances present appreciation of the accomplishments they manifest, that value might override retention of visible damage. The suitability of these options, of course, will vary with the amount of damage sustained, the possibilities for reconstruction, and the cultural standing of the object in question.

I am interested in cases where visible marks of assault become the very reason to preserve things in their damaged states, where destruction is so dramatically marked that damaged artifacts become memorials. This essay will examine the memorial role that damaged objects sometimes assume, and in so doing, draw attention to the particular affective power that real things can have, even in a fragmentary state. I hope to illuminate the perception and significance of partly destroyed buildings, ruins, and remnants that, in the words of artist Eric Fischl, are "objects that carry the scars of their survival" (Fischl 2006: 197). Examples include the Genbaku Dome in Hiroshima, artifacts from the World Trade Center Memorial in New York, and the bullet holes preserved from the American Civil War in Gettysburg, Pennsylvania, to name just a few. I call such objects *witness memorials*; their perceptually manifest destruction is the very feature that qualifies them for attention. They summon to mind the causes that brought them to that state by virtue of the fact that they *exemplify* the event that they memorialize, and therefore they possess a symbolic feature absent in more conventionally designed memorials. I begin with a general discussion of war memorials before turning to objects where damage is the proper object of attention and remembrance.

2. Memorials

A memorial is an object that is publicly presented to summon remembrance and to evoke affective attitudes such as respect, sorrow, resolve, and honor (Carroll 2010; Wolterstorff 2015). As Arthur Danto has noted: "We erect monuments so that we shall always remember and build memorials so that we shall never forget" (Danto 1985: 152). Erecting monuments in order to sustain collective memory is an ancient practice. According to art historian Alois Riegl:

> A monument in its oldest and most original sense is a human creation, erected for the specific purpose of keeping single human deeds or events...alive in the minds of future generations. Monuments can be either artistic or literary, depending on whether the event to be remembered is brought to the viewer's consciousness by means of the visual arts or with the help of inscriptions. Most of the time both genres are used simultaneously.
>
> (Riegl 1928: 21)

Like all monuments designed to commemorate, war memorials are highly symbolic, although the types of symbols employed vary quite a lot, indicating different modes of signification. (In this chapter, I use 'memorial' and 'monument' more or less interchangeably, though not all monuments are memorials and not all memorials are monuments.) Riegl calls attention to the combination of visual, often sculptural, elements that combine with inscribed text to convey meaning, usually in a straightforward fashion—for as public statements, memorials are intended to be readily understood. However, those categories can be analyzed further into a number of different referential devices. As we shall see, cultural artifacts damaged in war possess singular symbolic properties and, as a consequence, affective power that is different from the aesthetic and emotive effects of more intentionally designed monuments of the sort that Riegl has in mind. Before turning to artifacts whose damage endows them with memorial standing, I shall review briefly some other, more conventional, memorials, beginning with two that commemorate the American Civil War.

Probably the most familiar types of monuments are those made from materials such as stone or bronze. The durability of the substance is itself of basic symbolic significance because it lasts far longer than the persons or events commemorated. Kathleen Higgins states that stone actually has a metaphysical resonance: "Stone monuments combat oblivion...Stone adamantly proclaims our denial that death has had the final word" (Higgins 2020: 18). And Francis Sparshott, somewhat more pessimistically, remarks: "Only stone has the look of deliberate lastingness, and on a sufficient scale testifies to the futile stubbornness of humanity in its endeavor to win immortality through works" (Sparshott 1985: 92).

Conventional war memorials typically feature symbols of battle, either realistic or abstract, perhaps including names of soldiers among the fallen. Many such examples are situated at the Gettysburg Military Park in Pennsylvania, which itself is a multifaceted memorial, since it is the site of the famous battle where more than 7,000 men were killed in three days in July of 1863. The park contains dozens of monuments erected by different states of the once-divided nation to commemorate the regiments they sent into battle. A typical style features a standing soldier holding a weapon, who represents the many who fought in that regiment; inscriptions on the base list the other battles the regiment fought, along with a brief text summarizing its role at Gettysburg and the numbers of those killed in that battle. [Figure 1] Another device typical of war memorials includes in the descriptive text the individual names of the fallen.

Consider the types of symbolic devices at work in this sort of monument. First and perhaps most obvious, there is realistic representation, for the garb and weapons of a soldier are readily identified. Second, the single figure is a

Figure 1. Monument to the 72nd Pennsylvania Infantry, 2nd Brigade, Gettysburg Battlefield, Public domain. Photo #78309, Courtesy of Gettysburg National Military Park.
https://www.fhwa.dot.gov/byways/Uploads/asset_files/000/005/942/237_87jrfv2yte.JPG

kind of sculptural synecdoche, as one depicted man stands for the many men of the regiment. Third, there is descriptive text that labels the monument by referring to the regiment and to its other battles. Finally, the style itself is expressively symbolic, for its commanding vertical design indicates courage and resolve. In this park, some of the monuments may also be taken to signal the terrible losses the battle would take, for many portray a soldier preparing to attack with a swing of his rifle, suggesting that his ammunition is already spent.

The Eternal Light Peace Memorial on the same site features more abstract symbols. [Figure 2] It was intended to observe the fiftieth anniversary of the battle, but financial complications postponed its completion for another quarter century. Designed by architect Paul Philippe Cret and sculptor Lee Lawrie, and dedicated in 1938 by President Franklin Roosevelt, it commemorates the reunification of the country after the war that had divided it so grievously. A large inscription at its base reads *Peace eternal in a nation united*, and it is crowned with a perpetually burning fire, a so-called eternal flame. Lines chiseled on one side read: "An enduring light to guide us in unity and fellowship." The eternal light was at first lit from natural gas, which burned until 1979, when it was replaced by electricity; the gas flame was restored in

Figure 2. Eternal Light Peace Memorial (design: Paul Philippe Cret, sculptor: Lee Lawrie) Wikimedia Commons, photo credit: Veggies.
https://commons.wikimedia.org/wiki/File:Eternal_Light_Peace_Memorial_on_Oak_Hill.jpg

138 HERITAGE AND WAR

1988. The aptness of an actual flame as opposed to an electric light as a symbol of eternal vigilance is worth pondering. Evidently, electricity is out of step with the aesthetic function of a memorial because fire has longer and deeper symbolic meanings. One can contemplate an eternal flame but not an eternal light bulb. This is not mere cynicism but pertains to the emotional arousal appropriate for memorials, a subject to consider shortly. Use of an eternal flame partakes of ancient connotations of light, fire, and enduring vigilance. As such, the actual flame has more symbolic gravitas than would an electric light.

The images on the square column, two women and an eagle, symbolize unity of north and south in a nation restored. The eagle represents the United States and is a relatively recent symbol, historically speaking, for the choice of a bald eagle as the national bird dates from only the eighteenth century. The women, however, are depicted with older devices. They wear classical garb; the shield that one holds gestures to war, and the other carries a laurel wreath, ancient symbol of victory. (Presumably, peace is the victor, since only one side won the actual conflict.) A garland draped across the shoulders of both women emphasizes the nation's unity. Those symbols are both conventional and natural, in that the laurel wreath would not indicate victory without its use for that purpose in ancient Greece and continued cultural recognition of that meaning, but being bound together with a garland rather obviously suggests unity. There are other symbolic resonances of a general sort as well. As far as I can tell from scanning commentary about this monument, the meanings conveyed by the classical symbols have largely become forgotten in favor of a rather vague suggestion of a feminine principle of peace.

My point with these examples is to call attention to the various kinds of symbols that memorials employ in their commemoration of events from war. Just with these two we have realistic representation, images with abstract reference from at least two cultural sources (America and classical antiquity), textual descriptions (both names of participants in the war and declarations that express hope for peace), and expressive compositional style of a type that is often expected in commemorating sacrifice and bravery: a flame atop a structure that is vertical, upright, and stalwart. (One of the reasons that Maya Lin's Vietnam Veteran's Memorial was initially so controversial was the unfamiliarity of a dark, descending, horizontal design representing the pages of a huge open book rather than the more familiar towering monument.)

However, there is a particular kind of symbol that is absent from both examples—but that can be seen in another, far humbler, marker of the Gettysburg battle.

Throughout the town itself there are numerous scars and bullet holes, for while most of the conflict was waged on cleared farmland, on the third day of fighting it spilled over into the more densely built area. The most famous battle scar in town is to be found in what is known now as the Jennie Wade house. Jennie was making bread in her kitchen when a stray bullet penetrated her door and she was hit, becoming the single civilian casualty of the battle. While there are statues erected in her honor both in front of the house and in the graveyard where she is buried, it is the hole from the bullet that killed her that interests me. Bullet holes in the ordinary buildings of Gettysburg are not war memorials, but they command attention and arouse a vivid impression of the wounds of war, and in this respect their apprehension is comparable to encounters with memorials insofar as they keep alive remembrance of conflict, summoning images of battle by their very presence. Similarly, there are trees still growing on the battlefield that bulge with shells that lodged there during the fighting. These are chiefly objects of curiosity. But their important contrast with the monuments that were deliberately erected on the battlefield lies in the different symbolic function that they have in virtue of being the *real thing—actual scars from shots fired long ago*. Preservation and display of the real remnants of conflict return us to the damage that war wreaks on material cultural heritage and to memorials that preserve damage in order to commemorate its cause.

3. Memorials and Real Things

The Douaumont Ossuary in northeastern France is a memorial to one of the major battles of World War I. It contains the bones of more than 130,000 French and German soldiers who fell in 1916 during the protracted battle of Verdun. In a terrible irony, this monument also 'unites' former combatants, both symbolically and literally, because after ten months of fighting that claimed well over 700,000 lives, the unclaimed remains of the dead were too dispersed, mangled, and numerous to identify separately.[1] This memorial combines traditional abstract symbolism, most obvious with the large Christian cross on the tower, with the symbolic standing possessed by the *real thing*, the *actual remnants of war*, in this case the bones of the fallen—no longer signifying discrete individuals but disarticulated and piled in huge stacks behind glass.

---

[1] For an extensive analysis of burials and memorials to those killed in war, see Laqueur (2015: part III).

140 HERITAGE AND WAR

When a memorial displays the very object remaining from a war, it takes on a particular symbolic function that Nelson Goodman labeled *exemplification*. The term originates in the system of referential relations that Goodman developed in *Languages of Art* and that Catherine Z. Elgin amplified in *With Reference to Reference* (Goodman 1976; Elgin 1983). Goodman and Elgin gather together concepts such as denotation, representation, and expression into a system of symbols (their expansive use of the term) distinguished by the kinds of reference they manifest. While their schematic approach to referential relations and meaning may sound rather bloodless in the abstract, I have found it useful to distinguish the different cognitive functions that artifacts come to possess, thereby furnishing insight as to the singular power of damaged objects and the recognition of war's destruction that they inspire. I shall draw from their quite complicated schemata only a few, much simplified, points.

Exemplification was largely overlooked in philosophy of art—and in philosophy generally—until Goodman called attention to it. (In his Foreword to Elgin's work, he refers to "the almost universally overlooked referential relation of exemplification and its interconnection with denotation and expression" [Elgin 1983: 1].) Once noticed, however, it is obvious that exemplification functions crucially in both art and daily life, as his own quotidian examples demonstrate. Something that exemplifies both possesses a property and refers to that property, thereby highlighting its importance. Consider paint chips or fabric swatches. A swatch of upholstery fabric has many properties—such as being brocade, smooth, and yellow. These are characteristics it displays for someone seeking to reupholster furniture. Those particular properties refer to themselves in the interpretive context of sample books, for one uses samples in order to select the design, texture, and color of fabrics. The swatch possesses many other properties as well; it may be bound with a dozen others, be six-inches square, and weigh two ounces. It possesses these properties but does not exemplify them, because they are incidental to the practice that surrounds sample books. One does not upholster a chair with six inches of fabric, so whether the sample is six- or seven-inches square is irrelevant. Exemplified properties are recognized as such in the situations in which they are put to use. Paint chips clearly exemplify color because they are samples of color; they equally clearly do not exemplify being three inches on a side because they are not consulted for information about that property. What is more, they are literally samples, not imitations. With swatches, the exemplified objects are pieces of the actual fabrics, the colors on the paint chips are applied with the actual paint from a can you might purchase. They *refer* to what they *actually are*.

To put it simply: literal exemplification calls attention to what something *really is*. (Exemplification can also be metaphorical, which is the way Goodman analyzes expressive predicates.) This is highly useful when choosing paint or fabric. But exemplification also provides a vivid mode of recognition that can have profound meaning: including accidental calamity, such as Jennie Wade's fatal bullet, and loss of life on a colossal scale, as with the bones piled inside the Douaumont memorial. This *is* the mark of the lethal shot; these *are* bones that once supported men who died—and who died *here*. Places can also exemplify, for battlefields are, and refer to being, the very ground where the events commemorated took place.

Exemplification blends with other referential modes in the complex apprehensions aroused with memorials.

> Representation, exemplification, and expression are elementary varieties of symbolization, but reference by a building to abstruse or complicated ideas sometimes runs along more devious paths, along homogeneous or heterogeneous chains of elementary referential links.
>
> (Goodman and Elgin 1988: 42)

Memorials that include bomb debris, fallen roofs, crushed pediments, or bent weapons exemplify war-related injuries to material heritage because they literally possess those injuries, drawing attention to their partial destruction. The general property at issue here is *being damaged*, a visible feature that is hard to miss. One thereby apprehends more than the marks of material injury, for the reference continues to the conflict that inflicted damage (*being damaged from a particular attack*) and possibly even further to more abstract, general concepts, such as war itself and the hope of peace.

In addition to joining the list of symbolic references that memorials can exploit, exemplification furnishes a particularly moving and vivid sense of immediacy and presence that more formally designed memorials seldom attain. This claim presumes a thesis about the perception of damaged artifacts, which I hope will be persuasive after consideration of a few more examples.

4. Damage as a Perceptual Property

My grounding assumption relies on the intuition that the perception of damage entails immediate, virtually simultaneous, recognition of two things: that there was a prior condition of the object, a condition that might range from

142   HERITAGE AND WAR

new and pristine to ancient and already ruined; and that something caused the evident damage. Recognizing that the visible qualities of artifacts have causes is hardly unusual. One implicitly assumes that the design of a building, a tended landscape, or a painting was intentionally brought about. With qualities that signal material injury, that recognition is especially obvious because it is built into the perceptual property *being damaged*. Cause is embedded in the concept, if you will; if one perceives damage, then one recognizes at the same time that there was a prior destructive event. The exact nature of that event may be unknown or only vaguely sensed, but the mere notice of damage is *pro tanto* notice of some injurious cause.

Consider, for example, the experience of artifacts we now designate as ruins, such as the medieval abbeys to be found in Britain. You might not know exactly what brought about the destruction of Tintern Abbey, but seeing a large, old building without a roof entails realizing at the same time that something caused the roof to fall. There is even less remaining of what once was Shaftesbury Abbey, and one walks among remnants that are now little more than foundation stones outlining the abbey's original footprint. Taking note of foundations that now support no walls entails awareness that something brought down the entire structure. Without the double content to one's apprehension—effect and cause—one would not be noticing damage at all, just stones. Identifying such objects as damaged, indeed as ruins in these two cases, demonstrates awareness of some cause of their present state, although one might not know whether it was war, weather, or Henry VIII.

The perception of damage is relevant to considering the aesthetic aspects of artifacts that have fallen victim to conflict and figure among the casualties of war. By 'aesthetic aspect' I am not referring especially to artifacts such as sculpture or architecture and therefore as damaged works of art, although to be sure many art works are important examples of injured cultural heritage.[2] Nor do I mean the accidental formal beauty that damage sometimes leaves behind, such as delicate outlines of supportive arches now open to the sky. Rather, 'aesthetic aspect' pertains to any partially destroyed objects that exhibit compelling presence and carry perceptual impact. Their damage rivets attention on the causes of destruction, whether or not those objects were originally considered artistically significant. When damaged artifacts are presented as memorials they summon wonder, awe, sorrow, perhaps anger and a host of other difficult emotions as we contemplate what they have survived. They do so by exemplifying, by being the *real thing, literally damaged*. They

---

[2] Sandra Shapshay (2021) develops an account of the monumental as a distinguishable aesthetic category.

are "objects that bear the scars of their survival," to repeat Fischl's description. As such, they can be considered *witnesses* to their own destruction.

Consider the Hiroshima Peace Memorial, also known as the Genbaku Dome. [Figure 3] Designed by a Czech architect and completed in 1915, this European style building was never noted for its position in traditional Japanese culture, so it would not have counted as an object of cultural heritage before World War II. Rather, it was built as an Industrial Promotion Hall to encourage the modernization of Japan. Its significance today is entirely due to its freakish survival from the atomic bomb that was dropped over Hiroshima in 1945. Where all around was flattened rubble, the skeleton of this building alone still stood. For years there was controversy over whether it should be taken down or preserved. Not until the 1960s was the decision made to stabilize its remains and designate it as a memorial to the loss of life and the devastation of the attack, as well as an expression of hope for peace in future times. (In 1996, it was named a UNESCO World Heritage site.) Under these conditions, there was no question of repairing or reconstructing the structure. Its damaged state is precisely what commands attention and signals its meaning. As Yuriko Saito puts it, "The Dome asserts its existence for what it is and for where it is" (Saito 2020: 207).

Figure 3. Genbaku Dome, Hiroshima Peace Memorial Wikimedia Commons/ Oilstreet.2013.
https://commons.wikimedia.org/wiki/File:Genbaku_Dome04-r.JPG

144   HERITAGE AND WAR

Its status as a memorial to war begins with its literal properties: real damage from the bomb. Its standing as a symbol of peace relies on the declaration of this significance when the memorial was named and dedicated. Without the latter actions, it could equally well stand as a symbol of despair or warning, depending on the "more devious paths" of "referential links" invoked. As Nicolas Wolterstorff emphasizes, in order fully to come into being, a memorial requires an act declaring it as such (2015: 123–124). Any perceived damage may bring about recollection of a destructive cause. The Gettysburg bullet holes, for instance, are vivid reminders of the battle, but they are not memorials themselves. For damage to become a memorial in the most complete sense of the term, it must be formally recognized, usually by a ceremony of dedication, an occasion that can also expand its scope. The Genbaku Dome honors the dead of the 1945 attack and also, declaratively, the hope that peace will prevail and no such devastation will ever happen again.

The World Trade Center Memorial in New York contains multiple objects whose wreckage qualifies them as witness memorials to the attacks of 9/11. Like the Dome, many of the fragments here would never have been singled out for special attention were it not for the damage that they manifest. The huge slurry wall that is now on display, for example, would not have been visible, since it was constructed below ground as part of the foundation to form a barrier against flooding from the nearby Hudson River. The wall withstood the attacks and the collapse of the building, and it stands now as a symbol of endurance and resilience (Dunlap 2013). Here exemplification has two referents because it is both literal and metaphorical: the wall, being an exceptionally strong protective structure, was itself physically resilient; and therefore it is now taken to symbolize the resilience of a people and a nation.

The impact of the plane that hit the North Tower left some of the steel reinforcement structure bent into shapes that almost invite seeing them as abstract sculptures. [Figure 4] Doing so, of course, would require that one mistakenly misinterpret or deliberately overlook the property that makes them worthy of display: namely, being *damaged—not designed*. In their present twisted and jagged state, these objects exemplify the destruction of the attack: the cause of their shape and situation is immediately manifest to our perception. That awareness is, of course, guided; it is enhanced by the fact that one has entered a huge memorial site that contains a museum of artifacts from the attacks. The architectural fragments and the damaged rescue equipment within are not monuments that were intentionally designed as memorials, and so without the context of the site it would be easy to overlook their standing. That huge remnants of architectural infrastructure have been

WHEN DAMAGE BECOMES MEMORIAL 145

Figure 4. Section of Steel Façade, North Tower, Floors 93–96, World Trade Center Memorial, New York City. Photo by author.

grotesquely mangled would be obvious, but the specific cause of that damage might not be, and hence their meaning would not be recognized. The perception of damage that makes for memorial, therefore, involves certain background knowledge. We recognize the damage not only as indicating a prior cause, but as signaling a cause that is worthy of contemplation. If the cause remains unknown, the memorial function is incomplete.

Exemplification not only joins the list of symbolic references employed in the design of memorials, its special immediacy possesses a singular aesthetic impact (Young 2020). An object that truly bears the scars of its survival delivers a sense of *presence*—of being before the very thing, perhaps in the very place, where destruction occurred. I call a memorial that exemplifies damage a 'witness memorial' both because it testifies to war's devastation in virtue of its manifest damage, and also because, in a sense, we share in that witness by recognizing, standing before, the direct evidence of destruction. Both perceptual and emotive factors contribute to feeling this presence, for not only can one see actual damage, but when standing before the real thing

146 HERITAGE AND WAR

one could also, in certain circumstances, touch it, literally feel it. Even without direct contact, the sense of touch and the inner sense of proprioception heighten awareness of *where* one is (Korsmeyer 2019). The position of one's own body in relation to the physical thing engenders this experience.[3] Thus, there is a palpable awareness of *place* with memorials that display the real wreckage of war.

The Dome and the World Trade Center Memorial are large structures on sites that are wholly dedicated to a memorial purpose. To these we can add examples that incorporate damaged objects into other structures that take over the function of those that were destroyed. Some of these preserve the remnants of artifacts that were already recognized as culturally significant, such as churches. Unlike the pieces of infrastructure in the Twin Towers, which could not have had that standing prior to the attack, damaged objects that were once a noteworthy part of social activity are preserved because sustaining the presence of objects of important cultural heritage is, in itself, worthwhile. The Kaiser Wilhelm Gedächtniskirche (Memorial Church) in Berlin, for example, incorporates the tower of an older church that suffered bombing in 1943. Rather than either restore the original structure or tear down the remains, architect Egon Eiermann (responding to insistent public demand) incorporated the damaged tower into his new design (Visit Berlin n.d.).[4]

The original tower with its damage is rather easily recognized for what it was, but there are other aspects of damage and memorial that require quite specific historical understanding. Inside the Gedächtniskirche there is a metal cross. A cross is readily recognizable as a symbol of Christianity, but this particular cross is fashioned from three of the long, medieval nails that were used in the construction of England's Coventry Cathedral, founded in the fifteenth century. Coventry Cathedral was so damaged by German bombing in 1940 that it remains in ruins, but these nails were collected, made into crosses, and bestowed on other churches as symbols of peace, not only in Berlin but in Dresden and at other sites of Allied bombing (Welby 2016). Exemplification is again at work in the meaning of these objects, for a cross is an abstract symbol that can be made of any solid material, but only another artifact

---

[3] Following Brian O'Shaughnessy: "In touch we become aware of extra-bodily objects through becoming aware of the unique body-object. That is, in touch we gain epistemological access to the world at large through immediate epistemological access to one small part of it: our own body" (2000: 662).

[4] The original plan to raze the site and build an entirely new church met with so much public protest that the architect revised his designs in order to preserve part of the old one. I take this event to demonstrate widespread recognition of the importance of exemplification.

destroyed by war can be an actual instance of war's destruction. Their standing as memorials to peace requires dedication and acknowledgment as such, although a gift to a former enemy is readily noticed as a gesture of reconciliation.

The context needed to understand the import of visible damage can be provided quite simply as well, as with plaques that explain chips and fissures on a building that continues to function in its ordinary way. The Victoria and Albert Museum in London, for example, also sustained a good deal of bomb damage during World War II. One of the impact holes from the bombing, still visible on a façade, is next to a dedicatory plaque that reads "The damage to these walls is the result of enemy bombing during the blitz of the Second World War 1939–1945 and is left as a memorial to the enduring values of this great museum in a time of conflict" (V&A n.d.).[5] I surmise that the preservation of the marks of damage represents a spectrum from formal and somber memorials to traces known largely through informal transmission of local lore. All along that spectrum there is a special wonder invited by the real thing, which reminds us that we stand where terrible events took place.

The distinctive affective impact of real damage is borne out by (what I take to be) the obvious contrast with things that are made to look as if they are damaged, although in fact they are not. Given the technologies of reproduction now available, it is possible to create an exact copy of an object of cultural heritage that was targeted for destruction. The most famous case at present is doubtless the replicated Palmyra Arch. The original triumphal arch of Septimus Severus was erected when Syria was part of the Roman Empire, and to modern eyes it was always damaged, having fallen into ruin over many centuries. In 2015, it was among the classical ruins of Palmyra that were blown up by ISIS militants, the area also used as a site of execution of those who resisted the destruction. Because there were numerous photographs and measurements taken prior to its demolition, the huge object could be reproduced by means of scans and digital design programs, so that the classical ruin could be newly chiseled from marble, replicating (albeit on a somewhat smaller scale) its pre-2015 appearance down to the smallest cracks and breaks. (Both the accuracy and the ethics of the replication have been controversial [Khunti 2018].) But if I am correct that perceiving damage entails perceiving a cause that brought it about, then no matter how accurate the replication, the

---

[5] Thanks to Rumiko Handa for calling this example to my attention. There are numerous examples of war-ravaged artifacts that have been left in their damaged states and become memorials to the conflict that destroyed them.

148 HERITAGE AND WAR

appearance of the new arch differs from that of the original. Its apparent antiquity is recognized as the product of a clever computer program that marvelously presents what the arch was *like*, but not what it *was*.

Peter Lamarque observes that, "when perceived *under different categories* two otherwise indiscernible objects can come to look different" (Lamarque 2010: 134, emphasis in original). Ancient object and replica of ancient object are different categories. Therefore, this object—whatever its merits—bears the look characteristic of damage over centuries, but it is not itself damaged by the conflict that destroyed the original. Rather, its symbolic features represent and refer more remotely by means of imitation of the look of the original arch (now possibly destroyed beyond repair) and allusion to the cause of that destruction. (Elgin calls allusion "a form of referential action at a distance" [Elgin 1983: 142].) The grounding assumption to my argument—that perceiving damage entails recognizing some prior cause—calls into question a notion that has teased philosophy of art for some decades now, namely that exact copies can be perceptually indiscernible from their originals (Danto 1981). However, two things can initially and superficially *appear* the same and yet *be* so different that their appearance also alters. Perception involves recognition, so the fact that there are cognitive prerequisites for this claim should be no surprise. Memorials are, after all, highly complex artifacts requiring a degree of understanding for their apprehension and appreciation.

5. Absence Memorialized

Frequently, an act of war does more than damage cultural artifacts; it obliterates them. The painful erasure of objects valued for years or even centuries can be commemorated by memorials that exemplify absence, signifying that a building or a statue that once stood someplace is forever gone. Unlike a partially damaged artifact, which can be simply left in the state suffered after attack to refer to the event that caused its injury, absence requires design. Empty space by itself does not exemplify; it is too dispersed to indicate what it might refer to. Therefore, memorializing an artifact that has been utterly destroyed requires recognizable perimeters. Thus, to commemorate an absence necessitates delineation of the space where emptiness is now the object of attention.

The Twin Towers were huge buildings, and their complete loss is exemplified by the two reflecting pools that were constructed in the footprints of the towers. Titled *Reflecting Absence* and designed by Michael Arad, the pools—Arad calls them 'voids'—manifest several symbolic functions. They enclose moving water, peaceful, perpetually replenished; and their stone rims are inscribed with the names of all those who died in the 9/11 attacks. In addition to these conventional memorializing features, the pools refer to what no longer exists by exemplifying its absence. The air above them, formerly occupied by the towers, is now empty. One appreciative commentator remarks that "all who come to the Memorial...will acutely feel the Absence" (Denson 2017).

In this case, the place is retained, though what occupied it is gone. Another kind of absence that exemplifies obliteration in a more general way can be seen at Bebelplatz in Berlin. There, artist Micha Ullman designed an underground cube of empty library shelves to commemorate the Nazi burning of books by Jewish authors on October 10, 1933 (Scarre 2020: 30–31). These shelves, while literally empty, never held the books that were destroyed. Here emptiness is exemplified, but it refers to the many shelves from which books were removed and burned. It is, if you will, another visual synecdoche, the one type of thing referring to the many things. This stands in contrast to the reflecting pools, where the site of destruction is retained, carrying the sense of presence achieved by literal exemplification of the actual space where something once stood.

The empty gap that previously held something treasured can be extraordinarily moving, and I conclude with an example where the decision about how to address a grievous loss of cultural heritage is still pending. The famous Bamiyan Buddhas of Afghanistan, which kept vigil over their valley for well over a millennium, were brought down in 2001 by two weeks of artillery fire by the Taliban (Janowski 2020). The niches where they stood are still there, defining the empty space they formerly occupied. Whether the Buddhas can or should be reconstructed is still a matter of controversy. However, in 2019, a ghostly hologram of one of the giant statues was projected into the very place where its original stood for so long, both summoning it back and mourning its absence from the space that exemplifies its destruction. The sight was both awe-inspiring and heartbreaking. In one man's words: "The first time I saw this I cried. Every time I see it again I am so moved in new ways, and it is only 3-D. To think we had the real thing, and now it is gone" (Nordland 2019, quoting artist Arif Taquin).

The emphasis I have placed on the importance of the real thing—remnants of damaged physical artifacts—may sound as if I oppose repair, restoration, or replacement when cultural heritage is the victim in war. However, in many cases, damage will be so extensive that there is little worth retaining. And in

150   HERITAGE AND WAR

any event, shelter and functional buildings are needed for societies to continue, both during and after hostilities, and this need often overrides retention of things that used to be held dear. My defense of the memorial function of damage is not meant to freeze historical change, which is inevitable.

Nonetheless, I believe that calling attention to the distinctive, cognitively rich function of exemplification is important to bear in mind when pondering what to do about the destruction of war. At the very least, its power should mandate caution when the time comes to clear away and rebuild, and it also advises humility regarding the claims made for recreation of that which is destroyed. Even if damaged, real material things still have the power to connect people with their past, and thereby to sustain communities under siege.[6]

References

Carroll, Noël. (2010), *Art in Three Dimensions* (Oxford: Oxford University Press).

Danto, Arthur C. (1981), *The Transfiguration of the Commonplace* (Cambridge, MA: Harvard University Press).

Danto, Arthur C. (1985), 'The Vietnam Veterans Memorial', *The Nation* 241/5: 152–155.

Denson, G. Roger. (2017), 'Michael Arad's 9/11 Memorial "Reflecting Absence": More Than a Metaphor or a Monument', *HuffPost*, September 9, 2011, updated June 12, 2017, accessed April 20, 2020, https://www.huffpost.com/entry/michael-arads-911-memoria_b_955454.

Dunlap, David W. (2013), 'Looking to a Wall that Limited the Devastation at the World Trade Center', *The New York Times*, September 13, 2013, accessed February 13, 2020, https://www.nytimes.com/2013/09/12/nyregion/looking-to-a-wall-that-limited-the-world-trade-centers-devastation.html.

Elgin, Catherine Z. (1983), *With Reference to Reference* (Indianapolis, IN: Hackett).

Fischl, E. (2006), 'The Trauma of 9/11 and Its Impact on Artists', in E.A. King, and G.L. Levin (eds.), *Ethics and the Visual Arts* (New York: Allworth Press), 195–197.

Gamboni, Dario. (1997), *Destruction of Art: Iconoclasm and Vandalism since the French Revolution* (New Haven, CT: Yale University Press).

Goodman, Nelson. (1976), *Languages of Art*, 2nd edition (Indianapolis, IN: Hackett).

---

[6] Thanks to Sandra Shapshay, Derek Matravers, William Bülow, and Joshua Lewis Thomas for helpful suggestions on an earlier version of this chapter.

Goodman, Nelson, and Elgin, Catherine Z. (1988), *Reconceptions in Philosophy and Other Arts and Sciences* (Indianapolis, IN: Hackett).

Higgins, Kathleen. (2020), 'Life and Death in Rock: A Meditation on Stone Memorials,' in J. Bicknell, J. Judkins, and C. Korsmeyer (eds.), *Philosophical Perspectives on Ruins, Monuments, and Memorials* (New York: Routledge), 9–20.

Janowski, James. (2020), 'Bamiyan's Echo: Sounding out the Emptiness,' in J. Bicknell, J. Judkins, and C. Korsmeyer (eds.), *Philosophical Perspectives on Ruins, Monuments, and Memorials* (New York: Routledge), 215–227.

Khunti, Roshni. (2018), 'The Problem with Printing Palmyra: Exploring the Ethics of Using 3D Printing Technology to Reconstruct Heritage,' *Studies in Digital Heritage* 2/1: 1–12.

Korsmeyer, Carolyn. (2019), *Things: In Touch with the Past* (New York: Oxford University Press).

Lamarque, Peter. (2010), *Work and Object: Explorations in the Metaphysics of Art* (Oxford: Oxford University Press).

Laqueur, Thomas W. (2015), *The Work of the Dead: A Cultural History of Mortal Remains* (Princeton, NJ: Princeton University Press).

Matravers, Derek. (2020), 'The Reconstruction of Damaged or Destroyed Heritage,' in J. Bicknell, J. Judkins, and C. Korsmeyer (eds.), *Philosophical Perspectives on Ruins, Monuments, and Memorials* (New York: Routledge), 189–200.

Nordland, Rod. (2019), '2 Giant Buddhas Survived 1,500 Years. Fragments, Graffiti and a Hologram Remain,' *The New York Times*, June 18, 2019, accessed January 7, 2020, https://www.nytimes.com/2019/06/18/world/asia/afghanistan-bamiyan-buddhas.html.

O'Shaughnessy, Brian. (2000), *Consciousness and the World* (Oxford: Clarendon Press).

Riegl, Alois. (1928), 'The Modern Cult of Monuments: Its Character and Origin,' Kurt W. Forster and Diane Ghirado (trans.), *Oppositions* (1982), 21–52.

Saito, Yuriko. (2020), 'Reflections on the Atomic Bomb Ruins in Hiroshima,' in J. Bicknell, J. Judkins, and C. Korsmeyer (eds.), *Philosophical Perspectives on Ruins, Monuments, and Memorials* (New York: Routledge), 201–214.

Scarbrough, Elizabeth. (2020), 'The Ruins of War,' in J. Bicknell, J. Judkins, and C. Korsmeyer (eds.), *Philosophical Perspectives on Ruins, Monuments, and Memorials* (New York: Routledge), 228–240.

Scarre, Geoffrey. (2020), 'How Memorials Speak to Us,' in J. Bicknell, J. Judkins, and C. Korsmeyer (eds.), *Philosophical Perspectives on Ruins, Monuments, and Memorials* (New York: Routledge), 21–33.

Shapshay, Sandra. (2021), 'What Is the Monumental?' *Journal of Aesthetics and Art Criticism* 79/2: 145–160.

Sparshott, Francis. (1985), 'The Antiquity of Antiquity,' *Journal of Aesthetic Education* 19/1: 87–98.

V&A. (n.d.), 'The V and A at War: 1939–45,' accessed April 4, 2020, http://www.vam.ac.uk/content/articles/t/v-and-a-at-war-1939-45/.

Visit Berlin. (n.d.), 'Kaiser Wilhelm Memorial Church: A Memorial against War and Destruction,' accessed April 4, 2020, https://www.visitberlin.de/en/kaiser-wilhelm-memorial-church.

Welby, Justin, Archbishop of Canterbury. (2016), 'Building a More Christ Like World: The Story of the Cross of Nails,' accessed June 10, 2020, https://www.archbishopofcanterbury.org/priorities/reconciliation/cross-nails.

Wolterstorff, Nicolas. (2015), *Art Rethought: The Social Practices of Art* (Oxford: Oxford University Press).

Young, James O. (2020), 'How Memorials Mean,' in J. Bicknell, J. Judkins, and C. Korsmeyer (eds.), *Philosophical Perspectives on Ruins, Monuments, and Memorials* (New York: Routledge), 34–44.

9

Architecture and Cultural Memory

Robert Hopkins

1. An Immodest Proposal

According to John Ruskin, ancient buildings have a special role to play as repositories of cultural memory. Without architecture, he says, we may live and worship, but not remember (1849: 233). He takes the point seriously enough to make Memory the sixth of architecture's seven 'lamps', or guiding ideals. As Anthony Savile puts it, Ruskin's idea is that

> The building that has endured somehow encodes or embodies a past that pre-dates our individual memories and thereby keeps our common and social history alive. (2000: 92)

But what exactly is the relation between a culture's buildings and its collective memory?

Savile's answer is that the architecture of the past invites being seen in the light of thoughts about the culture that inhabited it; that doing so leads us to appreciate an otherwise hidden aesthetic aspect of the buildings, their 'aura'; and that perceiving aura requires that the thoughts that make it present to us be true. The result is an experience of the buildings that 'restitutes' the past to us, with that restitution lying in the experience itself, rather than in any other thoughts or memories to which it gives rise.[1]

I will attempt to go further, framing a position more ambitious than Savile's and more explicit than anything Ruskin proposes. Architecture is itself the vehicle of cultural memory. We collectively remember our past through the buildings that come down to us. As we remember our individual past through memory images, so we remember our shared cultural past through its architecture. In consequence, the loss of that architecture, in war or by other means, comes at a particular cost. We may still know our culture's past—after

[1] For a helpful summary, see Savile (2000: §6, 100; the idea of restitution is introduced on p.93).

Robert Hopkins, *Architecture and Cultural Memory* In: *Heritage and War: Ethical Issues*. Edited by: William Bülow, Helen Frowe, Derek Matravers, and Joshua Lewis Thomas, Oxford University Press. © Robert Hopkins 2023. DOI: 10.1093/oso/9780192862648.003.0009

154 HERITAGE AND WAR

all, there are many ways to retain information about it. But we will, as Ruskin says, no longer remember it.

2. Memory

Let's begin by setting architecture aside and considering memory in more familiar forms. There are various kinds of memory: compare remembering the chemical composition of salt, remembering your last birthday party, and remembering how to Escoffier an egg. Our focus will be the second sort of case, personal memory. It is memory for our individual pasts that best promises an analogy with the way architecture relates us to our collective history.

Personal memories are often for particular episodes, as when I remember receiving my A-level results over the campsite telephone while on holiday in Provence. They can also, however, be more general. I can remember what family holidays in France were like without remembering any particular episodes in any particular holiday. And I can remember what those Provençal campsites were like, or what my parents looked like at the time, without remembering any episodes at all. What unites personal memories is that their objects—be they events, people, places or things, and whether particular or merely representative of some type—all lie in my past, and are remembered as they then were. All memory is at root a matter of retaining information, and so requires a past in which it was acquired. But personal memory, unlike memory for facts or remembering how to do things, of necessity has the past at its subject matter.

If these are the contents of personal memory, what provides its vehicle? In paradigm cases that role is played by memory images. I remember receiving the exam results by picturing the cramped phone cabin, recalling the distant sound of my friend's voice, conjuring the anxiety I felt as the moment of truth arrived. (Note that images need not be visual.) This marks another difference between personal memory and other forms. In neither memory for facts nor remembering-how does the central case involve an image of what is remembered.

Still, it would be a mistake to take the paradigmatic to be universal. C.B. Martin and Max Deutscher (1966) describe a case of personal memory without memory imagery.[2] A painter finds himself depicting in some detail a farmyard. He takes it to be nothing more than his invention. His parents,

---

[2] The case that follows (which I have tweaked a little) is at pp.167–8 of Martin and Deutscher (1966).

however, recognise it as one he regularly visited when young. The artist need have no image of the farmyard as he draws—perhaps he just lets the lines develop in ways the initial marks suggest. Even so, it seems he is remembering the farmyard, a memory expressed only in the picture. Personal memory requires some kind of representation of the remembered, but that need not take the form of a memory image. Indeed, the representation at its core need not be mental at all.[3]

However, personal memory requires more than present representation of things earlier encountered. That representation must be derived in the right way from the past encounter. Suppose you were with me when I phoned for my results, and that at some point in the intervening years, confronted by my inability to recall it, you describe the scene to me. You do so in terms so vivid that thereafter I often picture the moment to myself. If my later images of that scene are due to your description, rather than my earlier experience, they don't count as my remembering the call. My images derive from the event— your description may be a truthful response to what took place that day. But they do so only indirectly, via your testimony. And that is the wrong kind of derivation for them to count as memories. Few have attempted to specify which derivations are right, but there is widespread agreement that only some are.[4]

One last point before I pull these threads together. Memory images are occurrent states—we have them at a time, for a given duration. But memory in all its forms is really a special kind of power, a capacity to bring about occurrences. That's why we can truthfully attribute memories to those who are not currently exercising the relevant capacities. Do I remember the chemical composition of salt, how to Escoffier an egg, or receiving the exam results, even when I'm asleep? In one way, yes, since going to sleep hasn't stripped me of the capacities in question. But in another, no, since they are capacities to judge the composition to be sodium chloride, to make the dish, and to recall hearing the results; and I do none of these things while in the land of nod. Personal memory, like the other forms, is a capacity: in this case, a capacity to form representations of one's past.

---

[3] For defence, see Hopkins (2014). The thought that the vehicles of memory may include external representations, such as pictures, is in sympathy with, though motivated independently of, the more general thesis of the 'extended mind' (see Clark and Chalmers 1998).

[4] For the testimony case, see Ayer (1956: 145–6); and Martin and Deutscher (1966: 168–9). For attempts to specify the appropriate derivations, see Martin and Deutscher (1966) and Dokic (2001: 213–32, esp. 228).

156   HERITAGE AND WAR

In sum, someone may be said to have personal memory of something, say family holidays in France, when (I) she has the capacity to represent those events; (II) she earlier experienced them (she was on those holidays); and (III) her capacity to represent them derives in the right way from her earlier experiences of them.[5]

3. Representation

Framing these conditions makes clear the challenges facing any attempt to argue that architecture also counts as memory. The most pressing arises from the fact that memory requires representation. Orthodoxy has it that buildings are not representational. Architecture is an art as abstract as music. In both, representational moments are possible—flutes may imitate birdsong, and a building may incorporate sculpture or even itself depict, as in drive-thrus shaped as burgers. But the vast majority of architecture, like most music, shuns representation altogether. How, then, can buildings represent the past, and in particular past culture?

However, every orthodoxy has its heretics, and in this case the most provocative is Susanne Langer. For Langer architecture offers a symbol, or what she sometimes calls an 'image', of an 'ethnic domain'. Since symbols are representations, and an ethnic domain is a central aspect of a culture, Langer's position promises precisely the resources we need (1953: esp. 92–103).

Let us begin with Langer's idea that buildings can be symbols. Talk of 'representation', like its close relatives 'meaning' or 'expression', covers a multitude of sins. We have various examples already before us: memory images, the painting of the farmyard, and the words I've used to describe them. We might also say that a dry cough represents the onset of a nasty illness, or that dark clouds mean rain. Langer first divides this messy terrain into 'symbols' and what I'll call 'traces'.[6] Traces are effects, from which, given enough knowledge, we may infer their causes. Their meaning what they do depends on their originating in those very factors. If the dry cough is in fact caused by high pollen levels, it doesn't represent the onset of the illness after all; and the dark clouds don't mean rain if they're the product of a distant fire. Symbols, in contrast, are tools we use to convey ideas. Their representing what they do

---

[5] Should we also require that her memories be accurate? She can remember an episode while misremembering some of its features, but mustn't she get at least some right? In fact, properly developed, the conditions above already contain the resources to secure accuracy (see Hopkins 2018: 46–71, esp. 51).

[6] Langer's term is 'signals' (1953: 25).

depends on how we use them, not what caused their deployment; and they retain their meaning whether or not it reflects the facts.[7] More precisely, a 'symbol is used to articulate ideas of something we want to think about' (Langer 1953: 28). Articulation is a matter of expressing understanding of the symbolised, of making manifest its internal structure. But the understanding a given symbol expresses need not precede, or be separable from, the symbol itself. Sometimes our representations make clear to us things we do not, perhaps cannot, articulate in any other way. As I'll put it, they can be the primary articulation of our grasp on whatever it is they capture.

Symbols in turn divide in two. There are the discursive symbols of language, where representation at root rests on conventional associations between elements in the symbol and elements in the world. Each element has a conventionally assigned meaning, or range of possible meanings; and the elements may be combined in specific ways to create larger units, the meaning of which depends on the elements and how they've been combined. But there are also non-discursive symbols, or 'images', such as pictures, vocal imitations, music and mime. Here no role is played by elements that bear their meaning as a matter of convention. Rather, the whole represents what it does by sharing that thing's structure or 'form'. We exploit that commonality of form in using the symbol to convey the idea of the symbolised. There are meaningful elements here, but each derives its significance from its place in the structure of the whole (Langer 1953: 30–31). This dot on the surface of the picture of the farmyard represents an eye only because it sits amid the curving lines that represent the cow's head—taken in isolation it is meaningless; put in another context it will represent something else. Architecture is a symbol of the non-discursive kind.

Images are as able as discursive symbols to serve as the primary articulation of a phenomenon. Just as I only grasp some thoughts when I put them into words, so I only grasp some feelings or atmospheres when I have a non-discursive symbol, perhaps a gesture or a piece of music, to act as an image of them. This will be of some importance below.

4. The Ethnic Domain

So much for representation. What of Langer's other idea, that what architecture represents is an ethnic domain? A domain, Langer tells us, is 'the sphere of influence of a function, or functions' (Langer 1953: 95). Function here is a

---

[7] Compare Grice on 'natural' vs. 'non-natural' meaning (1957: 377–88).

158   HERITAGE AND WAR

biological notion. It is organisms that have functions—to find food, consume it, sleep, reproduce, defend themselves, or nurture their young. Different organisms, with their differing functions and ways of discharging them, exhibit forms of life with different overall characteristics, rhythms, or tempi. Contrast the life of the lion, with long solitary periods of digestion and lazy watching, punctuated by moments of savage intensity in hunting and gorging, with that of the ant, restless and laborious at all times, and always part of a larger whole. However, at least for humans, it is not biology alone that dictates form of life. For us, what biology initially determines, culture then shapes. It moulds biologically determined life in the face of contingencies of environment, circumstance, and the need to bind socially. It is the patterns of life distinctive of particular cultures that architecture captures:

> The architect creates [a culture's] image: a physically present human environment that expresses the characteristic rhythmic functional patterns which constitute a culture. Such patterns are the alternation of sleep and waking, venture and safety, emotion and calm, austerity and abandon; the tempo, and the smoothness or abruptness of life; the simple forms of childhood and the complexities of full moral stature, the sacramental and capricious moods that mark a social order, and that are repeated, though with characteristic selection, by every personal life springing from that order.
>
> (Langer 1953: 96)

Thus architecture is the non-discursive symbol of a culture—of the form, or forms, of life that constitute it.

It is important to appreciate that there is a certain obliqueness in the way architecture provides a culture's image. What architecture symbolises, the 'rhythms' of culturally embedded life, are ultimately a matter of activities that people perform (provided activities include being inactive in distinctive ways). But architecture does not symbolise these activities through facilitating them—Langer denies that hooks for implements or well-placed benches play any part in the architectural symbol (1953: 98). Representation in architecture is not only far removed from the cheap mimicry of the drive-thru; it is also not a matter of reflecting cultural activities by providing means for their pursuit. Rather, architecture articulates an ethnic domain by sharing its structure. It is the 'strength and interplay of forms' that is the source of architecture's symbolising power; and what is captured is not the concrete details of communal life, but its overall tenor.

ARCHITECTURE AND CULTURAL MEMORY   159

Think, for instance, of the calm, rational yet industrious activity projected by the form of the modernist office block. (The exemplar is Mies van der Rohe's Seagram Building.) Or consider the dramatic shifts as one moves through the grand and expansive courts of an ancient college via the narrow and humble passages between. These echo in space the rhythms and atmosphere of the life they were built to house, a life in which periods of studious seclusion are punctuated by return to the wider worlds of public display, the shared meal and communal worship.

As this last example suggests, not all 'architecture' requires a figure recognised as its architect, and there is no reason to think Langer's claims apply only to a building that aspires to the condition of Art. Sometimes it is not individual buildings that symbolise the relevant form of life, but clusters of them, formed over time and with no guiding plan beyond the desire to harmonise with the existing context. The lively variety of a cathedral close symbolises the tenor of the secular life surrounding the great church, as surely as the purity of the cathedral itself captures that of the religious life within. Nor need anyone have independent sight of the character of the culture that its buildings express. Often, we don't identify that character and then build something to reflect it, but reach an understanding of the domain only through creating, or engaging with, the architecture itself. Buildings, as much as other 'images', may be the primary articulations of what they represent.

Thus, a building emerges from the culture, crystalising its character for builder and user alike. It is not a mere trace of that culture, unlike many of its other products, precisely because it is a tool for the culture's self-understanding. But what represents the present to the society that creates it can represent the past to those still to come. If architecture represents an ethnic domain, the first challenge to its acting as a vehicle for cultural memory is met.

5. Buildings and Memory Images

Still, it is people, not buildings, that remember; and, according to the first condition on personal memory, doing so requires that they have the capacity to represent the past. To remember is to be able to form a memory. We now see how to make sense of the analogue in the architectural case. Those who experience the building with understanding, experience it as symbolising an ethnic domain. This is true whether they built it or engage with it as inhabitants, and whether they are contemporary with its creation or later witnesses

160 HERITAGE AND WAR

to its survival. For all, the building can serve as a representation of the ethnic domain. They have the capacity to represent that domain, provided they are able to experience the building as the 'image' it is. And if they do come later, the capacity they enjoy is to represent a domain now past.

So it is not, strictly speaking, the building that constitutes the memory, but our experiences of it. We do the remembering, since both the occurrent representations of the past and the capacity to form them are ours. The buildings certainly play an essential role. The occurrent representations are precisely distinctive experiences *of the architecture*, experiences that could not occur without the buildings as their material support. And the buildings themselves certainly represent, else how could we accurately experience them as doing so? But perhaps, if we are to be precise, the buildings are not quite the vehicles of memory (Section 1) so much as essential components of them. They may not themselves constitute memories, but they are elements in them.

In this and related respects architecture contrasts with the mental images at the heart of paradigm cases of personal memory. A building may symbolise an ethnic domain while no one experiences it as doing so, and even while no one has the capacity for such experience. Perhaps all those who encounter it know too little of the culture from which it sprang, or are too insensitive to its expressive language. In contrast, a memory image cannot even exist without someone thereby remembering what it represents. (It is another matter whether that person recognises that this is what she is doing.) And while a building represents at all only because someone does, or is able to, treat it as doing so, memory images represent independently of how we respond to them. All of which really rests on a deeper contrast: that while buildings are things, memory images are not. To talk of them is to borrow the language of objects to describe what are really acts of remembering, where the remembered is represented in a sensory way.[8]

One moral of these contrasts is that memory images do not represent in either of Langer's senses. They are not traces, phenomena we treat as evidence of their causes. But nor are they symbols, tools for expressing our ideas. Their role is more fundamental: in effect, they are ideas themselves. To have a memory image is for one's mind to represent the past, and representation by the mind is different from, and the ground of, the representing that external representations go in for.

---

[8] See Jean-Paul Sartre (1938: ch.1). I will continue to use image talk, since it helps frame points in concise and accessible ways.

ARCHITECTURE AND CULTURAL MEMORY 161

Thus, occurrent memory, whether personal or cultural, involves a mind representing the past. Sometimes this is achieved by engaging with a symbol that itself represents the relevant object, sometimes not. Personal memory can take the first form (think of the painter and his farmyard) but need not. For architectural memory, only the first option is available: it always involves a symbol beyond the mind. Despite these differences, in both cases the first condition on memory, that we have a capacity to represent the past, is met.

6. Past Cultural Experience

What, though, of the other two conditions on personal memory? These were (II) that what is now represented was earlier undergone; and (III) that past experience and present representation are connected in the right way. Do they, too, have analogues in the architectural case?

If there is cultural memory, through architecture or otherwise, it will be interpersonal. Later members of the group will remember aspects of its life when others made up its number. So it would not be appropriate to require that the person who now represents the past be the same individual who earlier lived through that history; or to limit the legitimate connections between earlier experiences and later representations to those running within an individual life.[9] All this, however, is merely negative. Can we say anything more about the analogues of these conditions, and how they are met in the architectural case?

As far as condition (II) goes, it's enough to note that, if 'experience' is here required, it is experience in a very broad sense. The ethnic domain the building symbolises is one earlier members of the culture lived and breathed, rather than witnessed perceptually, or even stood back and contemplated. It was their form of life, and their engagement with it will be as various as that phrase suggests. It involves not only what they perceived, and how they felt, thought and acted, but also what they avoided perceiving, and how they

---

[9] Cultural memory may not require identity of individual, but does it at least require identity of group? Can we only remember earlier forms of life of the community to which we belong? Or can I, for instance, remember the pattern of existence in ancient Assyria, provided enough is captured in the buildings that survive?

Answering would require legislation as much as discovery. The conditions for identity of communities across time are unclear. Perhaps whatever past culture I can represent in ways meeting the other conditions this chapter describes already to that extent counts as mine. And even if not, if this is the only way in which my experience fails to count as memory, it may enjoy a status of almost equal interest. It would be the cultural analogue of Derek Parfit's 'q-memory' (1971, esp. 14–15).

162   HERITAGE AND WAR

refrained from feeling, thinking and acting. In principle it might include almost any aspect of their way of being in the world, provided that impinges in some or other way on their sentient lives. Indeed, with 'experience' so understood, the ethnic domain we seek to remember is not so much an object of experience as itself a vast body of experience—complex, variegated and communal in kind.

7. Derivation in Personal Memory

What about the third condition, governing the connection between earlier experience of the thing remembered and its later representation? To make sense of this for cultural memory, we first have to say more about the personal case.

We have before us one example of the wrong sort of connection, the case in which my later images of receiving my exam results derive from your description of the event (Section 2). Here's another. Suppose that after getting my results, I wrote about it in my diary. Years later, I reread the entry, which is sufficiently vivid to provoke images of the event it describes. I now have the ability to represent the episode. Even though that ability derives ultimately from the episode itself, there's no guarantee my images count as personal memories. If their immediate derivation is only from the diary entry, they aren't memories any more than were the images derived from your description.

Intuitively, in both these cases memory goes missing because the connection between past episode and present representation is insufficiently direct. But what does directness amount to? Not that derivation must stay within a single individual. That may be what's missing in the testimony case, where my images depend on your description; but cannot be the trouble with the diary example. Is the problem that both involve a key role for symbols? But in closely related cases symbols serve precisely to promote memory. We often use photographs, words and other external representations to refresh memory of an event. Indeed, that might be the effect on me of hearing your testimony or reading my diary. When it is, these cases, too, involve remembering. Refreshing memory is not replacing it with something else, but precisely giving it a new lease of life. If memory requires directness, directness cannot preclude symbols.

In a moment, I'll attempt to say what it is to refresh memory. First, consider a third example. We sometimes make use of external representations not to sustain memories, but to create them. Suppose that on results day I gave myself a running commentary on what I was experiencing and feeling. This might obstruct memory. If my commentary, rather than the experiences and feelings themselves, is the source of my later ability to picture the day, it's doubtful those images count as memories. Once again, directness goes missing. But things need not go that way. The commentary might instead fix my memories, helping to lay them down as the experiences unfold. Fixing memories is not failing to remember, any more than refreshing them is.

What positive account of derivation do these examples suggest? Their first lesson is that there are two stages to derivation. In the diary and testimony cases, the focus is on *propagation*: how later capacities to represent must relate to earlier ones. In the commentary case, the issue concerns *formation*: how the original capacity to represent the event relates to the subject's experience of it at the time.

The cases also show us what each stage requires. The commentary case suggests that formation goes well when our original capacity to represent the event is *immediately* caused by experience of that event. Where the commentary blocks memory, it intervenes between these two. The experience of the event causes the commentary on it, which in turn causes the capacity to represent it. In causing a cause of the capacity, the experience brings it about only remotely. Where, in contrast, the commentary fixes the memory, its causal role is different. It acts as an enabling condition, allowing the experience to bring the capacity into existence. In that case, neither the commentary nor any other cause intervenes between experience and capacity. The one is the immediate cause of the other.[10]

The other two cases contain lessons for propagation. We saw that leaning on symbols need not replace memory, but rather may refresh it. What's the difference? Intuitively, it turns on whether engaging with the symbols prolongs the life of our existing capacity to represent the past episode, or instead initiates a new capacity to represent it. Where the effect of the testimony or diary is deleterious to memory, that's because they leave us with new capacities to represent the episode of receiving my results, capacities deriving solely from those vivid descriptions of the day. Where their effect is beneficial, they instead serve to rejuvenate a capacity I already have.

If we run with intuition here, and combine it with our thoughts about formation, the result is the following condition:

---

[10] On causes, remote causes and enabling conditions, see Lombard (1990: 195–211).

164 HERITAGE AND WAR

(III)* S's current capacity to represent something E counts as a personal memory of E only if that capacity is immediately caused by S's earlier experience of E.

Where the experience is only the remote cause of the nascent capacity, formation goes wrong—the 'bad' commentary case. Where one capacity to represent the past is followed by another, propagation goes awry—the 'bad' diary and testimony cases. Where instead things go right, one and the same capacity that I now exercise was immediately brought about by my earlier experience of getting my results. The relation between them is direct in the sense that that very capacity was immediately caused by that experience. Only then, the suggestion goes, do we have memory.

This account is elegant and intuitive. Unfortunately, it rests on unsound foundations. Its treatment of propagation requires that my current capacity to represent the past be numerically identical with the capacity I enjoyed earlier. In the 'good' versions of the description and diary cases, this is so; in the bad cases it is not. But in all cases, what's at stake is a capacity of mine to represent results day. So, it would have to make sense to distinguish capacities, even when they're capacities on the part of a single person to do one and the same thing. And it's unclear this really does make sense. Suppose that while skiing I have an accident so serious that it forces me to learn to ski all over again. Is the result that over the course of my life I have two abilities to ski, one before the accident, one after? Or is my ability now just a later phase of one I enjoyed earlier? It's hard to know what to say, and the problem is that counting capacities in this fine-grained way isn't clearly meaningful. Better, if possible, to avoid it.

Still, a more resilient account lies near at hand. It may not make sense to ask whether my current and earlier capacities to represent results day are numerically identical, but it surely makes sense to suppose that I now have a capacity to represent it in part because I earlier did. We can understand directness in propagation as a matter, not of identity of capacities over time, but of causal connectedness between capacities at various times.

These causal connections might themselves be more or less direct. It might be that my earlier capacity is responsible for the later, but only via an intervening cause. This is so in the 'bad' diary case. My ability to represent getting my results brought me to write the diary entry, and reading the entry brought me to be able to picture those events. Here the earlier capacity is the remote cause of the later: it causes it by causing something else. But it need not be so. There are other ways for the earlier capacity to help bring about the later, ways that leave their connection more direct. Perhaps the earlier capacity is itself among the immediate causes of the later. Reading the entry is one such cause, the earlier capacity is another, and together they join forces as immediate causes of the later capacity. Perhaps instead the earlier capacity acts as an enabling condition: in its absence reading the entry would not exhibit any tendency to bring about the ability to picture the scene. Either way, the earlier capacity makes a causal difference to the existence of the later, but not by acting as a remote cause of it. When reading the diary doesn't replace memory, but refreshes it, one of these more direct connections is in play.

So, directness in propagation, as in formation, is a matter of non-remote causation. To have a personal memory is to have a capacity brought about in a distinctive way. The causal chain begins with earlier experience of the event, and goes via the subject's capacity, at various intervening times, to represent it. The experience immediately causes the initial capacity, and earlier capacities either immediately cause or enable their successors. What is key is that none of these causal relations is remote.

8. Derivation in Architecture

What would the corresponding condition on cultural memory be? Here any memory runs across individuals. That forces significant differences from personal memory. Even so, we can say something about what parallel condition holds, and how architecture meets it. We saw that derivation raises issues both of formation and propagation. Let's take them in turn.

As far as formation goes, the condition on personal memory transfers without difficulty. Cultural memory, too, must be immediately caused by experience. The capacity to represent the relevant cultural phenomenon must have experience of that phenomenon as its immediate cause. The experience helps bring about the capacity, but not by causing something else.

This is a requirement that architecture meets. Here the capacity to represent the ethnic domain is itself a matter of experiencing the building with understanding. The question is how that capacity relates to its builders' experience of the domain itself, their life in the culture it characterises. I said (Section 4) that often the building will be the primary articulation of the ethnic domain: its makers have no other way to articulate the domain. If so, there is no other representation that threatens to insert itself as the intermediate cause between living the domain and grasping it in architecture. What of the building itself? That is certainly crucial to the passage from life in the culture to the architectural experience that articulates it. But the building does not act as causal intermediary. For one thing, it figures in the architectural experience as component, not cause (Section 5). And for another, it is not complete until the architectural experience is. Rather than one bringing about the other, the two develop in tandem. Thus, nothing stands between the builders' lived experience of their ethnic domain and their capacity to represent it through architecture. The one is the immediate cause of the other.

What if the architecture is not the primary articulation of the domain? What if the architects do frame other ways to represent it, in thought or in symbols, and use those to guide their work? Even then, there need be no obstacle to memory. Those other conscious articulations are analogous to my running commentary on results day. Just as the commentary might fix memory or obstruct it, likewise here. The non-architectural articulation might help the architect translate her experience into stone, or it might intervene between that experience and the building she creates. The former will enable the architecture to sustain cultural memory; only the latter will prevent it.

Now consider propagation. Here matters are harder. Basic differences between personal and cultural memory force apart the conditions on derivation governing the pair.

Personal memory paradigmatically, and perhaps necessarily, concerns a single individual. In contrast, cultural memory is paradigmatically interpersonal: what is later remembered by one person was earlier experienced by someone else. We made sense of propagation in personal memory in terms of non-remote causation. The subject's earlier capacity to represent the past had to figure as either immediate cause or enabling condition of her later ability to do so. This condition is not one cultural memory can meet. It is very hard to see how one person's capacity to represent the past can bring about another's ability to do that, except remotely. Take the case in hand. Our architect creates a building that, experienced with understanding, enables her to represent her ethnic domain. With luck, that building also enables later generations, ourselves included, to grasp that domain. We gain the capacity she had, in key part because she had it. Perhaps the building embodies its meaning so clearly that alone it suffices to give us that ability. Or perhaps it can do so only with help from other resources—art historical knowledge, immersion in the history of the source culture, or the builder's own testimony as to what she was trying to achieve. Either way, her ability to represent the ethnic domain brings about ours only via the mediation of various representations: the building, her testimony and the like. Some of these representations are not traceable back to the architect. But even those that are intervene between her architectural experience and ours. Her grasp of the ethnic domain can cause ours only by causing something else that in turn instils that capacity in us. How else can she bridge the divide between herself and us? If the capacities are causally related at all, it will be only as remote cause and effect.

The problem here is not specific to architecture, but faces any candidate for cultural memory. So, if cultural memory is governed by the same condition on propagation as personal memory, there is no such thing. That, no doubt, will be the conclusion some draw. I suggest a different response. What the above shows is that the third condition must take different forms in the cultural and personal cases. In both, propagation can be more or less direct, and memory requires the latter. But what counts as directness varies.

The ideal at this point would be to frame a general account of direct propagation of capacities across people, to argue that directness so understood is required for cultural memory, and to show that architecture fits the condition thus imposed. However, that ideal is at present beyond my reach, so I offer something more modest. I describe two striking features of the architectural case and how they strengthen its claim to sustain cultural memory.

The first feature is that architecture propagates capacities through communication. It's not just that one person ends up with a capacity that another had because they communicated in some way. More, the capacity propagated is a capacity to represent a content (the ethnic domain), and one person passes on the ability to represent that content by showing the other a representation (the building) that has that particular content.

Why would this matter? It matters because it gives propagation through architecture a feature that memory also has—that it acts as a way of preserving knowledge.

In remembering, one knows now if and only if one knew earlier. This is true of memory in all its forms. The point is most obvious for remembering-that. Someone who knows the chemical composition of salt by remembering must also have known its composition when she originally acquired that belief. Remembering provides a way for her present state to tap the considerations that made her earlier state count as knowing. Even if she does not now remember the grounds for her original belief, retaining the content by remembering it allows her state now to benefit from her justification then. Something similar is true for personal memory. Someone who enjoys knowledge by acquaintance with an event, place or person can retain that knowledge in personal memory of that occurrence or thing. The factors that made that original encounter count as knowledge may no longer obtain, but their influence on her current epistemic status persists.

168 HERITAGE AND WAR

Propagating capacities through communication also promises to preserve knowledge.[11] Under the right conditions, communication enables the recipient, not just to grasp the content her informant offers her, but to inherit the informant's epistemic status with respect to that content. She knows if he does. Here, too, a person's mentally representing a content can receive epistemic support from factors beyond her ken. Only, here the transfer is effected between different people, rather than within a single person at different times.

Thus, propagation through communication shares a feature of all memory, that it preserves knowledge. Other ways to propagate capacities do not have that feature. This gives propagation through communication some claim to constitute the right sort of derivation to sustain memory. It won't always do so, of course. Your description of my getting the results communicates to me a capacity to represent that event, but the result need not be that I remember it. Personal memory involves conditions on derivation stronger than communication can meet. But we've seen that those stronger conditions are too demanding for cultural memory: there something weaker must govern. Preserving knowledge offers such a condition. It is something propagation through communication secures. And, of course, propagation through communication is precisely what architecture makes possible.

The other feature of the architectural case concerns, not the means of propagation, but its outcome. What is propagated is a capacity to form a complex representation. The complexity lies in the fact that, while the representation is a mental state, an experience, it is a mental state with an external representation among its components. It's an experience *of the building* as symbolising the ethic domain. Moreover, this component is common to the representational mental states, and thus to the capacities to produce them, that are propagated. Both we and our forebears grasp the ethnic domain by experiencing one and the same building in the same ways. So, it's not just that propagation occurs through communication. It's not even just that the symbol by which communication is effected is the same for earlier and later subjects, that we gain the capacity through engaging with the very symbol they created. It's also that the capacity in question retains that symbol at its core. What both we and our ancestors enjoy is a capacity to grasp the ethnic domain by experiencing *this building* a certain way.

Why would this second feature matter? We saw that personal memory requires propagation to take a certain form. The intuitive way to frame the

---

[11] See Burge (1993), Dummett (1993) and Owens (2000).

idea, encapsulated in (III)*, was as the persistence of a single capacity to represent the past. That idea was found wanting, since we cannot clearly count capacities in the way it requires. But the feature now before us offers an unproblematic approximation to the original intuitive idea. Having a crucial component in common does not render our capacity to represent the ethnic domain identical to the architect's. We may remain sceptical that counting capacities in this way makes sense. But sharing their central component does constitute one important connection between her capacity and ours. It is a connection through identity, and one that is certainly coherent. That is some reason to believe that this latter identity constitutes the kind of relation that memory—here cultural memory—requires.

In sum, the way architecture propagates capacities to represent ethnic domains has two features suited to memory: (i) the propagation is through communication, and (ii) it preserves some relation of identity across the capacities propagated. Architecture also involves suitable formation: the original capacity propagated is immediately caused by experience of that which it is a capacity to represent. The case thus made for our experience of architecture counting as cultural memory is hardly conclusive, but it carries some weight.

9. Monuments and Memorials

I am now in a position to explain why I've focussed exclusively on buildings, and said nothing about monuments and memorials. The omission may surprise. Representing the past is an obvious feature of most memorials, and central to their purpose. Some depict the events they commemorate; many record dates; outcomes and key participants. Aren't these more obvious vehicles for collective memory than architecture? Why ignore them?

Of course, what monuments and memorials commemorate is usually events and actors in them, rather than the form of life of the culture that produced them. But even with respect to what they do represent, they do not act as vehicles for cultural memory. At the least, to put the point more cautiously, two obstacles stand in the way.

Both concern formation. The condition on memory formation is that experience of the cultural past be the immediate cause of the capacity to represent it. The first obstacle is that those who create monuments usually did not witness the events memorialised. The monument's role is to engender a capacity to represent the past it commemorates. When its makers did not

170   HERITAGE AND WAR

themselves experience those events, that capacity cannot have such experience among its immediate causes.

What, though, if we concentrate on memorials that *are* built by witnesses to the events they commemorate? Here we encounter the second obstacle. While monuments and memorials symbolise the past, they do so only via a deliberate intention to represent it in a particular way. Their makers first formulate a view about the event commemorated, and then construct the memorial so as to convey it. The monument expresses their conclusions about that event, and captures nothing those conclusions omit.[12] Now, we saw that supplementary articulations of the past need not block memory. They may, like my commentary on results day in the 'good' case, merely enable experience to act as immediate cause of our capacity to represent. It is not impossible that the opinions of memorial builders play this role. It is, however, very hard to see how they can do so. Memorials seem not to articulate experience, so much as to be moulded to fit articulations already given in other terms. Those other articulations threaten to form a causal barrier in the passage of information from the event to its representation for posterity. Memorial and experience of the event memorialised will be related, at best, as remote cause and effect.

I do not say these obstacles are insuperable. Perhaps there are monuments that successfully negotiate them. Such cases, though, seem likely to be few and far between. It is hard for monuments and memorials to sustain the kind of access to the past that remembering requires.

10. The Loss of Memory

I have argued that buildings, experienced with understanding, offer us images of past ethnic domains. In their presence we have the capacity to represent those domains, to do so in a way deriving from the lived experience of those who inhabited them, and deriving in such a way that those capacities are both formed and propagated in ways as close as possible, given the interpersonal character of the cultural case, to the formation and propagation of personal memories. In thereby meeting conditions analogous to those governing

---

[12] Monuments may certainly encode information of which their makers were not aware. Like every other product of a culture, they provide evidence of the wide variety of causal forces whose traces they are. But traces are not symbols (Section 3), and inferring from them to how things were is not remembering.

ARCHITECTURE AND CULTURAL MEMORY   171

personal memory, architecture, appropriately experienced, provides the vehicle for collective memory of a culture's past.[13]

What, then, if the relevant buildings are lost to us, in war, redevelopment or through simple neglect? Along with the architecture, we will also lose the experiences of it that capture the past for us. Those experiences count as memories of past ethnic domains. It may be that, in general, architecture is the only artefact of previous ethnic domains that enables us to remember them.[14] Even if not, the durability of buildings, and their central place in the self-conception of many a culture, mean they will often be the only repositories of cultural memory for ethnic domains to come down to us. To lose the buildings is thus to lose our cultural memory for the tenor of previous forms of life. To the extent that we lack other sources of information about the relevant ethnic domain, it will be lost to us altogether. To the extent that we do have such sources, we may retain knowledge of it. But while knowledge may survive, memory will not. We will have suffered a distinctive kind of loss.

One last time, compare personal memory. Suppose you are told you will suffer selective amnesia for some of the people, places and events in your past. Perhaps medical science has advanced to such a point that the losses can be predicted far in advance, and with some precision. You thus have the opportunity to prepare. You can store photographs, make audio and video recordings, write diary entries, and pile up keepsakes to fill the blanks that memory will soon display. As far as retaining information goes, there's no reason why your preparations shouldn't be perfectly adequate. Our memories are sufficiently patchy and unreliable that technology easily matches them in the information it preserves. But consoling as this may be, it won't fully compensate your loss. In being forced to trade personal memories of these things for mere knowledge of them, however extensive, surely you

---

[13] Does this really go beyond Savile? He too appeals to the way thoughts about the past may transform present experience of old buildings. Moreover, he describes the result, the experience of aura, as a 'form of memory' (2000: 103). However, there are two reasons not to take this description literally. First, the experience of aura does not represent the past. This is clear from the example used to introduce the idea, a lonely valley in the Jura mountains (Savile 2000: 94–5; cf. Ruskin 1849: 231). This too, it is claimed, exhibits an aura, one we engage with when viewing it guided by thoughts of the history of the towns below. But surely the valley doesn't provide an image or symbol of the past. Its appearance may be subtly altered by thoughts of the skirmishes and sieges that took place nearby, but not in such a way as to put that past before us. Aura may in some sense reflect the past (and is certainly not a trace of it), but it hardly represents it. Second, Savile places no constraints on how our current experiences derive from those of our predecessors (beyond requiring that the thoughts that inform them be true). Thus, two central conditions on memory go missing.

[14] This may be Langer's view (1953), since she considers it architecture's special mission to provide us with an image of the ethnic domain.

172   HERITAGE AND WAR

lose something important. Memory has a value beyond that of the information it allows us to retain.[15]

In the architectural case, as in the personal, the seriousness of the loss depends in part on what other vehicles for memory are available. The loss of one ancient college leaves many others to represent the ethnic domain from which they sprang; the loss of all would be far more destructive of our memory for that world. And from the point of view of future memory of our corporate capitalist culture, the loss of a single office building, even one as emblematic as the Seagram, would hardly dent our successors' capacity to represent our own ethnic domain. A thousand imitations, and rivals, would remain.

Even where the loss is total, we may wonder whether it can be reversed. Provided they are sufficiently well documented, buildings can be rebuilt, as many were across Europe in the aftermath of the Second World War. Provided the replacement is true enough to the original, surely any experience of which the latter admits, the former will too. Does reconstruction promise a way to restore memory, to render its loss only temporary?

Perhaps, but there are grounds for doubt. For reconstruction to restore memory it must propagate the capacity to represent the ethnic domain into the future, and do so in the right way. In Section 8, I attempted to say what counts as right. I pointed to two features that support the claims of propagation through architecture to count. One was that the very same building is a component in all the representational states involved. Both its makers and those in generations to come represent the past through a distinctive experience of the building itself. Clearly, if we lose the building, this feature is lost with it. Reconstructions may allow for experiences just like those the original offered us, but by definition they sacrifice the identity of the object that sustains them. Only while the building survives can our experiences have at their core the very component that lay at the heart of the experiences of those who've gone before. Only then can those experiences lay claim to count as memory in virtue of the role in them for some form of identity.

Perhaps this loss of identity is not fatal to memory. Architecture's claims to sustain it did not turn on identity alone—the fact that capacities are propagated through communication also played a role. If reconstruction preserves that second feature, it will retain some claim to sustain memory. But, resting on one ground instead of two, that claim is significantly weaker than that the

---

[15] For a vivid imagining of what such loss would be like, see Christopher Nolan's *Memento* (2000). For an attempt to say what at least part of the loss amounts to, see Hopkins (2016).

original building enjoyed, and it's far from clear it remains strong enough. To that extent, at least, the loss of the architecture of the past threatens to be, not only distinctive, but irreparable.

References

Ayer, A.J. (1956), *The Problem of Knowledge* (Penguin).

Burge, T. (1993), 'Content Preservation', in *Philosophical Review* 102/4: 457–88.

Clark, Andy, and Chalmers, David J. (1998), 'The Extended Mind', in *Analysis* 58/1: 7–19.

Dokic, Jérôme. (2001), 'Is Memory Purely Preservative?', in C. Hoerl and T. McCormack (eds.), *Time and Memory* (Clarendon Press), 213–32.

Dummett, M. (1993), 'Testimony and Memory', in *The Seas of Language* (Oxford University Press).

Grice, H.P. (1957), 'Meaning', in *Philosophical Review* 66/3: 377–88.

Hopkins, R. (2014), 'Episodic Memory as Representing the Past to Oneself', in *Review of Philosophy and Psychology* 5/3: 313–31.

Hopkins, R. (2016), ' "Remember Leonard Shelby": Memento and the Double Life of Memory', in Julian Dodd (ed.), *Art, Mind, and Narrative: Themes from the Work of Peter Goldie* (Oxford University Press), 89–99.

Hopkins, R. (2018), 'Imagining the Past: On the Nature of Episodic Memory' in F. Dorsch, and F. Macpherson (eds.), *Memory and Imagination* (Oxford University Press), 46–71.

Langer, Susanne. (1953), *Feeling and Form: A Theory of Art* (Scribners).

Lombard, L.B. (1990), 'Causes, Enablers, and the Counterfactual Analysis', in *Philosophical Studies* 59/2: 195–211.

Martin, C.B., and Deutscher, Max. (1966), 'Remembering', in *Philosophical Review* 75/2: 161–96.

Nolan, Christopher. (2000), *Memento* (Summit Entertainment).

Owens, D. (2000), *Freedom Without Reason* (Routledge).

Parfit, Derek. (1971), 'Personal Identity', in *Philosophical Review* 80/1: 3–27.

Ruskin, John. (1849), *The Seven Lamps of Architecture* (Electric Book Company 2000).

Sartre, Jean-Paul. (1938), *The Imaginary*, J. Webber (trans.) (Routledge 2004).

Savile, Anthony. (2000), 'The Lamp of Memory', in *European Journal of Philosophy* 8/1: 89–105.

10

Heritage Tourism after Conflict

Starting Philosophical Thoughts

Penelope Bernard and Simon Kirchin

1. Introduction

Tourism to sites of war, conflict, terror and violence is hugely popular. All manner of tours and visits are organized worldwide, every day, to both current and historic conflict sites. Some are once-in-a-lifetime events, such as tours of current conflict sites in the Middle East or to the battlegrounds of the Second World War, some are routine family visits, such as day trips to local castles. Some visits focus on war and battles themselves, others focus on sites that were the centres of conflict in a broader sense, such as notorious prisons or torture chambers. This is part of a wider trend labelled 'dark tourism'—that is, tourism to sites of death and tragedy. Not only are conflict tourism and dark tourism popular, they are also big business. For example, a 2014 article in *The Atlantic* estimated tourism to conflict sites to be worth approximately US$263 billion. The figure will no doubt have increased in the years since (Kamin 2014).[1] Further to the phenomena, dark tourism is an established academic area, formed at the intersection of tourism studies, cultural studies and business studies.[2] This academic area considers the finances, cultural mores and norms, and human psychology related to sites of death and suffering.

What strikes us is the absence of sustained, critical attention to conflict tourism from philosophers. This chapter narrows matters into a more manageable form. We focus on the idea of tourist visits to conflict heritage sites, some of which are adapted for mass, regular, safe tourism. We treat 'war' and

---

[1] At time of writing, the COVID-19 pandemic beginning in 2020 halted travel and will have affected this figure. Assuming travel returns, so will the conflict tourism industry.

[2] Stone et al. (2018) is an excellent place to begin. It covers some of the ideas and examples we offer and could have been cited many more times over. See also the 2018 Netflix travelogue series *Dark Tourist*, written and presented by David Farrier. See also Lisle (2000, 2016), which focus on 'war tourism', and O'Rourke (1988), which is a popular account of the phenomenon.

Penelope Bernard and Simon Kirchin, *Heritage Tourism after Conflict: Starting Philosophical Thoughts* In: *Heritage and War: Ethical Issues*. Edited by: William Bülow, Helen Frowe, Derek Matravers, and Joshua Lewis Thomas, Oxford University Press. © Penelope Bernard and Simon Kirchin 2023. DOI: 10.1093/oso/9780192862648.003.0010

'conflict' together; for our purposes they raise the same or similar issues, and we use the term 'conflict heritage tourism' to cover all cases.[3] We focus on sites of past conflict, where the conflict is one of the main reasons for a site's being a tourist heritage site. We do not discuss tourism to current conflicts, nor past tourist visits to conflict sites that were contemporary to such visitors.[4]

Despite narrowing our focus we still have many complicated phenomena to discuss. In this chapter we have three aims: first, to raise awareness of the phenomena and show they merit sustained philosophical interest; second, to outline some relevant philosophical questions; third, to offer some initial responses to these questions. Our overall claim, voiced at various intervals, is that one can, at most, develop general, defeasible ideas both about the phenomena and about what one should do. We do not argue for anything more detailed than this. We make this claim both because there is a large range of conflict heritage sites and because such sites raise many issues to which site curators and philosophers need to be alive.

2. Some Examples

We begin with some illustrative examples of the phenomena.

English Heritage, Historic Scotland, Cadw and the National Trust in Great Britain operate numerous sites, many of which have a strong association with war and conflict. Yet, most sites are perceived to be nice days out, often seen and marketed as places of 'family fun' with associated merchandise and events. Here are two examples. The 950th anniversary of the Battle of Hastings held at the English Heritage site of Battle Abbey in 2016 featured plenty of activities for families to enjoy. The centrepiece was a mock battle between the Normans and the Anglo-Saxons, with the crowd encouraged to pick a side to cheer. English Heritage also organize World War II family fun days at Dover Castle, a site of military significance from Bronze Age times to the Cold War,

---

[3] 'War tourism' can be construed narrowly as tourism concerned only with battles and wars, whereas 'conflict tourism' also includes cases concerned with, for example, violence that falls short of war, such as state oppression.

[4] Both categories raise questions and contain rich examples. There are many companies that arrange visits to current conflict zones, raising complex issues concerning tourists being in harm's way and whether tour operators should profit from conflict. The history of war tourism also has interesting case studies. For example, many tourist companies grew or were created because of military conflict, and in some cases the military relied on local tourist operators. Some tour operators existed in sites of military conflict because earlier conflicts had become sites of historic interest. Lisle (2016) shows how the military and tourism relate, and explores whether and to what extent military personnel can be seen as tourists themselves.

seeing war and conflict on its own site and nearby, as well as being the centre of significant military decisions. These events offer visitors the chance to dress as soldiers and participants from the period, to view mock weapons and transport, and participate in educational activities such as code-breaking and rations-tasting. Such events are popular and routinely hosted by many heritage sites.

Internationally there are many other examples of past conflict sites that are important visitor attractions and which exemplify a range of approaches to presentation. For example, The Chinese Eighth Route Army Culture Park in Shanxi province is named after the communist military unit that fought the Japanese in the 1940s in the area. Visitors can dress as troops and blast each other with toy guns (Fung 2012). The park's entertainment aspect seemingly far exceeds any educational purpose; the main point seems to be nationalist propaganda. In contrast, consider the countless tours to sites such as Auschwitz and Hiroshima. The presentation of these sites clearly aims at remembrance, respect and education.

As indicated in the introduction, there are also numerous examples of sites and events that come under the heading 'dark tourism', from tours of disaster sites such as Chernobyl to tours of sites relevant to organized crime.[5] These examples raise issues similar to those raised by conflict heritage sites.

3. The Moral Tension

There is, plausibly, a moral tension involved in creating, sustaining and visiting conflict heritage sites. We can frame this tension as follows:

> *Moral Tension*: a moral tension arises when agents derive valuable benefits from moral wrongdoing or morally bad events, or act in particular ways in relation to such events.

Creating and visiting conflict heritage sites often produces morally valuable benefits, such as enjoyment and education. A tension arises because such benefits are intrinsically connected to bad things, such as conflict, suffering and death, and such things may be morally bad.[6] Similarly, whilst the very act

---

[5] Stone et al. (2018) discusses many examples from across the world.

[6] We distinguish between moral wrongs and bads in order to capture a broader range of suffering, for example, the killing of soldiers engaged in unjust wars might be morally bad but not morally wrong.

of creating a heritage site may be seen as positively morally valuable, no matter what the consequences, the act of creating a *conflict* heritage site may be seen as impermissible, because of the nature of the events depicted. Hence the tension arises again.

This disquieting tension animates much of our discussion and generates other questions. For example:

Creation: When and why is it morally acceptable to create, sustain and adapt conflict heritage sites for people to visit as tourists?

Participation: When and why is it morally acceptable to visit conflict heritage sites as a tourist?

Time: Does the passage of time make a moral difference to creating and participating in heritage sites? In other words, is there a morally significant difference between, say, visiting the site of a conflict that happened centuries ago and visiting the site of a more recent conflict?

Other matters arise, which we do not pursue. For example, assuming that part of the problem concerns respect for others, one can ask how respect should be shown to living individuals and communities affected by a site's events, and how one shows respect to one's ancestors. As in other arenas, one can ask what occurs or ought to occur when people show respect for the dead.

Throughout this chapter we speak of 'the tension's being resolved'. This resolution might take various forms depending on one's broader commitments. For example, and as just mentioned, some non-consequentialists might hold that the very nature of the creative and participatory acts in relation to *conflict* heritage sites renders such acts impermissible no matter what the benefits. The tension is resolved by prohibiting conflict heritage tourism. However, other possible resolutions support what strikes us as the intuitive verdict that such tourism is at least sometimes permissible. For example, some non-consequentialists might argue that whilst there is something bad about the tourism itself, this can, at least sometimes, be overridden when the benefits are sufficiently important. Similarly, some consequentialists might say that there is nothing wrong with the creation of, and participation in, conflict heritage sites provided that the creation of such sites produces more good than other treatments. There will be other stances, of course. We do not defend any particular resolution of the tension here, but rather, explore the kinds of benefit and forms of engagement that might bear on the permissibility of creating and participating in conflict heritage sites.

178 HERITAGE AND WAR

4. Creation and Participation

Why might people create, sustain and adapt conflict heritage sites, or visit such sites? Here are some suggestions:

    (i) education on specific matters (such as the history of the site or how people were affected in connection with that history);

    (ii) broadening horizons (related to the general history of a people or a time period);[7]

    (iii) specific remembrance and contemplation (such as remembering a relative who died, or how a whole people were affected);

    (iv) remembrance and contemplation about conflict in general;

    (v) pilgrimage and/or religious obligation;

    (vi) enjoyment and fun;

    (vii) relaxation;

    (viii) bonding as a family and/or as friends; creating a site in which these things can happen.[8]

In addition, there are various broader reasons. For example:

    (ix) financial reasons. Sites might exist, or be sustained and adapted, to generate money for investment in the site or relevant research, or for commercial gain. They might be supported by outside funds because having conflict heritage sites is good for the local or national economy. Similarly, there are some visitors who pay to visit so they can support the site and associated research;

    (x) political and national reasons. Some countries or groups might create sites in order to sustain or further political narratives and ideals. Similarly, some people might visit because of the messages conveyed;

    (xi) symbolic and identification reasons. Some sites are symbols of some general event, person or group, or fundamental idea, with which some tourists may identify;

    (xii) the site and/or its history need to be protected from hostile forces. This set of reasons will likely sit alongside (x) and (xi).

---

[7] Education is routinely given as one of the most important reasons for the existence of heritage sites; we ourselves have already mentioned it. The mission statement of one of the USA's most important sites, the Colonial Williamsburg Foundation, summarizes this well: 'That the Future May Learn from the Past' (Colonial Williamsburg 2022).

[8] We focus on people who want to visit a site, rather than cases of reluctant visitors who go because of other reasons, such as children who visit because they are bribed or coerced.

HERITAGE TOURISM AFTER CONFLICT 179

In many cases these reasons overlap. We do not pretend this list is exhaustive. Even so, it suffices to indicate some of the main explanations of both the creation and popularity of conflict heritage sites.[9] With these reasons in mind, we can turn to the question of whether and how the tension might be resolved, such that we can vindicate the view that both the creation of conflict heritage sites and visits to them are morally permitted (or, perhaps even obligatory).

Consider a general case so as to think about a starting question: what reason is there to create and sustain conflict heritage sites *at all*?[10] Imagine a bloody, long-running war that involved the horrific massacre of innocents, with survivors enduring arduous lives thereafter. Answering both *Creation* and *Participation* will be fairly straightforward, and will therefore help to guide action, since there is a strong set of overlapping reasons—normally pointing to moral permissibility, often to moral obligation—to educate people about the horrors of war, to memorialize people's suffering, and to create opportunities for reflection and remembrance. Better this than silence and forgetting. Of course, we have deliberately described a case which is horrific, but the general idea also holds in less dramatic cases. Whether conflicts are large or small, involving innocents or others, they are terrible. Their terrible nature gives us reasons to remember them. These reasons are sufficient at least to start us thinking that the moral tension of conflict heritage tourism can be resolved in a way that reveals such tourism to be morally permissible.

However, it is not clear that these reasons show that the site *itself* needs to be preserved and visited. Why not just read about the events in a book or watch a documentary? Why not have a memorial site elsewhere? We grant, of course, that things other than conflict heritage sites can be morally valuable in memorializing and educating about events. Our claim is not that conflict heritage sites are the only or even always the best way to achieve one's aims. Moreover, some conflict heritage sites do fail to memorialize or educate as they should, as we will show. Nevertheless, conflict heritage sites often *are* good ways of memorializing and educating. Further, they offer something that books, documentaries and memorials in other places simply cannot: a tangible connection to what happened through physical place.[11] In some cases this

---

[9] There is much written in heritage and tourism studies relating to the reasons listed, and much produced by heritage organizations themselves, both for conflict and other sites. For a flavour, see the following reports and policy documents: Advisory Council on Historic Preservation (2008), Global Heritage Fund (2010), and Historic England (2022). See also Poria, Butler and Airey (2004). It is worth noting there will be cultural differences, with groups and countries emphasizing some reasons more than others.

[10] In reality, many heritage sites are created *because* there are visitors, but we ask this question first.

[11] For insightful discussion of the significance of historical sites and artefacts, see Korsmeyer (2018).

itself will have positive (moral) significance. Nothing can substitute for being in the presence of the hills on which soldiers were massacred and upon which memorial stones now stand. Nothing can quite replicate the feeling one has when in the very courtroom where judgements were passed on innocents before they were taken out and shot. Handled in the right way, such sites can bring home to visitors what happened and thereby underline the significance of the events in a way that books or documentaries alone cannot do.[12] Similarly, remembrance can take on extra significance if it occurs in the place where people died, and might lose significance if undertaken elsewhere.

We now introduce more complications. The concentration camps of the Second World War seem to offer an obvious illustration of how *Moral Tension* is to be resolved. These sites seem to require preservation to remind us of the atrocities that occurred. They expect—*demand*—quiet respect and reflection, and this influences their presentation. They are places for education and memorialization of the horrors both of a particular war and of war generally. Indeed, these sites have been created, sustained and adapted to ensure these are the dominant themes. The opening remarks of the Auschwitz-Birkenau Foundation website summarize this well:

> If one Place could address the conscience of humanity in the 21st century, this Place is Auschwitz-Birkenau. The last of the enormous extermination centers which is tangibly preserved. The largest of all the Nazi German concentration camps. If the world we would like to build is to be safer, peaceful and more welcoming, it is imperative that we keep the authenticity of the Auschwitz-Birkenau Memorial viable and palpable. No one can change the past; however the future is in our hands. Help us to preserve the authenticity of Auschwitz-Birkenau. Help us to warn humanity against itself. Do not allow history to become a deafening silence. Save the memory.
>
> (Auschwitz-Birkenau Foundation 2022)

These remarks suggest that, far from being wrong, appropriate engagement with past wrongs can be morally demanded of us. However, even this straightforward example illustrates controversies. First, there is a debate about Auschwitz's preservation. There was a burgeoning tourist industry in the war's immediate aftermath, with former prisoners showing organized groups around the main parts of the site after it was partially destroyed. In the decade

---

[12] A further point. If one is morally queasy about heritage sites profiting from suffering and death, one can level the same charge at authors and documentary film-makers.

following the war, officials made decisions about how the site would be preserved, with some parts reconstructed out of the remains. No one thinks we should forget and obliterate all remains of the site, but some historians think that *the destruction* should be preserved and the site not altered for mass tourism: that this would make for a more powerful warning and better memorialize what happened. This taps into a question from above. Even in cases where a site should be 'preserved', what does this mean, and in what way and for what reasons should it be adapted?[13]

A second issue arises regarding the reasons for creating and visiting the site. Do we have moral reason to create, sustain and visit because we should memorialize the dead and, relatedly, because we should show respect for those who are still living who experienced these horrors? Or are the reasons different, as the passage above suggests? Rather than respecting past and present suffering, are we trying to educate and memorialize so as to prevent future suffering? This way of setting up the discussion seems right, even if philosophically clichéd. Plausibly, heritage sites based on concentration camps exist for a range of reasons, both retrospective *and* forward-looking. However, philosophers and curators need to ask of every site why it has been created and sustained, and how it is being visited.

Our purpose is not to resolve either issue just outlined, but rather to show that even in a case in which we might think *Moral Tension* is straightforwardly resolved, there is complexity. And, although we have started to appreciate the set of general reasons for creating conflict heritage sites, as we continue we will see these reasons come under pressure.

So, some sites may successfully resolve or navigate *Moral Tension* and address *Creation* and *Participation*. But there are some sites and visits that get things hopelessly morally wrong.

A case of a site which is created and presented such that the tension remains resolutely present is the aforementioned Chinese Eighth Route Army Culture Park. Despite its claims to be educational, reports suggest that it is little more than jingoistic entertainment. It involves live role-playing, in which the Japanese are portrayed as comedic villains at whom tourists are encouraged to take potshots. So, in keeping with our previous remarks, whilst it would have been possible to create a morally justifiable heritage site centred on the Chinese–Japanese war, this site does not seem to be it. Rather, we have a site of an atrocious war presented in a highly inappropriate manner whereby

---

[13] Lisle (2016: 130–141) discusses this general question and the details of both Auschwitz and Hiroshima.

182   HERITAGE AND WAR

visitors gain pleasure directly from imagining historic suffering. These benefits do not seem to respect the nature of the historical events. In addition, current tensions between the two nations may be exacerbated by the site. Both of these are the contraries of what is happening at Auschwitz.

What of morally inappropriate visits? The Culture Park appears to be intended to encourage visits that can be deemed inappropriate, but there are also inappropriate visits at Auschwitz, despite the sombre attitudes encouraged by its custodians. In recent years there have been problems with some tourists taking 'selfies' of themselves and friends, provoking outrage. Selfies speak of fun and enjoyment, and a focus on the individual and their experiences. A heritage site based around a concentration camp seems the very opposite of these things.[14] The outrage seems to reflect the mismatch between the reasons why these tourists visit and the site itself.

Even in seemingly straightforward cases, matters become complex. Education at a concentration camp can be viewed as a positive experience. Whilst such education can be positive under some descriptions, if done in the right spirit it will not be *enjoyable*. It will be disquieting or upsetting, and it is this that seems to be morally appropriate to the situation. But whilst there might be a range of acceptable visits and experiences, there is also a range of morally inappropriate experiences and visits, and not just visits where people are treating the whole experience as a fun time. One might be morally disquieted if, for example, tourists identify too readily with victims; a false association may be morally disrespectful. However, complete uninterest bordering on detachment is also inappropriate in the case of concentration camps, similar to the indifference that underlies selfies.

The character of the site also matters. A degree of indifference or fun might be wrong at one site but acceptable elsewhere. A further point is that, despite our earlier remarks, it may be that even if the educational aims or intentions around memorialization are positive, the history of the site and the majority of likely visits are such that it is morally safer not to create it. There may be no guarantee that visitors will appropriately respect the people who suffered and died. This is something that philosophers and site curators need to take seriously, human nature being what it is.[15]

---

[14] The phenomenon of selfies at Auschwitz and other sites has been lampooned, where that lampooning has itself come under attack, partly through misunderstanding. See, for example, Margalit (2014). Note, this is related to other modern phenomena, for example 'selfies at funerals'.
[15] As well as these types of case, there are other cases where authorities should discourage tourists despite a site's historic importance, such as sites where chemical weapons were tested.

We are beginning to identify some general ideas and issues which invite caveats as to how one should create and participate in conflict heritage sites. One might find that *Moral Tension* can be resolved, but such resolutions will need to address the specific character of the history of the site, the reception by certain visitors, the current social context, and other matters. It will likely be hard to arrive at principles which are exceptionless, widely applicable and detailed, demanding precise site presentations or ways of visiting, and which cover many or all cases. Perhaps there is simply some general injunction of creating and visiting conflict heritage sites in ways which are morally appropriate to the events with which a site is concerned, relying on judgement to adapt to features as one moves from case to case. Such features may help site curators focus on how to shape and present sites in morally justifiable ways. Even if true, this on its own may seem unsatisfactory when it comes to offering practical guidance. We have already mentioned education as a reason for creation and participation. To make a little more progress, then, we think briefly about some other reasons from our list above.

5. Enjoyment, Fun, Remembrance and Financial Gain

Enjoyment and fun are to be had at many conflict heritage sites, some of which we have mentioned above. The World War II fun day (or 'Fun Day') at Dover Castle is a good example. As well as recalling the Castle's significant military history, the hosting of a World War II Fun Day can be taken as marking the war generally. The Castle's Fun Days involve dressing up and displays of military hardware, plus permanent activities such as interactive events revolving around bombing raids in South-East England. There is an immediate moral issue here. Are such Fun Days, focusing on something that was the cause of so much suffering and death, morally permissible? Might they, or something like them, be obligatory?

In order to respond, consider first a different example. Consider comedic depictions of historic atrocities. No one can say the Spanish Inquisition was fun. Modern estimates put the number of people prosecuted at around 150,000 with around 3,000–5,000 executed. Yet many people also believe that it is morally permissible for *Monty Python* to use the Spanish Inquisition as a source of humour. Indeed, some might argue that comedic representation of such events is morally necessary. It may be a matter of psychological release or comfort to laugh at death and war, and it may be necessary to make fun of

184   HERITAGE AND WAR

authority figures. Further, it can be argued that many learnt about the horrors of the Spanish Inquisition only because of *Monty Python*.

As we know, *Monty Python*'s depiction of the Spanish Inquisition is part of a larger wave of comedic representation in the twentieth and twenty-first centuries, covering topics such as witch-burnings, human sacrifice, plague and poverty, as well as war and conflict. A good example is the popular twenty-first-century UK children's television show *Horrible Histories*, which uses sketches and songs to depict all manner of historic violence and suffering. The books on which the series is based are routinely sold at heritage sites with the stated aim of education about the past through humour, a well-respected and effective method of teaching.

This returns us to Dover Castle and the general idea of enjoyment at conflict heritage sites. An opening set of thoughts goes like this. People routinely enjoy many artistic depictions of negative things, including war and conflict, and believe that some such depictions and experiences are justifiable. Why single out conflict heritage sites for different treatment? Individuals learn, grieve, and react in many ways to negative events. Whilst not all reactions will be appropriate—amusement at depictions of Auschwitz, for example—anything that may be said in general about what responses are morally desirable at conflict heritage sites, and how they might be encouraged by presentations at such sites, needs to account for the range of ways in which we respond to events. We need to think, at least for some sites, in terms of a spectrum of responses that are morally permissible. (We come to obligations below.)

This is a powerful opening thought, which, we think, carries in the end: it can be morally permissible to create certain conflict heritage sites at which people have fun, even when this fun is robustly connected to morally significant harms. Correlatively, it can be morally permissible for tourists to have fun at such a site. But there is complexity here, which requires reflection. Sometimes having fun is not morally acceptable, despite what some curators and visitors might think. Here are four indicative points.

First, and echoing an earlier thought, there is at least one difference between conflict heritage sites and (other sorts of) fictional depictions of conflict. In the case of the former, one is typically having fun at the *very place* where the conflict, death and suffering happened. For some philosophers and others, this will make no moral difference: what matters is simply the nature of the suffering and death itself, not the place. For others, place will make a moral difference, often based on the fact that routinely people *do* think and feel that it makes a difference, even if it may be hard to rationalize such an everyday thought or reaction.[16] There are plenty of sites whose creation is morally acceptable, but where the custodians and presentation should not encourage fun or enjoyment, or at least certain sorts of enjoyment, and this seems to have something to do with the events having happened at the places themselves.

Second, we have talked generally about enjoying conflict heritage sites and concomitantly about how one curates a site to encourage such enjoyment. But what of *the source* of the enjoyment? It is one thing to admire some decayed, romantic battlements, but quite another to take enjoyment in death and suffering (and, similarly, to encourage such thoughts and feelings). One can be more specific than this. It might be fine to enjoy seeing an obviously fictionalized version of a battle with mock, over-the-top suffering just as one does in a theatre, but not fine to enjoy the thought of the *actual* suffering as depicted by actors.[17] 'Having fun at a conflict heritage site' is a broad phrase, disguising plenty. Again, this will require more thought, but one could easily imagine a general, defeasible principle emerging: 'It is normally fine to have fun at a conflict heritage site, so long as one is not *directly enjoying* the *actual* suffering that happened', and similar principles regarding a site's creation and presentation. Similarly, it might be morally fine to laugh along with *Monty Python's* surreal, exaggerated depiction of the Spanish Inquisition, but not to enjoy the thought of the *actual* horror.

Third, we have talked blithely about enjoying a heritage conflict site where there was suffering and death. But the identity and character of those who suffered may matter morally, or at least affect how one presents a site and therefore how one encourages visitors to engage. Even if one thinks that no one should enjoy suffering and death, no matter who died (be they a serving General or an innocent civilian), the differences between the people involved may affect how a site is presented. Perhaps some people in certain conflicts should not be depicted in cartoon panels explaining what occurred, but others may if handled sensitively.

Lastly and following on, we have talked in general about enjoying depictions and presentations. But, as we know, these come in a wide range, affecting visitor

---

[16] Consider the fact from our introduction that tourists visit current conflict sites. How would one feel having fun at a conflict *heritage* site compared with having a similar experience at a *live* conflict site? Would the Spanish Inquisition sketches have been as funny if *Monty Python* had deliberately recorded them at the very sites of torture and death?

[17] At this point we do not go further, but one might then reflect on whether and why people can enjoy fictional depictions of suffering (which undoubtedly people do, and which seems morally permissible) and how this contrasts with enjoyment of the actual suffering as depicted in fictions (which seems morally dubious). Thanks to Helen Frowe for encouraging us to raise this point.

186   HERITAGE AND WAR

reactions. When considering the moral permissibility of conflict heritage sites and the actual events of a conflict, philosophers would do well to consider them as part of a set of examples: historical books, 'factionalized' accounts, theatrical productions, people playing with model soldiers, historic enactors recreating battles, computer games, and the like.

These four points are important in and of themselves, and they also speak to the complexity we have indicated. They should not be seen as fatally undermining the idea that it is morally permissible to have fun at conflict heritage sites where the fun is connected to the conflict. The moral tension with which we started can be overcome in morally permissible ways. But there is much to consider in developing more specific ideas that can be useful as practical guides, and in deciding what one should do as a site curator.

One last point. Could one mount a case for a moral obligation to create a conflict heritage site which was developed so as to encourage people taking fun and enjoyment, and mount a concomitant case for there being a moral obligation to visit such sites? Quite possibly. One would need to address the points just made. One would be on shaky ground in talking about obligations to have fun deliberately aimed at the suffering of innocents, say. The most fertile route for arguing for such an obligation likely lies in other, previous thoughts, namely the educational benefit there is in such sites and in the fact that people often need education to be enjoyable in order to learn. One would also have to show, echoing an earlier concern, that the education value of the fun activity hosted at the site could not be easily replicated by alternatives because one would lose something important without the site itself.

These thoughts return us to the theme of sombre reflection and remembrance. The point of focusing on enjoyment is to show that not all (permissible) conflict heritage sites need be sites of such reflection or even sites of education offered and taken in that spirit. Whilst such attitudes have their place and are the most or only appropriate reactions in some contexts, such a *global* obligation seems incorrect. It can be fine for many reasons to enjoy in some fashion difficult past events which were themselves horrific. This is true in the case of historical sites of suffering and death, just as it is in the rest of our lives. Whilst some events involve suffering, there can be aspects that are humorous. Perhaps the person who loaded the cannon really was a buffoon who slipped and caused himself and others fatal injuries. We repeat the thought that humans often need humour for psychological reasons in case the enormity of the suffering overwhelms them. Humour, fun, and joy may all be justified even at a conflict heritage site. Such responses help us cope with what occurred and such responses can help us to better understand the site. Further, there is some obligation for historians and curators to tell the truth of what happened and to ensure their presentations tell much that is relevant. War and conflict often have amusing aspects. Why always leave them out?

Lastly in this section we turn to financial reasons for creating and visiting conflict heritage sites. Heritage sites cost money to create and run; conflict heritage sites are no exception.[18] Several questions follow, which again we merely raise. First, is it morally permissible to create a conflict heritage site simply or primarily to make money? We think not. Intending solely or primarily to profit from the suffering of others seems impermissible.[19] What does seem morally permissible is running a financially sustainable site where surplus is reinvested in the site (or research, or partner sites if part of a group), where the primary aims of the site are not financial. This may not be the end of the matter. It may also matter what or how one is memorializing. Earlier we listed 'political reasons'. The general guidance just given may look dubious if the main, non-financial reason for the site's existence and continuation is a controversial ideological view of history.

There are further difficulties when it comes to the wider economy. There are some conflict heritage sites that define their local area and dominate the local economy, with many other businesses dependent on tourists for their own trade. What moral obligations do conflict heritage sites have towards other organizations and businesses? In addition, an issue just mentioned returns in a different guise. Whilst the conflict heritage site may not exist to make a profit, the independent tearoom next door may well be trying to do so, and their trade arises because of the conflict. A full account of the relationship between heritage and financial gain will need to illuminate these indirect gains, as well as the more direct cases of profiting from conflict sites.[20]

6. The Passage of Time

If these issues were not enough, the passage of time adds further complications.

First, there is the issue of determining which conflict sites are 'in the past' and why. For example, whilst some conflict heritage sites are in the very

---

[18] Plenty of groups advocate for heritage sites based on economic benefits to a region and to support preservation of heritage generally. For example, see Maeer, Robinson and Hobson (2016: 20–28).

[19] The literature on war profiteering comes to mind (see Bazargan 2018).

[20] Elizabeth Scarbrough (2016) writes about a different but related case, namely so-called 'ruin tours' of inner-city Detroit. She considers the exploitation of current residents who have such tours in their city and how such exploitation can be avoided.

distant past, some sites are in the recent past, and some are past but have current effects. There are established tourist trails in Northern Ireland that visit sites of the worst of the Troubles, for example. Whilst it is true that some of the more extreme acts of war and violence are in the (recent) past, there are still localized outbreaks of violence, the causes of which may lie in the Troubles, even if these might not form part of any tourist trail.[21] Similarly, there are some places of conflict where there is currently no conflict occurring, but where there is a possibility of future conflicts erupting that can be seen as continuous with the recent conflict because the underlying reasons are the same. Even if one could rule out these cases, we may have other residual effects. Many people living in or near conflict sites of the recent past are likely to continue to suffer the indirect consequences of that conflict, such as poverty, displacement, and low levels of education and health. These cases still raise the question from above: is it permissible to visit and create tourist sites in places enduring the ongoing harms of a conflict?

Imagine, however, that we are considering cases where such worries have been satisfied and the conflicts and at least their immediate indirect effects are agreed to be 'in the past'. Even then there is a concern. At times it seems natural to think that conflict, death and suffering carry the same moral weight whenever they have occurred, and the passage of time makes no difference. Yet, sometimes it feels just as natural to think the opposite: the passage of time *does* matter. After all, it seems unlikely that every visit to every conflict heritage site is in some way morally dubious such that it needs some moral justification. So, should the passage of time affect visits to sites and whether the sites exist?

The broad answer to the question is, again, 'it depends'. It depends on what happened at the site, how those events are to be represented and what they did and now symbolize, how people may be affected by representations, and so on. We think, however, some points can be stated with a degree of certainty. First, there is, again, no exceptionless, specific principle of the form, 'it is easy to justify creating and visiting heritage sites based on past conflicts (certainly those from long ago) in a positive (for example, fun and enjoyable) way, but those in the recent past must be presented and visited in a sombre, reflective fashion'. Even some long past events have current resonance and can be

---

[21] The consequences of the Troubles in current criminal activity in N. Ireland is well-documented and a source of media reports. Even the Northern Ireland Direct (2022) government website on organized crime in the province acknowledges this by beginning, 'Organised crime involves a group of people involved in serious criminal activities, to make large profits. They use violence or the threat of violence. In Northern Ireland, organised crime groups might have paramilitary connections.'

reanimated, as we shall indicate. However, second, a similar principle, worded more generally and with some appropriate qualifier, *seems* more plausible. For example, one might plausibly claim the following: *by and large*, the further in the past the conflict which a heritage site represents, the easier it will be to justify creating and visiting it in a positive (for example, fun and enjoyable) way. Third, one likely has more latitude in how one represents and engages with matters in the distant past because these are matters that one cannot influence and which influence us far less; so much history has happened between then and now. Lastly, there is still the large question hanging over all of this. We may well engage in more positive fashion with brutal and horrible events of long ago, but should we? This is the broad point, already touched on, concerning the interplay between how in fact people feel and think and what any moral theory might prescribe.

To illustrate, consider some cases. First, we return to the Second World War and Dover Castle's Fun Day. Such days see large numbers of people; war re-enactment is a profitable business and a serious hobby. We visited such a Fun Day, and when we did so, most of the re-enactors were British, many of whom were dressed as Nazi officers and German soldiers. Most were in small groups in their own camps, dressed and displaying various war memorabilia. There is educational benefit to this and it lends a site atmosphere.[22] What was worrying and upsetting during our visit was the enthusiasm displayed by some dressed as Nazis who revelled in some assumed glamour.

A similar event in Haworth, England in 2012 was visited by residents of Hamm in Germany. The German visitors were upset by the presence of two people in Nazi uniforms, something which is illegal in Germany. The visitors reported the incident to the local authorities, leading to its being picked up as a national news item in both the UK and Germany (BBC News 2012).[23] We are sure the German visitors would have been similarly appalled by what we saw at Dover Castle.

From these examples one can see how a conflict's effects can resonate and how they can reanimate a site. There are, broadly, matters of offence that can easily slip into matters of harm, particularly where the issue of Nazism is concerned.[24] That such issues and presentations have the power to offend and

---

[22] The educational benefit can be high but can also sometimes be doubtful as the presentations may not be scrutinized by anyone other than those in the groups.

[23] One local councillor is quoted as also being appalled. One of the organizers, who also notes it is distasteful, defends the action because the UK is a free country. He also points out that there were only two people in Nazi uniforms out of around 20,000 attendees. (The Dover Castle event we refer to had quite different numbers.)

[24] See Feinberg (1984, 1985) for a classic modern discussion of harm and offence.

190   HERITAGE AND WAR

harm, even after a number of years, is clear. This general point is sharpened when one considers how a site should be presented and responded to, particularly once one realizes that there has to be selectivity of both presentation and memory.[25] This has added significance again once one realizes that historic sites, if they are to have educational value, have a role to play in both advancing and challenging memories and historical narratives.[26] The presentation of a site and its perception show the multiple tensions we have discussed. How does one remain faithful to a site and its history, and respect the dead and those who feel a connection to the site, whilst allowing for a (reasonable) range of reactions, some of which might include explicit displays of enjoyment, thus creating a site that people want to visit?

More specifically, these examples indicate how an overall view of each example can be reached. For a start, there might be good reason to have people in Nazi uniforms at a Second World War event, but one can distinguish Dover from Haworth. From what we can see of the two examples, there may be far more reason to have people present in Nazi uniforms at the Dover event, since it is trying to display and balance a range of different military units and cover 1940s wartime generally. In contrast, the Haworth event seemed to be a recreation and celebration of the war *in* Haworth and its surrounds, so a Nazi party presence is inappropriate. A second point is that any such events should be alive to the fact that the Allies in the Second World War can also be accused of atrocities. Indeed, whilst it may be a difficult balancing act in what is supposed to be a family event, some acknowledgement of the horrors of war and the tragedies that some groups faced seems necessary, especially given that the events mentioned here are within living memory.[27] Similarly, the overall aim of such events, and how they are marketed and presented, sets the tone. Are we aiming to *commemorate* a set of discrete events? Are we *celebrating* the culture of the period and the positive changes that occurred? Plenty of Second World War event days are simply celebrations of 1940s culture, with singers and bands appropriately dressed. (The Haworth event seems closer to this, which is why the presence of people in Nazi uniform seems wrong.)

---

[25] These and other themes are explored in Harrison, Bergqvist and Kemp (2016).

[26] At time of writing there is controversy in the UK and elsewhere concerning how various organizations deal with the historic associations that sites have with the slave trade. An extended version of this chapter would consider more examples, discuss the nature of commemoration, and show how memory and presentation affect each other. Auschwitz and Hiroshima are key examples of commemoration and memory, much discussed and debated in tourism studies (again, see Lisle 2016 and Stone et al. 2018), but there are many examples worldwide.

[27] At a large site there is more scope for this to happen, of course.

We have used the phrase 'living memory', which requires further specification. It might mean only that there are people alive who were directly affected by the events depicted at a site. It might be extended also to cover people who have personal memory of a now-departed relative or friend who was directly affected by the events. However this phrase is specified, many events at conflict heritage sites are not within living memory, but that does not mean one has complete moral latitude to act as one wants. It also means that one should pay heed to the '*by and large*' qualifier given above when considering how sites are presented and visited.

Some more examples illustrate this and other points above. If one takes our suggested principle, it implies two things: that, by and large, the nearer in time an event of war and conflict is to living memory, the more one should err on the side of sombre reflection or education and, correlatively, that pleasure-seeking is best suited for conflict sites that are settled and far in the past. Whilst one can think of illustrative examples in both categories, we can show why the principle is nonetheless defeasible and needs to be applied appropriately. For example, no one could think that the 1746 Battle of Culloden was in the recent past. However, the current interpretation of the site errs on the side of respect and reflection. The reason is that Culloden is seen as a touchstone event in the history of Scotland, emphasizing its importance as a nation. A few people may overly politicize this for current and future purposes, but it is a good example of when it is important to mark events in a certain way so they remain in the memory.[28] An example of a recent conflict, certainly one within living memory (with attendant local consequences), where a site privileges enjoyment but does so in a justifiable manner is again found at Dover Castle which hosts a Cold War 'escape room', marketed as an interactive, fun experience, targeted at families and friendship groups.

Even when marking events of the distant past, such as the 950th celebrations of The Battle of Hastings at Battle Abbey, one cannot do whatever one wants. There has to be respect shown for the brutal events and their aftermath, even if one is celebrating and not (only) commemorating. This was another celebration we visited. The mock battle really was a piece of theatre, and no one was encouraged by the site or the events of the weekend to revel in the thought of the actual suffering experienced. The materials provided to the visitors reflected the details of the battle itself, the historical build up to the

---

[28] Thanks to Jeanette Kennett for the example. Derek Matravers gave us another example, the storming of Clifford's Tower in York in 1190, which has a modern anti-Semitic resonance and which seems to resonate in a way the Battle of Hastings does not.

192 HERITAGE AND WAR

Norman invasion and its consequences, and did so in a sensitive way, whilst incorporating some measure of enjoyment. Imagining oneself into the lives of those who lived through the battle, for example, can be of educational benefit. With that said, there are some difficulties. If someone had come forward who took offence because of the enjoyment gained from the site and the weekend's events, and furthermore made the case that they were psychologically harmed as a result because they claimed some long-dead ancestor from the conflict, we would think they had an unusual reaction.[29] But what if a retired soldier, who had experienced a very harrowing and recent conflict, had had the same reaction, concerned that the death of soldiers was being treated merely as a form of entertainment?[30] This latter reaction might also be unusual, but the matter of which reactions require adaptions to a presentation, or even the cancelling of events or closure of sites, still requires consideration.

No doubt further reflection on the significance of the passage of time will identify more complicating factors and we imagine there is much to take issue with in what we have said. But the passage of time nevertheless generates a rich vein of debate and demonstrates our claim that, at most, one can develop general, defeasible principles about conflict tourism to help guide judgement and action.

7. Conclusion

Every heritage conflict site presents a complex range of moral issues, sometimes unique or rare, and each must be judged on its merits. Nevertheless, in raising many questions we have outlined some fundamental ideas and considerations that have general, if defeasible, applicability and which both aid understanding of the moral tension connected to conflict tourism and potentially serve to reduce or resolve it. Even the limited number of examples that we have considered show the breadth and complexity of the issues that arise and the potential for further philosophical exploration of the idea of conflict heritage tourism. Such tourism raises important moral issues concerning

---

[29] Unusual but not unheard of. Some people do struggle in such situations, such as some children with special needs. This point and others (such as the range of inappropriate reactions at Auschwitz) call to mind the philosophical literature on sentimentality. See, for example, Tanner (1976–1977). Thanks to Derek Matravers for this thought.

[30] Thanks to Helen Frowe for the example.

profit, education, commemoration, celebration, pleasure and grief, all of which would benefit from more philosophical attention.[31]

Bibliography

Advisory Council on Historic Preservation. (2008), 'ACHP Policy Statement: Archaeology, Heritage Tourism, and Education', adopted 15 August 2008, https://www.achp.gov/sites/default/files/policies/2018-07/ArchPolicy.pdf.

Auschwitz-Birkenau Foundation. (2022), *Homepage*, accessed 10 January 2022, http://www.foundation.auschwitz.org/.

Bazargan, Saba. (2018), 'Noncombatant Immunity and War Profiteering', in Seth Lazar and Helen Frowe (eds.), *The Oxford Handbook of Ethics of War* (Oxford: Oxford University Press), 358–382.

BBC News. (2012), 'Nazi SS Uniforms at Haworth 1940s Event "Offensive"', 14 June 2012, https://www.bbc.co.uk/news/uk-england-leeds-18443126.

Colonial Williamsburg. (2022), *Homepage*, accessed 10 January 2022, https://www.colonialwilliamsburg.org/.

Feinberg, Joel. (1984), *Harm to Others* (Oxford: Oxford University Press).

Feinberg, Joel. (1985), *Offense to Others* (Oxford: Oxford University Press).

Fung, Brian. (2012), 'Japan Invades China!…Year-Round at this Theme Park in Shanxi', in *The Atlantic*, 29 October 2012, https://www.theatlantic.com/international/archive/2012/10/japan-invades-china-year-round-at-this-theme-park-in-shanxi/264180/.

Global Heritage Fund. (2010), '2009–2010 Biennial Report: Saving our Global Heritage for Future Generations', accessed 10 January 2022, https://globalheritagefund.org/ghfwp/wp-content/uploads/2016/08/GHFAnnualReport20092010v7.pdf.

Harrison, Victoria, Bergqvist Anna, and Kemp, Gary (eds.). (2016), *Philosophy and Museums: Essays on the Philosophy of Museums* (Cambridge: Cambridge University Press).

Historic England. (2022), 'Heritage Conservation Defined', accessed 10 January 2022, https://historicengland.org.uk/advice/hpg/generalintro/heritage-conservation-defined/.

---

[31] Thanks to Helen Frowe and Derek Matravers for several comments on earlier drafts, and to those who responded to social media posts: Chris Armstrong, Jan Bell, Zsuzsanna Chappell, Vybarr Cregan-Reid, Daniel Elstein, Ian Evans, Arabella Garvey, Max Khan Hayward, Jeanette Kennett, Tim Toepritz and Lee Walters.

Kamin, Debra. (2014), 'The Rise of Dark Tourism', in *The Atlantic*, 15 July, https://www.theatlantic.com/international/archive/2014/07/the-rise-of-dark-tourism/374432/.

Korsmeyer, Carolyn. (2018), *Things: In Touch with the Past* (Oxford: Oxford University Press).

Lisle, Debbie. (2000), 'Consuming Danger: Reimagining the War/Tourism Divide', in *Alternatives: Global, Local, Political* 25: 91–116.

Lisle, Debbie. (2016), *Holidays in the Danger Zone* (Minneapolis, MN: University of Minnesota Press).

Maeer, Gareth, Robinson Amelia, and Hobson, Marie (2016), 'Values and Benefits of Heritage: A Research Review', *Heritage Lottery Fund Strategy and Business Development Department*, accessed 10 January 2022, https://www.heritagefund.org.uk/sites/default/files/media/research/values_and_benefits_of_heritage_2015.pdf.

Margalit, Ruth. (2014), 'Should Auschwitz Be a Site for Selfies?', in *The New Yorker*, 26 June 2014, https://www.newyorker.com/culture/culture-desk/should-auschwitz-be-a-site-for-selfies.

Northern Ireland Direct. (2022), 'Organised Crime', accessed 10 January 2022, https://www.nidirect.gov.uk/articles/organised-crime.

O'Rourke, P. J. (1988), *Holidays in Hell* (Washington, DC: Atlantic Monthly Press).

Poria, Yaniv, Butler, Richard, and Airey, David (2004), 'Links between Tourists, Heritage and Reasons for Visiting Heritage Sites', in *Journal of Travel Research* 43: 19–28.

Scarbrough, Elizabeth. (2016), 'Visiting the Ruins of Detroit: Exploitation of Cultural Tourism', in *Journal of Applied Philosophy* 35: 1–18.

Stone, Philip R., Hartmann, Rudi, Seaton, Tony, Sharpley, Richard and White, Leanne (eds.). (2018), *The Palgrave Handbook of Dark Tourism Studies* (Basingstoke: Palgrave Macmillan).

Tanner, Michael. (1976–1977), 'Sentimentality', in *Proceedings of the Aristotelian Society* 77: 127–147.

11

Stoics on Stuff

Stoic Consolations on the Destruction of Cultural Heritage in War

Nancy Sherman

1.

Let me begin with a sober historical event that involved massive destruction of cultural and sacred artifacts. It may have been the work of an enemy, internal not external, though history is not decisive here. I have in mind the Great Fire of 64 A D, the fire that devastated Rome. Whether or not Nero "fiddled while Rome burned," let us assume, for argument's sake, the arson was the act of an internal enemy, resulting in a fiery apocalypse that destroyed vast numbers of religious and heritage sites.[1] The question I want to pose is how ancient Greco-Roman Stoics, such as Seneca (Nero's tutor, as it happens) force us to rethink our attachment to cultural objects and our valuation of them as a central part of flourishing.

Pushing the Socratic view to an extreme, the Stoics hold that virtue alone is sufficient for happiness. External goods, including material objects and edifices, among them the historic and ritual monuments of a culture or religion, are classified as "indifferents," to be preferred rather than dispreferred, but themselves not the kinds of things that can make or break our happiness. Rome may burn under Nero's hand, the most precious tombs and monuments may be leveled by war, the glories of Greece demolished by battle—all are disasters, but for the wise person or advanced moral aspirant, they amount

---

[1] Griffin (1984: 141) and Champlin (2003: 178–209, esp. 191) take the view that Nero was responsible for the fire. For the view that the Christians may have been the arsonists, see John Pollini (2017). Our ancient sources are Tacitus in the Annals (1942: 15.38–44) who wrote in the early second century, and later authors Suetonius (1914: 38) and Dio (1925: 62.16–18). The latter two point the finger at Nero. Tacitus cautiously says: "A disaster followed, whether accidental or treacherously contrived by the emperor, is uncertain, as authors have given both accounts" (1942: 15.38).

Nancy Sherman, *Stoics on Stuff: Stoic Consolations on the Destruction of Cultural Heritage in War* In: *Heritage and War: Ethical Issues*. Edited by: William Bülow, Helen Frowe, Derek Matravers, and Joshua Lewis Thomas, Oxford University Press. © Nancy Sherman 2023. DOI: 10.1093/oso/9780192862648.003.0011

196 HERITAGE AND WAR

to a different kind of injury from that of losing, or failing to cultivate, one's goodness.

The view strikes many of us as inhumane and an expression of the overly austere side of Stoicism. We may rehearse evils in order psychologically to protect ourselves against actual harm. But to claim there are no real harms or moral injuries, individual or collective, in the wake of actual cultural devastation is quite another matter. Moreover, to muster Stoic views in defense of failures to protect against the destruction of heritage in war seems to give too much credence to Stoicism's strange value system of discounting all goods that are not inner virtue, as not genuine goods (Sherman 2021: 46–48).

Still, the Stoic view gives us space to wonder if we don't at times fetishize material stuff, including even ritual sites invested with history and the long-standing practices of a culture. Is there something problematic about heritage in general, when it puts so much emphasis on *things* outside our control? The Stoics don't take up the contemporary question of whether all sites are equally valuable, irrespective of the values for which they stand. Instead, they ask a broader-stroked question about what we value as good in a good life, and the appropriateness of our reactions when we lose those things. The Stoics, popularized in history, are famous for advice about how to cultivate attitudes of acceptance about the loss of things we care about. It is at the heart of their exhortative essays about managing grief and anger. But the stronger doctrinal view is that we should change what we care about so that we can reduce the impact of the loss of things outside of our control. Fetishizing stuff, when we should be caring about virtue, is a flawed way of living and leads to attachment emotions hard to control. If we want to go on valuing stuff, then, at least, we should find ways to accept loss that can promote calm.

Despite the initial harshness of the Stoic challenge to revalue our attachments, and short of that, our reactions, it makes some sense when we consider cultural heritages that are the source of constant strife. Think here of the Temple Mount in Jerusalem (Har Habayit and Haram-Al Sharif) one and the same site with competing cultural narratives and identities—and a flashpoint for violence.[2] Stoic meditation on our relationship to things and our investment of value in them may give us some "calm" to think about how we value and ritualize objects, to what lengths we go to defend them, and what our shared moral obligations to protect them are. Seeing through a Stoic lens is a way to sharpen our focus about what and how we value things in a good life. It may give insight into how, as combatants and non-combatants, theoreticians

---

[2] I owe thanks to conversation with Michael Gross for this example.

and practitioners in war and after war, we prepare for human and cultural loss and protect ourselves in the face of it.

But first, a caveat. I am not here trying to refine the criteria of just war or post-bellum reparations. As with much of my recent work, in a trilogy of war books, *Afterwar*, *The Untold War*, and *Stoic Warriors*, I explore the moral psychology of immersion in war, and how to protect and heal. My work has been about how servicemembers go to war and then return from war, trying to recreate a sense of meaning away from the urgency and operational tempo of deployments. They carry the moral burdens of having survived their buddies or being the cause of accidents and collateral killings that have left tragedy and horror in their wake. They return stateside, where so few go to war and civilian gratitude often comes in a thin crust of etiquette delivered at an airport lounge: "Thank you for your service." The poet Marianne Moore once said, "There never was a war that was not inward" (1944). My own work has been about those inner wars, fought in training for war, downrange, and long after servicemembers leave war and try to come home.

My plan is this: I continue my remarks (in Section 2) with Stoicism's view of material goods, such as cultural artifacts, and what is meant by valuing those goods as indifferents. I then (in Section 3) discuss the Stoic account of emotions, especially forms of moral injury and distress, and frame them in terms of P.F. Strawson's (1962) famous account of reactive attitudes. I then (in Section 4) turn again to Seneca's letters on loss and consider some implicit moral attitudes and asymmetries in moral perspectives toward self and others. I conclude (in Section 5) with a contemporary example of the destruction of cultural heritage and pause to see it through a Stoic lens.

2.

So how do the Stoics view cultural and religious monuments? Do they hold, as most of us do, that they figure in a conception of good and human flourishing? The Stoics don't take for granted the architectural sites and edifices that enable the conditions of their lives, even, presumably the *stoa poikile*, the painted colonnade where they taught and that gave its name to their philosophy. In the mold of Socrates and later the Cynics, the Stoics are anti-conventionalists. The Cynics famously flout, in the street theater of their day, culture and custom and all its accretions. "Cosmopolitanism," Diogenes the Cynic's terminological invention, meant not just being a citizen of nowhere and everywhere, but not being wed to the coinage and customs of local

198   HERITAGE AND WAR

habitus. It meant, for him, sleeping naked in a bathtub in the middle of the agora, and scorning material luxury and unnecessary aesthetics. Nature not culture becomes the source of norms, however hard it is to interpret nature's norms. The Stoics lighten up on the austere asceticism and street theater of Cynic practice. But they continue to take seriously how attached we are to goods external to our inner selves, even those that may be the finest presentations of our inner excellence. And so, the Greek and later Roman Stoics develop a highly systematic way of protecting against losses from outside. We are to learn how to weather the vicissitudes of fortune. At the center is an axiology of goods supported by a highly sophisticated and multi-tiered descriptive conception of emotions and a prescriptive account of their management and training.

The Stoics, as I said, revive the Socratic claim that virtue alone is necessary and sufficient for happiness. Still, they never fully abandon the view elaborated by Aristotle that we need externals in that life. Rather, they rightly recognize that Aristotle fudged on just what role they would play and how they were to be ranked or constrained within the mixed composite of happiness. And so, in a sense, the Stoics want to have their cake and eat it too. Externals are "indifferents" that don't make a difference to individual or collective well-being. Only virtue, inner goodness, can make that difference and is the only genuine good. But demotion to "indifferents" doesn't mean adopting a psychological state of indifference or apathy.[3] Rather, we are to prefer and disprefer certain indifferents, just as we would the externals to which most of us commonly assign positive or negative values in a good life. We prefer as beneficial, for the most part, health over disease, wealth over poverty, the safety and security of our loved ones over their endangerment. Even though only virtue is good and vice evil, we specify moral value concretely through our selections of indifferents (Epictetus 1995: 1.29.2). And here, the Stoics teach that we are to be guided by nature, hence the ancient Greek Stoics' linkage of logic, physics, and ethics as interrelated areas of philosophical study. We make informed selections following reason and the *logos* of nature (Cicero 2001: Bk.3). Nature, of course, does not make its moral laws explicit. But the Stoics hold a view that comes to influence later moral philosophy, that the moral law is as if the work of universal reason written in nature. Kant's view, after all, is that the moral law for humans, the Categorical Imperative, has as one of its formulae, the formula of the law of nature.

---

[3] See "Stoic Interludes" in Sherman (1997).

But what then of a specific way of life and its cultural heritages? Is preservation, for the most part, a preferred indifferent? Does the qualification depend on the kind of life in which the cultural inheritances figure—a life dedicated to philosophy and virtue, as a Stoic sage might envision it? Or are the Stoics anti-establishment, anti-conventionalist Cynics at heart who would strip down cultural aesthetics to ascetic, bare bones?

Certainly, outright asceticism is not the practice of the Roman world in which Stoicism comes to be the dominant philosophy in imperial palaces such as that of Nero and Marcus Aurelius. True, there may be aspirations to the simple life, notably, in Marcus Aurelius's *Meditations*, which bear witness to the influence of his spiritual mentor, Epictetus, a former slave who turns to the inner freedom of reason as the real form of moral freedom. Epictetus does promote a harsh asceticism reminiscent of external slavery. But Marcus is ambivalent. In his diary, penned to himself in the quiet hours of the Germanic campaigns (169–175 CE), he shuns gold and glory. But it was likely the victories of those campaigns that occasioned the commissioning of the famous equestrian monumental statue that has survived to this day and that then, and for some now, is the site of a kind of glory worship.[4]

Seneca, with his incomparable oratorical high style, famously struggles with the contradictions of his life of material and aesthetic production and consumption as "minister" of Nero and his lifelong aspirations to Stoic simplicity. He tells of how he aspires for the simple life in diet, "forswearing oysters and mushrooms forever... for they are just relishes designed to make the sated stomach go on eating"; in mattress choice, "that doesn't hold an imprint"; in avoidance of the caldarium, the hot bath that boils down the body only to "sweat it thin"; in foregoing use of perfumes that disguise "the best scent for the body [which] is no scent at all."[5]

This may give us warning that asceticism is the enemy of aestheticism for a Stoic like Seneca, and that religious and cultural edifices, at least of the sort built by coffers of wealth, are not an obvious "type" of preference. Various remarks by Seneca push in this direction: "I am not telling you to give yourself airs if you look down on golden couches and bejeweled cups. What's the virtue in scorning superfluities? Admire yourself when you look down on necessities" (Seneca 2015: 110.11, p.440). Don't be fooled by "the glitter and gleam of wealth" or the "false glare of high repute and great power" (115.7,

---

[4] Perhaps preserved because it was mistaken as a statue of Constantine, who legalized Christianity in the Roman Empire (Musei Capitolini, 2020).

[5] *Letter* (108.22, 15), here translated by Wilson (2019: 53). For full text, see Seneca (2015).

200   HERITAGE AND WAR

p.459). Learn to see virtue as what's really beautiful, even when coated in dirt
and grime (Seneca 2015: 115.6, p.459):

> Only then will we be in a position to understand what worthless items we
> admire. We are just like children, who set great store by their playthings and
> care more about any cheap trinket than they do about a sibling or even a
> parent. As Aristo says, how are we different from them, except that we with
> our statues and paintings have a more expensive form of silliness. They delight
> in smooth pebbles found on the beach with specks of different colors; we
> delight in patterned marbles imported from the deserts of Egypt or the wilds
> of Africa, broad columns supporting some hall or dining pavilion large
> enough for an entire town.   (Seneca 2015: 115.8)

If cultural heritage is built with that patterned marble—in imperial columns
and arches that fill a forum—then Seneca seems to be saying that we are being
schooled in false glory. We need to recast glory, so that virtue and its exempla,
in a Cato or a Socrates, come to inspire in the way that triumphal pageantry
and monuments do (Newman 2013: 323).

3.

That's a harsh asceticism. And not the full picture. But it's a jumping-off
point for Seneca's remarks about a conflagration that can wipe out a city's
cultural edifices, let alone annihilate a population. The fire he writes about in
a letter to Lucilius is not of Rome, but of the Roman colony of Lugdunum
(modern Lyon). The conflagration may have taken place shortly after the
Great Fire (Seneca 2015: n.91.1). Seneca's letter gives us a sense of how he
likely viewed the Roman conflagration. But more critically, it allows us to
take stock of Stoic notions of anticipating distress and loss, the place of grief
in the Stoic emotional profile, both for a sage and a moral progressor, and
consoling or consolation letters of moral counsel in coping with tragedy.
Seneca doesn't distinguish between destructive fire caused by an act of war or
nature. Stoic psychic preparation and armor is meant to cover both cases. The
letter opens showing the gentler side of Seneca's Stoicism:

> Our friend Liberalis is quite upset at news of the fire that has completely
> consumed the municipality of Lyon. The catastrophe could have shaken

anyone, let alone a person deeply devoted to his native land. It has left him searching for the mental toughness with which he had undoubtedly armed himself against what he thought were possible objects of fear. I'm not surprised, though, that he had no advance fears of this disaster, so unforeseen and virtually unimaginable, because it was unprecedented. Fire has troubled many cities, but not to the point of completely annihilating them. Even when buildings have been set alight by enemy action, many places escape destruction...

Such a range of splendid structures, any one of them capable of embellishing a city all by itself—and a single night has leveled them all!

(Seneca 2015: 91.1–2)

Seneca continues with lessons on what the Stoics refer to as the "pre-rehearsal of future ills"—preventive measures for managing and mitigating disabling emotions, a kind of stress inoculation: "Although our friend Liberalis is no weakling in facing his own troubles, he is quite depressed by all of this. It's no wonder...When one is unprepared for a disaster, it has greater effect: shock intensifies the blow...Exile, torture, war, shipwreck—keep rehearsing them in your mind" (Seneca 2015: 91.3).[6]

There are several points to note. To begin with, we have here a conversation with and about non-sages, or better, advanced moral progressors, who have taken seriously Stoic tonics and have developed, over time, considerable grit and resilience. And, we should note, *en passant* here, that these individuals are doing it together, as Stoics, with concern for each other, as friends and addressees in epistolary relationships.[7] So Stoic grit and resilience, contrary to some popular views about Stoicism, are not sheer self-reliance. The Stoics advocate a community, a cosmopolitan city, across borders, of humans and god; even the wisest are fellow citizens. In the later Stoic-influenced Philo Judaeus, the Aristotelianizing claim about our natural sociality is especially bold (Schofield 1999: 108).

Still, Stoic discipline has left Seneca and his friends unprepared for this overwhelming and unprecedented disaster. Pre-exposure to scenarios of threat and loss, regularly rehearsing the "bads" that can befall you, would unlikely have included anything of this magnitude. Perhaps virtual reality training would have helped here. Or what psychologists now use to mitigate and prevent severe anxiety disorders, such as posttraumatic stress—attention bias

---

[6] For Cicero on pre-rehearsal, see Cicero (2002: 3.28–31).
[7] Liberalis is the addressee of *De Beneficiis*, a name there suited to the topic at hand.

202 HERITAGE AND WAR

modification training (Badura-Brack et al. 2015; Lazarov et al. 2019; Wald et al. 2013). But the claim is that even if some of the shock could have been mitigated, grief and mourning would still remain, and moreover, be fitting, at least for us non-sages who haven't risen to the lofty perch of divine-like sagacity.

But this then raises the question of how we are to understand Stoic emotions of distress, such as grief, for things or persons. How can we cultivate a form of grief that isn't at root crippling? For that, after all, is the best gloss on the Stoic promise: to learn a kind of resilience that allows us to feel without being undone by our vulnerability.

The Stoics develop a sophisticated multi-layered conception of our affective experience and its expression. Their view anticipates cognitive theories of emotions as well as the idea that there are "low road" and "high road" emotions—quick response emotional arousals that bypass more complex neural and cognitive circuitry and those that, in varying degrees, are more cognitively mediated (LeDoux 1996).

At the center of the account are ordinary emotions, directed at future and present (or past) "goods" and "bads"—that is, externals. Since the Stoics are cognitivists (the Stoic psyche is just "tensions of reason"),[8] the core of an emotion is an impression, say of a loss, as in the case of grief. For a full-blown emotion to form, we need to take mental action, "assent" to the impression, cognitively "grasp" and accept the impression as true. With that assent, belief or judgment is formed. More specifically, two beliefs are formed, both of which are evaluative. The first is that the loss is damaging and chips away at one's happiness. The second is that certain reactions are appropriate behaviors, such as mourning, shedding tears, going into seclusion, visiting a mausoleum or shrine, making sacrifices, etc. The push to action means emotions are beliefs that are "umphy"—they impel us to action. Put otherwise, emotions are cognitive impulses, belief-laden umphs. Moreover, they are voluntary. Assent is a volitional act. As Seneca puts it in *On Anger*, an emotion "is not a mere impulse of the mind acting without our volition" (Seneca 1995a: 2.1.5).

Ever eager to draw bright stripes and clear classifications, the ancient Greek Stoics hold there are four main genera of emotions, under which all ordinary emotions fall: fear directed at a future bad or threat; desire directed at a future good; pleasure directed at a past or present good; and distress (of which grief is a species, and possibly anger[9]) directed at a past or present bad.

---

[8] And so unitary, not tri-partite, as in Plato's conception of the psyche in the *Republic*.
[9] Though, anger is often thought of in the ancient world as desire for revenge; so in Aristotle's Rh. II.2, it is also classified as a desire.

That's the heart of the descriptive account of the emotions in our ordinary emotional lives. They are: evaluative cognitions, volitions, and behaviors. But, of course, ordinary emotions can be disabling. Often, they are acquisitive, not only umphy but sticky, getting us overly attached to things we desire, frustrated and angry when we can't get those things or bring about desired outcomes, depressed in the face of what we have lost, especially when the losses are great and of things of importance. In short, everyday emotional experience lays bare the hazards of not learning Stoic lessons: namely, that external goods aren't the real good. If we were to view externals as indifferents to be selected or deselected but not as the objects of sticky attachment, or panicky avoidance or depressive sorrow, then we would have a better chance of weathering the vicissitudes of life.

And so, the Stoics hold, now prescriptively, that ordinary emotions are false evaluations of good and evil. They are irrational in their valuation. They get the world wrong. In addition to false valuations, they do their bidding with excess and so, contrary to the Aristotelian view, they can be hard to moderate. The metaphors for recalcitrance are telling: Ordinary emotions are like a runner who can't stop once in full stride. Or they are like stepping off a precipice: there is no going back once the momentum begins (Galen 1981; Long and Sedley 1987: 65J; and Seneca 1995a: 1.7). By and large we are to get over these emotions, but as we've seen, grief seems to slip through, at least in Seneca's letter that we've looked at and in other letters and consolations he wrote.

But before returning to the case of grief, we need to consider the more complete complement of emotional experience. There are two additional layers of emotional phenomena, one "low road," we might say, the other quite "high road," which most of us won't achieve. The first are protoemotions (*propatheiai*, or as Seneca dubs them, preludes to emotions *proludentia adfectibus*)—starts and startles, blushes and sweats, shivers and shakes, arousals that we can't be impugned for because they are involuntary; they come quick and may not be fully cognitive. We can often nip them in the bud, that is, not assent to the impressions which would lead to full-blown emotions. Even a sage, or those near to the highest rungs of virtue, will experience some of these emotions with impunity: a sage may turn green in a shipwreck (Gellius 1927), "the fiercest soldier tremble a little as the signal is given for battle," "a great general's heart is in his mouth before the lines have charged against one another," the most seasoned and "eloquent orator goes numb at the fingers as he prepares to speak" (Seneca 1995a: 2.3.1–3). But a sage can quickly recover composure. Even if he experiences some of those affects, they may be felt more like scars, inscribed by the body and mind, *madeleines* that remind

204   HERITAGE AND WAR

him of how he used to react in non-sage days, albeit with more indulgence back then and in ways that could easily lead to ordinary emotions.

But what is specific to the emotional profile of the sage are the good, or eugenic correlates of ordinary emotions. These are not only fully cognitive and volitional emotions, "high road" emotions, but normatively good ones. And they are good because they are directed at virtue and avoidance of vice—in place of desire, is rational desire; in place of fear, rational caution; in place of pleasure, rational joy. We might think of these as the attitudes of pursuing virtue and avoiding vice. They are directed at indifferents in so far as the wise selection of indifferents (the material content of virtuous choices) will be manifest in these good attitudes. But significantly, what there is no room for in the sage's emotional profile is a correlate for distress, and specifically, moral distress of the sort caused by one's own wrongdoing. For that's not a possibility if you are perfectly virtuous.

But what about distress as victim of others' ill will and enmity—what P.F. Strawson famously labeled personal reactive attitudes, such as resentment? Or moral distress on behalf of others who suffer others' ill will—Strawson's vicarious reactive attitudes, such as moral indignation? Or moral distress as agent/perpetrator of ill will or wrongdoing—Strawson's self-reactive attitudes, such as guilt and shame? In *Afterwar* and the *Untold War*, I have recast this trifecta of attitudes as central to the emotions of moral injury, so pervasive in war. We can think of moral injury as an exacerbated and often traumatic form of moral distress—wrenching moral anguish with symptoms often overlapping those of other trauma syndromes, such as posttraumatic stress. I return to resentment and moral indignation in the next section. But for now, consider the self-reactive attitudes of holding the self to account. And in particular, shame.

Cicero, a sympathetic Stoic redactor, urges Stoics to leave room for the distress of shame, particularly at the level of moral aspirant. "Suppose a person is upset about his own lack of virtue—his lack of courage, say, or of responsibility or integrity. The cause of his anxiety is indeed an evil." Shame is a spur to moral progress, an "impulse toward virtue itself" (Cicero 2002: 3.77, pp.34–35). Cicero directs his complaint against Cleanthes, the second head of the Greek Stoic school whom he says "doesn't take sufficiently into account the possibility that a person might be distressed over the very thing which [he] Cleanthes himself counts as the worst of evils"—namely, vice (Cicero 2002: 4.61, pp.61–62). The later Roman Stoics, immersed as they were in civic life, have their focus less on theory than on public moral improvement. The sage and the restrictive class of good emotions is an ideal, but not one that gives clear guidance for those whose lives may still be bumpy, morally and otherwise. And so, the moral distress of shame is an emotion, Cicero implies, that should be given space.

Cicero writes the *Tusculan Disputations*, from which the above quotes are drawn, in the throes of his own deep distress—here not moral distress, but profound grief over the loss of his beloved daughter Tullia in childbirth. Distress (*lupē*) comes in many species, moral and non-moral. The Stoics list "malice, envy, jealousy, pity, grief, worry, sorrow, annoyance, mental pain, vexation" (Long and Sedley 1987: 65E), and also the "distraction and mental confusion"—the ruminating and distorting, as they describe it, that can come with grief or shame and that can prevent one from seeing situations in perspective (Laertius 1970: 7.112). Some Stoics call attention to the Greek etymology of distress—from a verb, meaning "to dissolve"; distress, as they put it presciently, can cause "people to disintegrate."

As disabling as mental distress can be, Cicero argues for something short of full extirpation. He opts for behavior modification, how we comport ourselves in reaction to what causes distress, whether through wrongdoing or loss. He now focusses on loss: "It is this latter belief that gives rise to all those despicable forms of mourning such as smearing oneself with dirt, scratching at one's cheeks like a woman, and striking oneself on the chest, head, and thighs." Or tearing hair in grief—"as if baldness were a cure for sorrow!" (Cicero 2002: 3.62).[10]

Recall, Cicero is turning to Stoicism at this point in his life, not simply as an academic exercise, but as self-help for his onslaught of tears and self-imposed seclusion from public affairs: "I try all I can to bring my face if not my heart back to composure" (Cicero 1999: 12.14).[11] He is eager for a discipline that will restore decorum. But not at the cost of denying the genuine value of his loss: "I pass over the method of Cleanthes, since that is directed at the wise person who does not need consoling. For if you manage to persuade the bereaved person that nothing is bad but shameful [i.e., vicious] conduct, then you have taken away not his grief, but his unwisdom. And this is not the right moment for such a lesson" (Cicero, 2002: 3.77). In short, there may be a time for lessons in wisdom, but even Stoic addresses of consolation need to begin by acknowledging the genuine impact of significant loss. Whether the "bad" is due to natural cause or human evil, and a damage to persons or things,

---

[10] Cicero here quoting Bion of Borysthenes, as Graver notes in her commentary on the text, "the third-century satirist and wit," and for a time, a Cynic philosopher (Cicero 2002: 112).
[11] For more on Stoics and "permission to grieve," see Sherman (2005: esp. 130–149).

206 HERITAGE AND WAR

the preliminary belief that a bad has taken place, should not be dismissed. This is no time for wisdom that downgrades it to a dispreferred indifferent. Timing is everything in psychotherapy, even in Stoic psychotherapy.

4.

With Cicero's warning in mind, it's time to return to Seneca's consolations on cultural destruction. After acknowledging his own tremendous shock about events in Lyon, and expressing heartfelt sympathy for what Liberalis must be going through, Seneca moves on quickly to stock Stoic themes and lessons, too quickly, as Cicero might add, in undoing "unwisdom." This is the gist of his remarks: Fortune can be indiscriminate in its sweep; death is an equalizer; a quick but capacious scan of the hazards of fortune makes clear that those ills to do with epidemics, natural disasters, and war—are all suitable subjects for Stoicism's calm. We need to remember that a short duration on earth, and even a ghastly, fiery end, is not itself a harm; only vice is (Seneca 2015: 91).

We should note in all this that Stoic moral discipline is, by and large, a personal project, even if collectively taught in schools, writings, and letters to friends. It is about our own virtue, the good will, as Kant will go on to put it, in a way that retains the Stoic primacy of our will and agency as the real subject of moral judgment. Kant's point is that even if the heart is opaque, the study of our own conscience through first personal reflection allows for more transparency than possible in our judgments of others. Approval and disapproval of the actions of others interpersonally or from the point of view of an impartial judge represents, historically, a different moral psychology track; and similarly, so, the reactive attitudes, as Strawson goes on to develop them, with an implicit debt to Hume, expressed in taking up the interpersonal or vicarious stance and the personal stance of self as object of others' good or ill will.[12]

This may strike some as odd. In thinking about the trauma of moral injury and lesser severe moral distress, why focus only on one's own wrongdoing and not on what other people do to you or the cultural heritages of your collective identity? Or again, why not focus on you as witness and the stance you take on behalf of others? In short, why focus only on what you do, and not what's done to you or to others or to their beloveds, whether things or persons?

---

[12] On this, see insightful discussion in Deigh (2018: especially, his chs. 4 and 5: "Psychopathic Resentment" and "Reactive Attitudes Revisited: A Modest Revision"), and Sherman (2022).

This is, in part, a Socratic inheritance, that no harm can come to the good person, in the sense that the ideally good person can't be made vicious or corrupted from outside (see Brickhouse and Smith 1995: 122). However psychologically implausible the view, the doctrine sets Stoics on their agenda for the perfection of our own virtue. To the degree to which the sage is such a model for all persons, we are to take seriously the discipline of virtue and its exercise; hence, all the Stoic exercises to do with strengthening will and mastery, such as in pre-rehearsing evils, or trying to prevent frustration at failure by tagging onto our intentions' tacit reservation clauses: "if nothing happens to prevent it" (Seneca 1995b: 4.34.4).[13] These are cognitive exercises to be taken up with the same vigor that we would with daily strenuous physical exercise. They are self-protective, of persons as agents.

Emotions too, as we've said, are, both psychically and behaviorally, actions on which to practice control. The Stoic sophisticated descriptive theory of emotion is meant to have prescriptive pay-off. Harms to self and those things that represent self in our collective identities, in our cities, their edifices and religious and cultural heritages, through injustice, incite for the ordinary person not only grief but anger, and the payback emotions that come with the sense of being wronged. Retributivist anger is, primitively at least, aggression, even if conventionally, at times, a justified defense. It's a "bite-back" mechanism that feeds on new provocations. And on the Stoic normative view, it isn't reparative. This is the well-rehearsed theme of Seneca's *On Anger*: "no plague has cost the human race more…cities of the greatest renown, their very foundations now scarcely discernible," "buildings set alight and the fire spreading beyond the city walls, huge tracts of territory glowing in flames that the enemy kindled…deserts, mile after mile without inhabitant—anger emptied them" (Seneca 1995a: 1.2.1–3). Anger is an enemy of reason. It's a perversion of judgment, like all ordinary emotions. But it is an emotion especially hard to turn off once turned on. Once it takes grip, it "tightens its noose" (Seneca 1995a: 3.16.1). If there is an emotion on which to practice Stoic abstention, it is anger.

I can't take up here the plausibility of the view or ways of domesticating it, as, say, Martha Nussbaum has recently in her notion of "transitional anger." "Transitional anger," on her construction, is an emotion type that harnesses the bare impulse of retributivist anger but then transforms it into more pacific and constructive form (Nussbaum 2015). In earlier work, in particular in *Stoic Warriors* (2005: esp. ch. 4 "A Warrior's Anger," 64–99), I have argued against the Stoic extirpation of anger. For our purposes here, it is worth

---

[13] See also Epictetus (1995: 2.6.9–10), and Arius Didymus (1884: Ecl. 21115.5–9). See Inwood (1985: 121).

208   HERITAGE AND WAR

noting that while the Stoics *may be* willing to see the benefit of the moral distress of shame, and, we might add, guilt, in the life of a moral aspirant, it's harder for them to see a comparable benefit for outward directed anger, that is, resentment or moral indignation. And so, even if the self-reproach of shame is at its core a form of anger, distress and anxiety for the sake of self-improvement seems a more permissible kind of anger for the Stoics than anger directed at others, on behalf of oneself or others. For anger directed at others, they think, can unleash a hard-to-stop volley. That's one of Seneca's complaints. The bite-back mechanism feeds on itself.

But if hard-to-stop excess is the worry, then moral anger against self hardly guarantees self-imposed limits. Moral injury experienced as agent, whether to do with real or apparent commissions or omissions, can be every bit as overproductive as anger directed outside oneself. This is a theme that emerges over and over again in my interviews with service members, and that I explore in *Untold War* and *Afterwar*. Self-compassion sometimes requires switching perspectives, imagining if one would reproach others as harshly as one reproaches oneself. Trading places may be therapeutic precisely because the perspectives of reactive attitudes are not symmetrical.[14] In practice, we don't move seamlessly within the trifecta of reactive attitudes, as Strawson seems to suggest. We may get to one only by moving through another. Servicemembers may let up on their own, sometimes suicidal, self-blame only by imagining, in the safe haven of therapy, if they would judge others every bit as harshly, or if others would judge them with the same lack of mercy with which they judge themselves.[15]

5.

Moral distress, then, takes many forms, often laced with anger, pointed inward and outward to self as agent and victim. Are moral distress, rage and resentment, and moral indignation appropriate reactions to the destruction of cultural heritages in war? Seneca's response seems to be "no." We are to loosen the attachments to things, even if they are sacred and vital to a communal identity. Shy of radical re-evaluation of our attachments, we should try

---

[14] Here I am grateful to a paper delivered by Lisa Tessman in a joint keynote we did on moral injury at West Point, October 2019 (Tessman 2019). I develop these themes in comments (Sherman 2022) on John Deigh's chapters on reactive attitudes.

[15] For clinical work on forgiveness and compassion in treating moral injury, I am grateful to conversations with Brett Litz, Shira Maguen, Bill Nash, and their VA and DOD colleagues, over the years (see Litz 2014, 2019; Litz, Lebowitz, Gray, and Nash 2016; Maguen et al. 2017).

to modify our reactions so we can come to accept loss and move forward with greater equanimity and resilience. Strategies for accepting loss are part of the Stoic scheme for building grit.

To many, seeking equanimity of either sort in the face of the destruction of cultural heritages in war seems to acquiesce to injustice. It is giving up morality for the sake of calm. If that is the cost of equanimity, then it may be a false equanimity, every bit as false a value as the glory and fame the Stoics would have us shun. Seneca might reply that this is the necessity of survival under a tyrant's thumb. In a consolation to his mother, written during his exile in Corsica by Claudius, he says hardship and Heraclitean flux is the way of the world: "the human race is constantly rushing to and fro," "the foundations of new cities are laid," older ones "blotted out or lost by annexation with a stronger" (Seneca 1932: 7.4–8). Cultures and civilizations are layered neatly in archaeological lines, and calm comes with the settling of the shards and dust. This is a son talking to a mother, trying to rest her nerves, but also, a son preaching Stoic wisdom.

Should this give us solace as we watch the first-century Temple of Baalshamin at the ancient ruins of Palmyra in Syria destroyed by the Islamic State in August 2015? Shouldn't we be morally outraged at the obliteration of history, the record of a civilization, and a cultural center of the ancient world, contemporaneous with Seneca's own times? I have read Seneca, and explored his words, precisely because the record remains. He wrote with an eye to history and posterity. Shouldn't we view other culturally and historically precious "stuff" in the same way?

I am not advocating the Stoic position. I have been exploring it and suggesting that it gives us space to reassess both what we value and how we are attached to what we value through emotions that can often control us rather than we them. That is the critical Stoic lesson: to explore the moral psychology of what and whom we value in life and how we do that valuing so that we can come up with solutions that allow us to go on as partners in the cooperative endeavors of a cosmopolitan community. Even the noblest of our artifices, that represent the best of our selves and cultures, can distract us from our shared humanity. "Let us cultivate humanity," Seneca exhorts in his famous final injunction of *On Anger*. The plea should give us some space, as I have tried to find, to reflect on how and why we value what we do in a good life.[16]

---

[16] I am grateful for comments by Helen Frowe, Joshua Lewis Thomas, and William Bülow on an earlier draft of this chapter. And I am grateful to Katherine Ward for editorial assistance along the way. Views in this paper are more fully developed in Sherman (2021). That book was written after this paper was originally penned.

References

Arius Didymus. (1884), "Epitome of Stoic Ethics," in C. Wachsmuth and O. Hense (eds.), *Ioannis Stobaei anthologium* (Berlin: Weidmannsche Buchhandlung), 57–116.

Badura-Brack, A. S., Naim, R., Ryan, T. J., Levy, O., Abend, R., Khanna, M. M., McDermott, T. J., Pine, D. S., and Bar-Haim, Y. (2015), "Effect of Attention Training on Attention Bias Variability and PTSD Symptoms: Randomized Controlled Trials in Israeli and U.S. Combat Veterans," in *The American Journal of Psychiatry* 172/12: 1233–1241.

Brickhouse, T., and Smith, N. (1995), *Plato's Socrates* (New York: Oxford University Press).

Champlin, E. (2003), *Nero* (Cambridge, MA: Harvard University Press).

Cicero. (1999), *Letters to Atticus*, D. R. Shackleton Bailey (trans.), 4 vols., Loeb Classical Library (Cambridge, MA: Harvard University Press).

Cicero. (2001), *On Moral Ends*, R. Woolf (trans.), J. Annas (ed.) (Cambridge: Cambridge University Press).

Cicero. (2002), *Cicero on the Emotions: Tusculan Disputations 3 and 4*, M. Graver (ed.) (Chicago, IL: University of Chicago Press).

Deigh, J. (2018), *From Psychology to Morality: Essays in Ethical Naturalism* (New York: Oxford University Press).

Dio, C. (1925), *Roman History, vol. 8* (Cambridge, MA and London: Loeb Classical Library).

Epictetus. (1995), *The Discourses*, R. Hard (trans.), C. Gill (ed.) (London and Vermont: Everyman).

Galen. (1981), *On the Doctrines of Hippocrates and Plato*, P. De Lacy (ed. and trans.) (Berlin: Akademie Verlag).

Gellius, A. (1927), *The Attic Nights*, J. C. Rolfe (trans.) (Cambridge, MA and London: Loeb Classical Editions).

Griffin, M. T. (1984), *Nero, The End of a Dynasty* (London: Batsford).

Inwood, B. (1985), *Ethics and Human Action in Early Stoicism* (Oxford: Oxford University Press).

Laertius, D. (1970), *Lives of Eminent Philosophers, vol. 2* (Cambridge, MA: Loeb Classical Library, Harvard University Press).

Lazarov, A., Suarez-Jimenez, B., Abend, R., Naim, R., Shvil, E., Helpman, L., Zhu, X., Papini, S., Duroski, A., Rom, R., Schneier, F. R., Pine, D. S., Bar-Haim, Y., and Neria, Y. (2019), "Bias-Contingent Attention Bias Modification and Attention Control Training in Treatment of PTSD: A Randomized Control Trial," in *Psychological Medicine* 49/14: 2432–2440.

LeDoux, J. (1996), *The Emotional Brain* (New York: Simon & Schuster).

Litz, B. (2014), "Clinical Heuristics and Strategies for Service Members and Veterans with War-Related PTSD," in *Psychoanalytic Psychology* 31/2: 192.

Litz, B. (2019), Moral Injury Special Issue, *Journal of Tramautic Stress: Moral Injury Special Issue*.

Litz, B., Lebowitz, L., Gray, M. J., and Nash, W. (2016), *Adaptive Disclosure: A New Treatment for Military Trauma, Loss, and Moral Injury* (New York and London: Guilford Press).

Long, A. A., and Sedley, D. N. (1987), *The Hellenistic Philosophers, vol. 1: Translations of the Principal Sources with Philosophical Commentary* (Cambridge: Cambridge University Press).

Maguen, S., Burkman, K., Madden, E., Dinh, J., Bosch, J., Keyser, J., Schmitz, M., and Neylan, T. C. (2017), "Impact of Killing in War: A Randomized, Controlled Pilot Trial," in *Journal of Clinical Psychology* 73: 1–16.

Moore, M. (1944), "In Distrust of Merits," *Poetry Nook*, accessed February 22, 2022, https://www.poetrynook.com/poem/distrust-merits.

Musei Capitolini. (2020), "Equestrian Statue of Marcus Aurelius," accessed March 3, 2022, http://capitolini.info/scu03247/?lang=en.

Newman, R. J. (2013), "In umbra virtutis: Gloria in the Thought of Seneca the Philosopher," in J. Fitch (ed.), *Seneca: Oxford Readings in Classical Studies* (Oxford: Oxford University Press), 316–338.

Nussbaum, M. C. (2015), "Transitional Anger," *Journal of the American Philosophical Association* 1/01: 41–56.

Pollini, J. (2017), "Burning Rome, Burning Christians," in S. Bartsch, K. Freudenburg, and C. Littlewood (eds.), *The Cambridge Companion to the Age of Nero* (Cambridge University Press), 212–236.

Schofield, M. (1999), *The Stoic Idea of the City* (Chicago, IL: University of Chicago Press).

Seneca. (1932), *To Helvia On Consolation*, J. W. Basore (trans.) (Cambridge, MA and London: Loeb Classical Editions).

Seneca. (1995a), *On Anger*, in J. M. Cooper and J. F. Procopé (trans.), *Moral and Political Essays* (New York: Cambridge University Press).

Seneca. (1995b), *On Favours*, J. M. Cooper and J. F. Procopé (trans.), in *Moral and Political Essays* (New York: Cambridge University Press).

Seneca. (2015), *Letters on Ethics to Lucilius*, M. Graver and A. A. Long (trans.) (Chicago, IL and London: University of Chicago Press).

Sherman, N. (1997), *Making a Necessity of Virtue: Aristotle and Kant on Virtue.* (Cambridge; New York: Cambridge University Press).

Sherman, N. (2005), *Stoic Warriors: The Ancient Philosophy Behind the Military Mind.* (New York: Oxford University Press).

Sherman, N. (2021), *Stoic Wisdom: Ancient Lessons for Modern Resilience.* (New York: Oxford University Press).

Sherman, N. (2022), "Shame & Guilt: From Deigh to Strawson & Hume, and Now Back to the Stoics," in *Philosophy and Phenomenological Research,* 104(3), 768–776. Book Symposium on John Deigh's "From Psychology to Morality: Essays in Ethical Naturalism."

Strawson, P. F. (1962), "Freedom and Resentment," in *Proceedings of the British Academy* 48: 1–25.

Suetonius. (1914), *The Lives of the Twelve Caesars: The Life of Nero* (Cambridge, MA and London: Loeb Classical Library).

Tacitus. (1942), *The Annals* (New York: Perseus; Random House).

Tessman, L. (2019), "Moral Injury and Moral Failure," paper presented at *Ethics of War and Peace Conference*, United States Military Academy, West Point, October.

Wald, I., Degnan, K. A., Gorodetsky, E., Charney, D. S., Fox, N. A., Fruchter, E., Goldman, D., Lubin, G., Pine, D. S., and Bar-Haim, Y. (2013), "Attention to Threats and Combat-related Posttraumatic Stress Symptoms: Prospective Associations and Moderation by the Serotonin Transporter Gene," in *JAMA Psychiatry* 70/4: 401–408.

Wilson, E. (2019), *The Greatest Empire: A Life of Seneca* (New York: Oxford University Press).

Index

For the benefit of digital users, indexed terms that span two pages (e.g., 52–53) may, on occasion, appear on only one of those pages.

Absence (as memorial) 148–9
Aggressors, culpable 55–7
Al–Azm, Amr 2, 99–100
Ascherson, Neal 100–1
Augustine 20–1
Aurelius, Marcus 199
Auschwitz–Birkenau 180–2

Bamiyan Buddhas 43, 54, 149
Bebelplatz (Berlin) 149
Bernard, Penelope 8–9
Blue Shield 2, 39, 41, 117
Bokova, Irina 2, 92, 103
Bülow, William 5–6

Chinese Eighth Route Army Culture
 Park 176, 181–2
Christianity 20–5
Cicero 204–6
Civilians, risk to 40–3, 45–7, 57–60, 63–9
Combatants, risk to 37–41, 47, 60–9
Connelly, Nina 2, 40–1, 44–6, 62, 92, 97,
 103, 106
'Cultural denizen' 5, 73–4, 83–4, 88–90
Cultural self-determination 58–60
Culture: (dead) 118–20, (embedded)
 118–20, (iconic) 116–20,
 (living) 119–24
Cunliffe, Emma 39, 41–2, 96–8
Cuno, James 44–5

Damage, collateral 35, 54–5
Damage, intentional 35, 54
Damage, as perceptual property 141–50
Displaced populations (return
 of) 100–2, 106
Dorsey, Dale 5
Douaumont Ossuary 139, 141
Dover Castle 175–6, 183–4, 189–91
Duties, negative (duties not to harm) 53–4
Duties, positive (duties to prevent
 harm) 53–4

Eaton, Jonathan 98–9
Education (use of heritage in) 98–100,
 178–80
Egypt (ancient) 118–19
Elgin, Catherine Z. 140–1, 148
El–Mecky, Nausikaä 2
Emotions (Stoic view of) 202–9
Enjoyment (at sites of conflict) 183–7
Eternal Light Peace Memorial 137–8
'Ethnic domain' (as articulated by
 architecture) 157–9
Exemplification 140–1, 144–9

Farchack Bajjaly, Joanne 42–3
Feasible alternative, (see also
 'necessity') 35–7, 45–7
Fox, Paul 39, 96–8
Frowe, Helen 55–6, 62

Gettysburg Military Park 136–8
Goodman, Nelson 140–1
Greece (Ancient) 13–19, 195–6

Hadžić, Lejla 98–9
Hague Convention on the Protection of
 Cultural Property in Time of Armed
 Conflict (1954) 4, 13–14, 34–9, 45–7,
 117, 119–20
Haydar, Bashar 4–5
Heritage for Peace 39
Higgins, Kathleen 135
Hiroshima Peace Memorial (Genbaku
 Dome) 143–4
Hopkins, Robert 7–8

'Indifferents' (Stoic term) 198–9
'Inseparability Thesis' 1–4, 33–47, 92–3, 103
Intergenerational significance (of
 culture) 121–4
International Criminal Court 1
International Humanitarian Law 13–15,
 24–5, 45–6

214 INDEX

Intervention, military 40–1, 61–9
Israel 6–7, 113–31

Jus in bello 12–13
Just cause (of war) 5, 40–1, 53–69

Kaikkonen, Tuukka 3–4
Kaiser Wilhelm Gedächtniskirche
  (Memorial Church) 146–7
Kant, Immanuel 83–4, 198, 206
Kirchin, Simon 8–9
Korsmeyer, Carolyn 7

Lamarque, Peter 148
Langer, Suzanne 7, 156–60
Looting 1, 41–2
Lostal, Marina 41–2
Lydda (Lod) 6–7, 113–31
Lyon (Lugdunum) 200–1, 206

Matravers, Derek 55–6, 62
Memorials (cf. monuments) 7, 134–50,
  169–70, 179–80
Memory 7–8, (loss of) 170–3
Menegazzi, Cristina 2
Middle Ages 16–22
Military necessity (military advantage) 35–6
Modern Period 24–5
Monuments (cf. memorials) 134–7,
  169–70, 197–9
Muhesen, Nibal 41–2

Necessity (*see also* feasible alternative)
  35–6
Notre Dame, Cathedral of 52–5, 57, 61,
  76–7, 116–18, 121–2
Nussbaum, Martha 207–8

O'Driscoll, Cian 3–4
Opportunity costs 104–5

Palestine 6–7, 113–31
Presence 145–6, 149, 179–80
Problematic heritage 106–7
Proportionality 4–5, 36–43, 51–69, 72,
  88–90, 102–4

Reanimation (of a heritage site) 189–91
'Reconciliation Thesis' 5–6, 92–109

Reconstruction (of heritage) 107, 133–4,
  147–50, 172–3
Reductivism: (welfarist) 75–7, (aesthetic)
  75, 77–9, (historical) 75, 79–80
Rehabilitation (economic) 97–8, 106
Remnants of conflict 139
Representation 156–7
'Responsibility to Protect' (R2P) 40–1
Response to wrongdoing 125–31
Riegl, Alois 134–5
'Right of return' (of Palestinians) 126–31
'Role Principle' 85–90
Rome (Ancient) 16, 18–21, 195–6
Ruskin, John 153–4

Saito, Yuriko 143
Sanctuary 3–4, 12–26
Savile, Anthony 153
Seneca 9, 199–204, 206–9
Sherman, Nancy 9
Slavny, Adam 125–6
Sparshott, Francis 135
Stilz, Annie 121
Stone, Peter 2, 39, 96–8
Strawson, P.F. 204, 206, 208
Sui generism (about value) 80–2

Tadros, Victor 6–7
Thomas, Joshua Lewis 5–6
Timbuktu 1, 38
Time (influence on the way we view
  heritage sites) 187–92
Tourism 8–9, 106, 187–9
Tupajić, Milan 100–1

UNESCO 39, 51
Uniacke, Suzanne 93–4

Value 37, 43–5, 55–7
'Value-based view' (of heritage) 82–4
Victoria and Albert Museum, London 147

Wade, Jennie (bullet hole) 139, 141
Weiss, Thomas 2, 40–1, 44–6, 62, 92, 97,
  103, 106
'Witness memorial' 145–6
Wolferstan, Sarah 99
Wolterstorff, Nicolas 144
World Trade Center Memorial 144–5, 148–9